# PRISONERS OF CONSCIENCE IN THE USSR:

## Their Treatment and Conditions

Published by Quartermaine House Ltd
Windmill Road, Sunbury, Middx, UK
for Amnesty International (British Section)
8 Southampton Street, London WC2E 7HF, England

First edition, November 1975
Second edition, April 1980
Copyright © Amnesty International Publications, 1975
ISBN: 0 905898 09 5
Printed by: Unwin Brothers Ltd, Old Woking, Surrey, England

# PRISONERS OF CONSCIENCE IN THE USSR:

## Their Treatment and Conditions

**An Amnesty International Report**

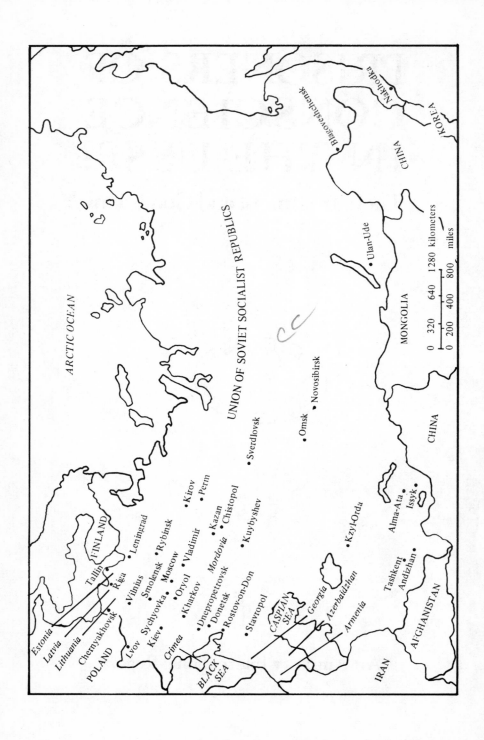

# CONTENTS

Introduction                                                                  1

1.  Soviet Law and Prisoners of Conscience                                    3
    *The USSR Constitution (1977)*                                            3
    *Soviet Criminal Law: Background*                                         7
    *Freedom of Expression*                                                   9
    *Freedom of Association*                                                 19
    *Freedom of Religion*                                                    30
    *Freedom of Movement*                                                    45
    *Imprisonment of Conscientious Objectors
    to Military Service*                                                     51
    *Application of Non-Political Articles of Criminal Law
    to Dissenters*                                                           56
    *Administrative Surveillance of Released Prisoners
    of Conscience*                                                           60

2.  Arrest, Trial and Sentencing                                             65
    *Arrest and Pre-trial Confinement*                                       65
    *Defence Counsel*                                                        71
    *Trial*                                                                  74
    *Sentencing*                                                             78
    *Appeal, Review and Other Means of Relief from Sentence*                 82
    *The Death Penalty*                                                      86

3.  Corrective Labour Legislation                                            89
    *Theory*                                                                 89
    *Socialist Legality*                                                     94
    *Categories and Places of Imprisonment*                                  98
        *a) Imprisonment in prison and colonies*                            98
        *b) Exile, Banishment, Corrective Work Without
        Imprisonment and Assigned Labour*                                   101

4.  Maintenance of Prisoners                                                106
    *Transport of Prisoners*                                                106
    *Prisoners' Accommodation and Other Facilities*                         110
    *Food*                                                                  112
    *Medical Conditions*                                                    122

5.    Reform of Prisoners    134
    *Work*    135
    *Political Education*    145
    *Vocational Instruction*    148

6.    Relations between Prisoners and Administrators    151
    *Security, Discipline and Prisoners' Rights*    151
    *Punishments*    157
    *Beatings and Physical Ill-Treatment of Prisoners*    165
    *Legal Controls over Colony and Prison Administrations*    167

7.    Compulsory Detention in Psychiatric Hospitals    172
    *Formal Procedures for Compulsory Confinement*    173
    *Criminal Procedure for Compulsory Psychiatric Confinement*    174
    *Civil Procedures for Forcible Commitment*    178
    *Diagnosis*    181
    *Treatment in Psychiatric Hospitals*    189
    *Special Psychiatric Hospitals*    189
    *Ordinary Psychiatric Hospitals*    196
    *Treatment with Psychiatric Methods*    196
    *Release and After Release*    200

    Index    205

    Amnesty International Publications    214

# INTRODUCTION

This report is an updated and revised edition of the Amnesty International publication *Prisoners of Conscience in the USSR: Their Treatment and Conditions*, published in 1975.

In the 1975 edition, Amnesty International made important and detailed recommendations to the USSR authorities for improvements in legislation and practice relating to official intolerance of freedom of conscience, the conditions under which convicted prisoners serve sentences of imprisonment, the forcible confinement of people to psychiatric hospitals and their conditions and treatment in psychiatric hospitals.

The USSR authorities rejected the findings in Amnesty International's report and attributed it to "anti-Soviet" motives on the part of the organization. The authorities did not respond in substance or detail regarding the human rights violations described in the report. The authorities have not, as far as is known to Amnesty International, made any of the changes in legislation and practice which Amnesty International had recommended.

During the past four years the abuses documented in the first edition of this report have remained part of official practice in the USSR. Dissenters in various categories have been arrested and imprisoned for non-violent exercise of their human rights and sentenced to imprisonment, frequently under criminal legislation which explicitly restricts the non-violent exercise of human rights. Amnesty International has learned of more than 400 people who were tried and sentenced to imprisonment, internal exile or other punishments involving physical restriction or who were forcibly confined to psychiatric hospitals for exercising their human rights during the four years after the writing of the 1975 edition (June 1975 to May 1979). Reports of fresh arrests and trials were reaching Amnesty International as the second edition went to print in late 1979.

Amnesty International believes the real number of prisoners of conscience in the USSR to be much larger than the known number. However official censorship and secrecy regarding penal practices and the permanent threat of arrest of those who speak out about political imprisonment make it difficult to attempt an estimate of the total number of prisoners of conscience.

Amnesty International still has not heard of a single case in which a Soviet court has acquitted someone charged with political or religious offences.

Inmates of the country's penal institutions are still subjected to a regime of chronic hunger, inadequate medical care and difficult, often dangerous compulsory labour. Inmates of psychiatric hospitals are still deprived of virtually every right that would enable them to protect themselves against ill-treatment by medical or other methods. Soviet citizens who expose and protest against these human rights violations risk imprisonment, now as before 1975.

Amnesty International is also concerned about the continued use of the death penalty. Soviet law prescribes death by shooting for 18 different offences in peacetime, some of these being non-violent economic or political offences. Each year official Soviet news media report approximately 30 death penalties, but Amnesty International believes the annual number of executions to be much higher.

It was in view of the continuation of regular violations of Soviet citizens' human rights that Amnesty International decided to publish a second edition of the report *Prisoners of Conscience in the USSR: Their Treatment and Conditions*. Amnesty International's concerns remain unchanged, and this volume follows the outline of the 1975 report: examining first the laws and practices by which people come to be arrested, tried and sentenced for exercising their human rights; describing the country's penitentiary (or "corrective labour") legislation and the actual conditions in penal institutions; and devoting a separate chapter to the forcible confinement of people to psychiatric hospitals because of their exercise of human rights rather than for authentic medical reasons. This second edition brings the report up-to-date to mid-1979 and goes into greater detail regarding the laws and other institutions of the USSR which relate to the imprisonment and treatment of prisoners of conscience.

In preparing this report, Amnesty International has relied primarily on two types of sources: officially published materials and accounts by prisoners themselves, their relatives and friends.

Officially published sources include legal texts, official commentaries on them and works by Soviet jurists and scholars whose writings bear the official approval necessary for publication. Such sources have provided Amnesty International with essential information regarding official norms in prosecuting dissenters and the principles and mechanisms governing the operation of the country's penal institutions.

However, official sources have severe limitations. In the USSR, as in other countries, such sources provide almost no reliable information about legal proceedings against dissenters or about conditions in the country's camps, prisons and psychiatric hospitals. Such information must be sought in statements by prisoners and ex-prisoners and their relatives and friends. This type of material is mostly available in the form of *samizdat*, writings published privately without official sanction or censorship. In recent years scores of former prisoners of conscience have left the USSR and have added their accounts of their personal experiences to what is known from *samizdat* sources about the treatment of prisoners of conscience.

Translations from the RSFSR Criminal Code and Code of Criminal Procedure are taken from Harold J. Berman and James W. Spindler, *Soviet Criminal Law and Procedure: The RSFSR Codes*, Harvard University Press, Cambridge, Massachussetts, 1972.

# CHAPTER 1

# Soviet Law and Prisoners of Conscience

## The USSR Constitution (1977)

The USSR abstained in the United Nations General Assembly vote on the Universal Declaration of Human Rights in 1948. However, since that time the USSR has adhered to a number of international human rights instruments, including the United Nations International Covenants on Civil and Political Rights (1966) and on Social, Economic and Cultural Rights (1966). These Covenants came into force in 1976.

The USSR Supreme Soviet promulgated a new Constitution in October 1977 to replace the one which had been in effect since 1936. In a submission to the United Nations Human Rights Committee, set up under the International Covenant on Civil and Political Rights, in January 1978 the Soviet Government said that the new Constitution "fully guarantees and ensures the practical implementation in the Soviet Union of all the principles enshrined in the Charter of the United Nations, the International Covenant on Civil and Political Rights, the International Covenant on Economic, Social and Cultural Rights and other international instruments of the United Nations concerning human rights".[1] In Amnesty International's view, the new Constitution, like that of 1936, institutionalizes unjustifiable restrictions on Soviet citizens' human rights.

Article 34 of the 1977 Constitution proclaims that citizens of the USSR are equal before the law "without distinction as to origin, social or property status, race or nationality, sex, education, language, attitude to religion, type and nature of occupation, domicile or other status". This article repeats almost verbatim the proclamation of non-discrimination in Article 26 of the International Covenant on Civil and Political Rights. However, Article 34 of the USSR Constitution deviates from the United Nations model by not prohibiting discrimination on grounds of "political or other opinion".

Article 39 of the new Constitution, which opens the chapter dealing with the rights and duties of Soviet citizens, states that citizens may not exercise their rights "to the detriment of the interests of society or the state". Other articles make plain that it is not the individual but official bodies which determine "the interests of the state".

According to Article 50, Soviet citizens are guaranteed freedom of expression in various forms. However, as in the 1936 Constitution, this guarantee is prefaced by the statement that these rights are guaranteed "in accordance with the interests of the people and in order to strengthen and develop the socialist system". The right to freedom of association (Article 51) has a similar preface. Soviet judicial and other authorities have made plain that the prefacing statement restricts the manner in which these rights may be used.

Article 52 states that Soviet citizens are guaranteed "the right to conduct religious worship or atheistic propaganda". Just as in the 1936 Constitution, the choice of words signifies that religious believers do not have the right to conduct religious propaganda. In law and in practice, this entails restrictions on the right of believers to preach their religious views and to instruct their children in religion.

Article 62 states in part: "Defence of the Socialist Motherland is the sacred duty of every citizen of the USSR". Nowhere in the Constitution is provision made for those who, for reasons of conscience, are unwilling to perform military service.

These and other provisions of the Constitution sanction retention of penal and other legislation permitting the imprisonment of Soviet citizens solely for exercising their human rights. Amnesty International has in the past publicly called on the Soviet authorities to repeal such laws.[2] Nevertheless, in its submission to the United Nations Human Rights Committee in 1978 the Soviet Government referred to the "highly developed character of Soviet legislation relating to human rights and freedoms" and indicated that domestic legislation would not be changed in the light of the country's internationally-assumed human rights undertakings.

In other contexts Soviet spokesmen have come close to acknowledging the Soviet Government's restrictive attitude to Soviet citizens' human rights. Leonid Brezhnev, the General Secretary of the Central Committee of the Communist Party of the Soviet Union (and since June 1977 Chairman of the Presidium of the USSR Supreme Soviet), said in his speech to the World Congress of Peace Forces in 1973:

> Soviet laws afford our citizens broad political freedoms. At the same time,
> they protect our system and the interests of the Soviet people from any
> attempts to abuse these freedoms.

Mr Brezhnev went on to infer that the "abuses" to which he referred were of the sort foreseen in the limiting clause of Article 19 of the International Covenant on Civil and Political Rights:

> And this is in full conformity with the International Covenants on Human
> Rights, which say that the rights they enumerate "shall not be subject to
> any restrictions except those which are provided by law, are necessary to
> protect national security, public order, public health or morals, or the rights
> and freedoms of others . . .".

Commenting on Mr Brezhnev's statement and on international human rights guarantees, a Soviet author said in early 1974 in *Partiinaya Zhizn* (*Party Life*), the fortnightly journal of the Central Committee of the Communist Party of the Soviet Union:

> It is a norm of our life that the exercise of rights and freedoms is
> inseparable from citizens' fulfilment of their obligations to society.

He went on to describe the reciprocal relationship of rights and obligations between the Soviet state and its citizens, and said:

. . . a man must live and act in correspondence with the highest humanistic goals and ideals of society—to fulfil the norms and rules of socialist life at work and at home, to struggle with violations of these norms, in all ways to support everything that corresponds to the nature of socialism and to help speed up the movement of society towards communism.[3]

These statements reflect the prevailing official Soviet view that not only should freedom of expression be restricted so as to prevent its being abused to the detriment of Soviet society and state, but its exercise should be of positive value to the public interest as defined in official policy.

The same official norm that civil rights must be exercised in a particular way to the exclusion of other ways appears in the official interpretation of the Constitution of the USSR. Article 50 of the USSR Constitution (1977) states:

In accordance with the interests of the people and in order to strengthen and develop the socialist system, citizens of the USSR are guaranteed freedom of speech, of the press, and of assembly, meetings, street processions and demonstrations. Exercise of these political freedoms is ensured by putting public buildings, streets and squares at the disposal of the working people and their organizations, by broad dissemination of information, and by the opportunity to use the press, television and radio.

This article of the 1977 Constitution is essentially identical to Article 125 of the 1936 Constitution.

Officially-approved descriptions of these constitutional guarantees are unanimous in stating that these freedoms may be exercised only in restricted ways. The nationally prominent Soviet jurist G.Z. Anashkin said in 1977 in a booklet published officially for mass distribution, entitled *The Rights and Obligations of the Citizen of the USSR*:

Our legislation, which rejects the exploitation of man by man, forbids the "freedom" to slander socialist democracy and the Soviet system.

Socialist society gives no one the freedom to commit actions aimed at restoring bourgeois ways or to propagandize bourgeois ideology, or the right to commit anti-social acts.

It is forbidden to create anti-Soviet organizations, or to use national survivals or religious prejudices for criminal goals.

A recent officially-published university textbook, *The Constitutional Rights and Obligations of Soviet Citizens*, by L.D. Voevodin, is also typical of official commentary on this article of the Soviet Constitution. (This volume was written when the 1936 Constitution was still in effect, but the passages cited are of continuing relevance.)

Mr Voevodin observes that Article 125 (equivalent to Article 50 of the 1977 Constitution, cited above) deals with freedom of opinion. He observes that every person's opinions reflect the interests of his or her social class:

It follows that genuine freedom of conscience (*mneniya*) is not any un-hindered dissemination of ideas, opinions, etc., but only the dissemination of progressive, revolutionary ideas and opinions which respond to the interests of the popular masses—the bearers of social progress, the moving force of history. Only under this condition can one speak about real freedom of conscience, in particular about freedom of speech, press, assembly, etc.

In short, Mr Voevodin explains that freedom of expression applies only to certain kinds of ideas. Like all official commentators, he argues that the Constitution itself stipulates such restrictions:

> . . . in guaranteeing to citizens freedom of speech, press, assembly, meetings and street processions and demonstrations the USSR Constitution demands that they be implemented ''in accordance with the interests of the working people with the goal of strengthening the socialist system''.

The author concludes:

> If someone uses these freedoms to the detriment of the Soviet people, and if their exercise does not facilitate the strengthening of the socialist system, then in accordance with the Constitution and the laws promulgated on its basis the Soviet Government and its competent organs are obliged not to allow such activity but to stop it. The person who commits serious violations of the aforementioned provision of the Constitution can, in accordance with the law, be held responsible before the courts.

It is the criminal law which lays down penalties for exceeding the limits of approved freedom of expression.

Amnesty International knows of more than 400 persons who were tried and sentenced to imprisonment or analogous punishment or confined to psychiatric hospitals on account of their non-violent exercise of their human rights during the period 1 June 1975–31 May 1979, the interval between the times of writing the first edition and the second edition of the Amnesty International report *Prisoners of Conscience in the USSR: Their Treatment and Conditions*.

At the time of writing, this figure is growing constantly as fresh information trickles out of the USSR. It is Amnesty International's experience that many prisoners of conscience become known only years after their arrest and trial or confinement to psychiatric hospitals.

This figure does not include all persons who are known to have been prisoners of conscience during the four years prior to the writing of the report. For one thing, it does not include the hundreds of people who are known to have been sentenced administratively to short terms of imprisonment. Second, this figure does not include the many hundreds of known persons who were prisoners of conscience during this four-year period but were sentenced prior to 1 June 1975.

The more than 400 persons known to have become prisoners of conscience during this four-year period do not include the large number who may be prisoners of conscience but on whose cases Amnesty International lacks sufficient information to categorize them as such.

Observers inside the USSR learn of prisoners of conscience for the most part only with difficulty. The official media are subject to complete government censorship and have mentioned only a tiny proportion of the prisoners of conscience known to Amnesty International from unofficial sources. The authorities also surround places of imprisonment and psychiatric confinement with great secrecy. In the past decade there have been efforts by some Soviet citizens to report human rights violations. However, these efforts have scarcely penetrated most parts of the country or most places of imprisonment.

As the present report shows, Soviet citizens who do obtain and circulate information about prisoners of conscience are themselves liable to imprisonment for precisely this activity, and whatever information has become available to Amnesty International has been obtained at considerable risk to the compilers and distributors.

For all these reasons, Amnesty International believes that the figures for known prisoners of conscience are far from complete.

## *Soviet Criminal Law: Background*

The Criminal law currently applicable in the USSR is set down in the criminal codes enacted in each of the country's 15 Union Republics in 1960 and 1961 on the basis of the Fundamentals of Criminal Legislation of the USSR and the Union Republics, which came into force in 1958.

Criminal procedural law is set down in the codes of criminal procedure which were enacted in each of the 15 Union Republics of the USSR after 1958, when the Fundamentals of Criminal Procedure of the USSR and the Union Republics came into force.

This report refers in detail primarily to the codes of the RSFSR (Russian Soviet Federated Socialist Republic), the largest of the Union Republics. Generally there is little difference in content between the codes of the different Union Republics.

The RSFSR Criminal Code came into force in 1960. The 1960 criminal code replaced criminal legislation that had been in existence since 1926. The 1926 code was devised in part as a class weapon in the fledgling Soviet state's years of struggle. It made a distinction between ordinary and "counter-revolutionary" (political) crimes and called for much stronger penalties for the latter.

Article 58 of the 1926 code provided blanket charges against anyone even remotely suspected of representing a threat to the survival of Bolshevik rule. Some provisions in the 1926 code made legal the arrest and sentencing of people who were known to have committed no crime. This legislation sprang from the primacy assigned to the interests of the state and to the survival of Bolshevik power. The law was an instrument of political power. Interpretation and application of its provisions were always subject to the political demands of the moment. The leading jurist A.A. Piontkovsky, writing in 1947, made it clear that, for political reasons, people could be sentenced under criminal law in the absence even of suspicion that they had committed a crime:

> Of course, sometimes for these or those considerations of a political nature
> it is necessary to apply compulsory measures to people who have not
> committed any crime but who on some basis or another (their past activity,
> their ties to a criminal environment, etc) are socially dangerous.

The 1926 criminal code was amended many times between 1929 and 1953, and in such a way as to make it increasingly repressive. The infamous Article 58, proscribing "counter-revolutionary crimes", was used to cover the arrest of countless people, often on no logical basis other than the convenience of the police organs. From 1934 until Joseph Stalin's death in 1953 a three-member special board of the NKVD (People's Commissariat of Internal Affairs) was empowered to arrest, investigate, try, sentence and execute sentence on people suspected of political opposition. The special board worked in secret in the absence of the accused and without need to consult any regularly-constituted court.

After Stalin's death in 1953 there was a strong reaction against the arbitrary terror from which no one had been secure. Various piecemeal reforms were undertaken until the new criminal legislation was formulated at the end of the 1950s. The 1960 Criminal Code represented a major transformation of the Soviet legal system.

The 1960 Criminal Code is not a "revolutionary" document—that is, it is not overtly intended as a weapon for one faction, party or class but as a law to be applied equally to everyone in Soviet society. One consequence of this is that the 1960 code does not explicitly distinguish between criminal and political offences. To do so would be to hint at the continuing existence of political opposition in the USSR, whereas according to official doctrine there is no social basis for such opposition.

Unlike its predecessors, the 1960 code stipulates that a person can be sentenced only if he or she has been tried in a court of law and proved guilty of an act specifically designated by law as a crime at the time of its commission. The 1960 Code of Criminal Procedure also contains many guarantees of the rights of the accused. For example, the revulsion against earlier practice is very clearly expressed in the prohibition of night-time interrogation. The code limits the types of crimes which the KGB (Committee of State Security) and MVD (Ministry of Internal Affairs) are empowered to investigate and stipulates that all investigations must be under the supervision of the Procuracy (a judicial agency that in law is accountable only to the Supreme Soviet). The crimes which the KGB can investigate are mostly to be found in the section of the Criminal Code titled "Especially Dangerous Crimes Against the State" (Articles 64-73). Many political prisoners have in recent years been convicted under articles in this section.

The role of the courts, their manner of functioning and their jurisdiction are laid down in another statute, the Law on Court Organization of the RSFSR, which came into effect in 1960.

The strong role of the Procuracy in assuring observance of legality is affirmed by the 1960 Criminal Code and the 1960 Code of Criminal Procedure. The Procuracy is a highly centralized organ, with the USSR Procurator General (since 1953, Roman Rudenko) appointed by and responsible only to the USSR Supreme Soviet. The Procurator General appoints all procurators at Union Republic level. In turn, the procurators of the Union Republics appoint the local, regional, city and district procurators. The officially-stated reason for this strong centralization is to free the Procuracy from the control of local organs and thus enable it to exercise an autonomous supervisory function. This independence of the procurators is required specifically in Article 168 of the USSR Constitution (1977).

The law (especially the 1955 Statute on Procuracy Supervision) gives the Procuracy considerable power of supervision of the execution of justice. The Procuracy can protest against any official order, instruction or decree which it considers to be in breach of the law. It can protest against the conduct of investigations and prosecution in criminal cases. In fact, the Procuracy itself conducts the investigation of most kinds of criminal cases. In all criminal investigations, the officers of the Procuracy, according to the law, must satisfy themselves that the law is being rigorously observed and "strictly watch out that not a single citizen is subjected to illegal or unfounded criminal prosecution or to any other unlawful restriction of rights". Finally, the Procuracy has broad supervisory rights over court procedures and decisions and over the operation of places of imprisonment.

Nonetheless, both the written Soviet law and its application are still subject to considerations of political "expediency" which often dictate that legal and constitutional principles must be sacrificed to current political goals.

## Freedom of Expression

The criminal codes of the Union Republics of the USSR contain in identical form two articles which explicitly circumscribe freedom of expression. In the RSFSR Criminal Code they are Article 70 and Article 190-1.

Article 70 states:

### Anti-Soviet Agitation and Propaganda

Agitation or propaganda carried on for the purpose of subverting or weakening the Soviet regime (*vlast*) or of committing particular, especially dangerous crimes against the state, or the circulation for the same purpose of slanderous fabrications which defame the Soviet state and social system, or the circulation or preparation or keeping, for the same purpose, of literature of such content, shall be punished by deprivation of freedom for a term of six months to seven years, with or without additional exile for a term of two to five years, or by exile for a term of two to five years.

The same actions committed by a person previously convicted of especially dangerous crimes against the state or committed in wartime shall be punished by deprivation of freedom for a term of three to 10 years, with or without additional exile for a term of two to five years.

The sense of this article is explained in some detail in the official Commentary to it.[4] There are official Commentaries to the legal codes in each branch of Soviet law. These Commentaries are official documents, written by eminent legal specialists. Their purpose is to make clear the elements of the text of each article of the given legal code and to explain how the article should be applied. The Commentaries, which are not readily available to most Soviet citizens, are indispensible reference works for practitioners of Soviet law. For example, the current *Commentary to the Criminal Code of the RSFSR*, published in 1971, "is meant for workers of the court and the Procuracy, for lawyers, for workers of the Ministry of Internal Affairs and for students and correspondence students of higher judicial institutions and intermediate level specialized courses."

The official Commentary to Article 70 states that the following actions constitute anti-Soviet agitation and propaganda:

  a) agitation or propaganda carried on for the purpose of undermining or weakening the Soviet regime;
  b) agitation or propaganda carried on for the purpose of committing particular, especially dangerous crimes against the state;
  c) disseminating, for the purpose of undermining or weakening the Soviet regime or with the purpose of committing particular, especially dangerous crimes against the state, slanderous fabrications which defame the Soviet state and social system;
  d) disseminating, for the same purpose, slanderous literature which defames the Soviet state and social system;
  e) preparing, for the same purposes, literature of the aforementioned character;
  f) storing, for the same purposes, literature of the aforementioned character.

The Commentary further elaborates that agitation and propaganda may be carried out orally or by circulating written materials or pictorial art. "Agitation" consists of disseminating materials of anti-Soviet character to a "small" group of people, while "propaganda" consists of disseminating such materials to a "larger" group of people.

Section 3 of the Commentary states:

Agitation or propaganda carried on for the purpose of undermining or weakening the Soviet regime—this is disseminating within a more or less sizeable circle of people opinions or ideas which communicate hatred towards the Soviet state or social system and an effort to overturn the Soviet regime, to renounce the conquests of the socialist revolution to the benefit of the restoration of capitalism and similar actions committed to the advantage of anti-socialist forces.

Section 5 states:

Distributing for the same purposes slanderous fabrications which defame the Soviet state and social system—this is passing on to other people by one means or another (verbally, by printed means, through pictures) information which is known not to correspond to reality and which is aimed at discrediting the Soviet regime, the Communist Party, Soviet democracy or socialist social relations to the advantage of anti-socialist forces.

These passages make clear that the purpose of this law is to make punishable by imprisonment the dissemination of ideas or information on the grounds that their dissemination is inimical to the established political order.

The Commentary to Article 70 includes stipulations which would have the ameliorating effects of at least restricting the application of Article 70 and requiring stringent standards of proof for convictions under it. Section 10 of the Commentary states:

Anti-Soviet agitation or propaganda is a crime committed with the direct intention and the special goal of undermining or weakening the Soviet regime or of committing particular, especially dangerous crimes against the state. *While committing the crime the culprit (vinovny) is aware* that it is with the aforementioned purpose that he is disseminating anti-Soviet ideas and opinions or slanderous fabrications which defame the Soviet state or social system, or *is conscious* that he is disseminating, preparing or storing literature of such content and that in this *he aspires* to the undermining or weakening of the Soviet regime or to the commission of particular, especially dangerous crimes against the state. (Emphasis added by Amnesty International.)

Thus, according to the Commentary, people can be convicted of anti-Soviet agitation and propaganda only if it can be proved that in disseminating any material it was their considered intention to undermine or weaken the Soviet state, or if it can be proved that at the time of their actions they knew that the material which they disseminated or stored contained slanderous falsehoods against the state.

In practice, these restricting clauses have not been observed by Soviet courts when dealing with cases of "anti-Soviet agitation and propaganda".

Similar to Article 70 is Article 190-1 of the RSFSR Criminal Code. This article states:

*Circulation of Fabrications Known to be False which Defame the Soviet State and Social System*

The systematic circulation in an oral form of fabrications known to be false which defame the Soviet state and social system and, likewise, the preparation or circulation in written, printed or any other form of works of such content shall be punished by deprivation of freedom for a term not exceeding three years, or by corrective tasks for a term not exceeding one year, or by a fine not exceeding 100 rubles.

According to the official Commentary to Article 190-1:

The crimes dealt with in Article 190-1 are distinguished from anti-Soviet agitation and propaganda (Article 70) by the absence in the guilty person of the goal of undermining or weakening the Soviet regime or the purpose of committing any particular, especially dangerous crimes against the state.

Both the text of Article 190-1 and the Commentary to it[5] are clear on the point that dissemination of opinion is not an offence under this article, and that only wilful and repeated dissemination of what the author or distributor knows to be false and slanderous of the Soviet state and social system may be punished under it.[6] The Commentary states:

Fabrications which are known to be false and which defame the Soviet state and social system are fabrications about purportedly true facts and circumstances which the culprit already knows do not correspond to reality when he disseminates such fabrications. The dissemination of fabrications which the person who disseminates them does not know to be untrue, and equally the expression of mistaken evaluations, judgments or suppositions, do not constitute the crime designated by Article 190-1.

Further:

The preparation or dissemination of works which express the negative attitude of the person who has prepared them toward Soviet reality, but which do not contain fabrications which are known to be false and are of the above-mentioned character, does not entail responsibility under Article 190-1.

In spite of the formal differences between Article 70 and Article 190-1, the authorities are equally liable to apply either article to any given case involving expression of opinion or information. In choosing which of these articles to apply in a given case, the authorities appear to be guided not, for example, by the existence or non-existence of an element of "anti-Soviet intent" in the case, but by considerations of how severe the punishment should be.

Article 70 carries a penalty of up to 12 years' imprisonment and exile for a first offender and up to 15 years' imprisonment and exile for a second offender. It is one of the most severe articles under which prisoners of conscience are likely to be convicted. By contrast, someone who had carried out the same actions but was charged under Article 190-1 would face a maximum of three years' imprisonment. (In a number of trials for "anti-Soviet agitation and propaganda" defence lawyers have pleaded—usually unsuccessfully—for the charges to be reduced to "dissemination of fabrications known to be false which defame the Soviet state and social system".) Amnesty International knows of no case in which someone convicted under Article 190-1 has been sentenced merely to "a fine not exceeding 100 rubles".

Hundreds of Soviet prisoners adopted by Amnesty International as prisoners of conscience have been sentenced to imprisonment under either Article 70 or Article 190-1. Amnesty International knows of approximately 100 people who have been tried and convicted under one or another of these articles during the four years (June 1975 to May 1979) since the first edition of this report was written. This figure does not include cases in which people were charged with these offences but officially ruled to be "non-accountable" because of mental illness and confined to psychiatric hospitals instead of being brought to a normal trial. The texts of the indictments or court verdicts in many of these cases are available to Amnesty International, as are detailed unofficial accounts of the charges and trials.

Participants in virtually all the various strains of dissent in the USSR have been tried and sentenced to imprisonment for either "anti-Soviet agitation and propaganda" or "dissemination of fabrications known to be false which defame the Soviet state and social system". People active in disseminating information about human rights violations in the USSR have been especially liable to such charges, since it is official policy to deny that such violations occur and to label such information as "slanderous". Members of minority nationalities who criticize the official nationalities policy or advocate greater autonomy or cultural rights for their national group have been accused of "slandering" nationalities policy, "sowing enmity" among the peoples of the USSR or showing "anti-Soviet intent" by advocating "bourgeois nationalist" views which could undermine and weaken the Soviet state system. In recent years Lithuanians, Latvians, Estonians, Georgians, Armenians, Moldavians, Russians, Crimean Tartars and—most frequently—Ukrainians have been tried on such charges and sentenced to imprisonment for expressing non-violent national views. This is in spite of the fact that Article 72 of the USSR Constitution (1977) proclaims that "each Union Republic of the USSR has the right freely to secede from the USSR".

Members of minority groups—particularly Soviet citizens of German origin—who have applied to emigrate have been convicted of "dissemination of fabrications known to be false which defame the Soviet state and social system", often because their accounts of their reasons for trying to emigrate have been ruled "slanderous". It is notable, however, that in recent years almost none of the Soviet Jews who have been imprisoned after applying to emigrate have been convicted under either of these explicitly political articles of criminal law. Although a number of Jewish would-be emigrants have been warned of possible prosecution for "anti-Soviet" activity, the authorities have almost invariably preferred ostensibly non-political charges or, in a number of cases, charges relating to refusal to serve in the armed forces. Sometimes members of religious minorities—especially Protestant groups—have been charged and tried under Article 70 or 190-1 in addition to articles relating specifically to religion because of their criticism of religious persecution.

A number of individuals have been imprisoned under these articles for individual complaints to the authorities or to others, without being involved in general advocacy of human rights or other public causes.

It is most exceptional in the cases known to Amnesty International for the use or advocacy of violence to figure in the charges brought under Articles 70 or 190-1 of the RSFSR Criminal Code.

The Soviet authorities regularly assert that trials under these articles do not involve punishment of people for their dissenting opinions and that the courts sentence people only for specific criminal offences. In fact, trials under these articles of law have the sole effect of punishing people for their exercise of their right to freedom of expression. Such trials are commonly characterized by violations of the legal requirements of Articles 70 and 190-1 as described above, in spite of the fact that even if these two articles were applied literally they would still have unconscionably broad application to people exercising their right to freedom of expression.

To understand how the substance of the law is violated in the trials known to have been conducted in cases of people charged under these articles it must be remembered that the articles themselves require proof that the subject's intention was to weaken or undermine the Soviet system (Article 70), or that he or she prepared, distributed or stored literature in the knowledge that it contained falsehoods slandering the Soviet system (both Articles 70 and 190-1). Defendants in such trials normally do not deny their responsibility for the literature in question, but nonetheless plead not guilty to the charge on the grounds that they did not have as their aim to undermine the Soviet system and that they believed at the time that the material was not false and slanderous. Soviet courts have not required the prosecution to establish proof of either of these necessary elements of the case; invariably the courts have convicted people accused under these articles without such proof. Furthermore, the courts have consistently refused to allow thorough examination in court of the literature specified in the charges.

The net effect is that virtually any unauthorized criticism of official actions or policy or distribution of information on "forbidden" subjects may lead to imprisonment.

The following are illustrations of cases under Articles 70 and 190-1 of the RSFSR Criminal Code. In almost all of these cases the complete texts of the indictment or court judgment is available outside the USSR.

Balys Gajauskas was tried by the Lithuanian Supreme Court in April 1978 and sentenced to 10 years' imprisonment and 5 years' internal exile for "anti-Soviet agitation and propaganda". He had been released from imprisonment in 1973 after serving a 25-year sentence for "counter-revolutionary activity" in the form of participation in Lithuanian resistance to Lithuania's becoming part of the USSR as a result of territorial changes brought about by the Second World War. After his release in 1973 Gajauskas was active in trying to help prisoners and their families, especially through a fund being operated for that purpose by Alexander Ginzburg, another former prisoner, who was subsequently sentenced to 8 years' imprisonment for such activity. According to the court judgment against Gajauskas in 1978 (a complete copy of the judgment is available outside the USSR), Gajauskas' offence consisted of "storing anti-Soviet literature" (principally volume 1 of Alexander Solzhenitsyn's book *GULag Archipelago*), storing and distributing literature relating to the Lithuanian partisan movement of the late 1940s and early 1950s and compiling lists of prisoners. Gajauskas denied that he had distributed Lithuanian partisan movement literature; it has been reported elsewhere that he collected such materials and that he intended to write a book on the subject. Most significant from a legal point of view is the fact that the court judgment includes no proof of the "false, slanderous" content of the literature listed in the charges against Gajauskas, and describes as proof of Gajauskas' "anti-Soviet intent" his alleged knowledge that these materials would be published abroad and used there "for anti-Soviet agitation and propaganda".

Another case is that of Sergei Kovalyov, one of several Soviet citizens sentenced to imprisonment on charges which included that of publicizing the case of Leonid Plyushch, a Ukrainian cyberneticist who was confined to a special psychiatric hospital between 1973 and 1976 after being arrested for "anti-Soviet agitation and propaganda". Others convicted for their statements on behalf of Plyushch have been Andrei Tverdokhlebov, Yury Orlov and Alexander Podrabinek. At the time of Kovalyov's trial in December 1975 there was already a large body of evidence showing not only that Leonid Plyushch was confined to a psychiatric hospital for writing *samizdat* (uncensored) materials on human rights themes rather than for authentic medical reasons but that his health was seriously undermined by ill-treatment with drugs. Plyushch was finally released in January 1976 in the midst of a massive international campaign which had recently culminated in public statements of concern by the French Communist Party. Although Soviet official media at the time said that Plyushch had "recovered" from his mental illness only shortly before his release, testimony from Plyushch himself and his family, as well as evidence given by psychiatrists from several countries who examined him immediately after his release, bore out the long-standing complaints that Plyushch was a victim of psychiatric abuse.

Nonetheless, in December 1975, only weeks before Plyushch's release, Kovalyov was tried for "anti-Soviet agitation and propaganda"; one of the main charges related to his complaints about Plyushch's mistreatment.[7] As in several other cases where complaints about Plyushch's treatment have formed the basis of charges of "slander", the authorities brought as a witness a doctor, L.A. Lyubarskaya, who was in charge of the ward at the special psychiatric hospital where Plyushch was being held. Dr Lyubarskaya testified that Plyushch was confined after being properly diagnosed as mentally ill. She also testified that Plyushch's conditions were "comfortable", that his drug treatment "had no side effects" and that Plyushch himself had not complained. From the unofficial transcript of the trial it is clear that Dr Lyubarskaya refused to answer a number of the questions which Kovalyov put to her in court and that the judge prevented any cross-examination of her testimony. The judge also refused Kovalyov's request that Plyushch's wife be called as a witness.

In summing up the case against Kovalyov the prosecutor stated that in the USSR "the confinement of healthy people in psychiatric hospitals is completely excluded". He went on:

> One could think, from some of the statements of the defendant and his questions to witnesses, that all his arguments on this subject consist of the subjective opinion of some individual people not competent in psychiatry, of some relatives of patients such as, for example, Plyushch's wife. . . .
> How can we characterize Kovalyov's position? I can find no other characterization than that it is slanderous. Only a slanderer can write that in our country psychiatry can be utilized for the punishment of objectionable people.
> Esteemed colleagues: reactionary bourgeois propaganda does not scruple. Its basic function is lies, slander, misinformation.

The other specific charges against Kovalyov related to various appeals by him on behalf of prisoners of conscience in the USSR; involvement in two *samizdat* human rights journals, *A Chronicle of Current Events* and the *Chronicle of the Lithuanian Catholic Church*; and involvement in an effort by another person to photocopy parts of Solzhenitsyn's *Gulag Archipelago*. The prosecution argued that this literature too was false and slanderous in describing human rights violations.

The prosecutor noted before closing his summary of the case against Kovalyov that "during the preliminary investigation the defendant stated that throughout his activity he did not have as his aim the undermining of the Soviet regime, and that the question of the strength or weakness of the regime was a matter of profound indifference to him". The prosecutor rejected the argument that Kovalyov's aim was "the defence of the rights of man and democratic freedoms" in the country. The prosecutor asked that Kovalyov be sentenced to 7 years' imprisonment and 5 years' internal exile, saying.

In deciding the question of the measure of punishment, one must take into account . . . the consequences of the crime which Kovalyov has committed; these consequences are in my opinion very grave. I have in mind the damage which has been done to the prestige of the Soviet Union in the international arena in the eyes of world public opinion. For the materials transmitted by Kovalyov have provided nourishment for bourgeois propaganda.

Kovalyov was found guilty and sentenced to a total of 10 years' imprisonment and exile.

The following cases are also typical of those in which Soviet citizens' expressed opinions have been arbitrarily labelled "slanderous".

Pavel Bashkirov, a museum worker from Siberia, was travelling to visit Andrei Tverdokhlebov, the secretary of Amnesty International's Moscow adoption group (who was serving a sentence of exile after having been convicted under Article 190-1), when he was searched by police officials and found to be in possession of two issues of *A Chronicle of Current Events*. Pavel Bashkirov was subsequently arrested and charged under Article 190-1. He was tried in September 1976 and convicted of distributing George Orwell's novel *1984*, a verbatim record of an officially-sponsored public meeting in 1966 at which Stalin was criticized and various *samizdat* works by and about Alexander Solzhenitsyn. He was sentenced to 18 months' imprisonment.

Heinrich Reimer and Lily Furman, two Soviet citizens of German origin, were also convicted of "anti-Soviet slander". Both were among the numerous Soviet Germans who had applied unsuccessfully for permission to emigrate to the Federal Republic of Germany; both had taken part in the movement of Soviet Germans to obtain the right to leave the country. In the summer of 1976 they were arrested. They were subsequently charged with writing appeals to Soviet and international authorities complaining that Soviet citizens of German origin were victims of discrimination and with circulating lists of Soviet Germans who wished to emigrate from the USSR. At their trial in Kazakhstan in September 1976, it was not proved that their complaints constituted "slanderous falsehoods" but both were found "guilty" and sentenced to terms of imprisonment: Heinrich Reimer to 3 years and Lily Furman to 18 months.

A further example of application of this legislation was the case of the poetess Yuliya Okulova (whose pen name is Yuliya Voznessenskaya). She was one of several Leningrad residents subjected to criminal investigation after slogans appeared on the walls of several public buildings in that city in 1976 calling, for example, for the freeing of the prisoner of conscience, Andrei Tverdokhlebov. She was eventually charged not with participation in the slogan-writing but with "systematically writing and distributing in written form fabrications known to be false which defame the Soviet state and social system". Among the documents named in the indictment was a collection of poems and drawings which, according to the official text of the indictment, "contained the deliberately false fabrication that freedom of speech, the press and creative art are absent in the USSR." Yuliya Okulova was tried at the end of 1976 and sentenced to 5 years' internal exile.

In both the Gajauskas and Kovalyov cases, as in many others, there was indication that the prosecution and courts are especially quick to identify "anti-Soviet intentions" in the dissemination of opinions and information which will arrive abroad and be used in publicity about human rights violations or other problems within the USSR. However, the courts have frequently convicted people of "agitation and propaganda" with "anti-Soviet intent" where the literature involved in the case was not at all known abroad. For example, Boris Monastyrsky was charged with "anti-Soviet agitation and propaganda" in 1976 while he was already serving a sentence of 3 years' imprisonment imposed on him in 1973 for "dissemination of fabrications known to be false which defame the Soviet state and social system". The "agitation and propaganda" in the new charge consisted of letters, complaints and poems which he had sent to various Soviet authorities and public agencies from his place of imprisonment. The text of the judgment of the Donetsk Regional Court in his case also cites as evidence of his guilt a letter written by him to his mother. Many of the letters listed in the court judgment did not even reach their addressees, having been confiscated by the censor in Monastyrsky's corrective labour colony. The court also ruled that he had committed "anti-Soviet agitation and propaganda" by showing some of his writings to fellow prisoners and communicating his "hostile fabrications" to them. Monastyrsky denied that his intention had been to weaken or undermine the Soviet system, but the court ruled that he had foreseen "that as a result of his agitation and propaganda the undermining or weakening of the Soviet regime was possible", and sentenced him to another 6 years' imprisonment.

Other prisoners of conscience who in recent years have been sentenced to imprisonment under Article 70 or Article 190-1 for letters and statements which they wrote while imprisoned include the Armenian Paruir Airikian and the Crimean Tartar spokesman Mustafa Dzhemilev.

In other cases people have been imprisoned under these articles for writing documents which they had shown to no one.

It is not uncommon for Soviet citizens to be prosecuted under one or other of these articles for letters they have addressed to Soviet government authorities. This is in spite of the fact that Article 58 of the USSR Constitution (1977) guarantees the right of Soviet citizens to lodge complaints against the actions of officials and state and public bodies.

In August 1978 a court in Stavropol territory (in the south of the RSFSR) sentenced the Russian worker, Nikolai Shatalov, to 18 months' imprisonment for "dissemination of fabrications known to be false which defame the Soviet state and social system". Shatalov and his family had been applying for permission to emigrate since at least 1976. His wife Tatyana was forcibly confined to a psychiatric hospital for four months in the autumn of 1976 after she visited the embassy of the United States of America in Moscow for advice regarding their application to emigrate. Their son Vasily was sentenced in March 1977 to 2 years' imprisonment for refusing to respond to call-up for obligatory military service. Nikolai Shatalov was subsequently arrested in August 1977. According to the official indictment against him, "the basis for opening a criminal case against Shatalov was a letter which N.P. Shatalov had written and mailed to the General Secretary of the Central Committee of the Communist Party of the Soviet Union, Comrade Brezhnev, which contained slanderous fabrications known to be false which defamed the Soviet state and social system". The indictment went on to mention other letters by Shatalov to the RSFSR Supreme Court and the USSR Procurator General.

According to the court judgment, the slander in the letters consisted of statements that human rights are systematically violated in the USSR and general criticism of the Soviet system of government. The indictment said that Shatalov had admitted sending the letters but defended himself on the grounds that he had not sent them with the goal of carrying out slander but had only expressed his opinions and criticized the existing situation. In finding him guilty and sentencing him to imprisonment the court rejected this defence.

Letters to friends have also counted as "dissemination" of "anti-Soviet slander", for example in the case of Yevgeny Buzinnikov, a worker who was sentenced to 3 years' imprisonment by a court in the Byelorussian SSR in 1978. In at least one case where the full text of the official indictment is available, that of the German would-be emigrant Erhard Abel in the Kazakhstan SSR in 1974, conversations in the presence only of the defendant's wife and children have counted as "anti-Soviet slander". Abel was sentenced to 3 years' imprisonment.

In most trials for "anti-Soviet agitation and propaganda" or "anti-Soviet slander" at least several writings or other statements by the accused person are cited as specific instances of the crime. However, this is not apparently an obligatory requirement of the courts, even in cases under Article 190-1, where the action must be "systematic" to constitute an offence. In 1978, when Alexander Podrabinek was tried under Article 190-1 and sentenced to 5 years' internal exile, only one statement by him was cited in the indictment: his *samizdat* book, *Punitive Medicine*, an account of abuses of psychiatry in the USSR. The Latvian painter and art historian Jurgis Skulme was tried under the same article in Riga in August 1977. In his case only one statement was mentioned in the court's judgment against him: a 12-page letter which he had written to someone abroad and which had come into the hands of the Soviet authorities. According to the court, the letter contained fabrications to the effect that there had recently been strikes and other protests by workers in Latvia. The court found Skulme guilty and sentenced him conditionally to 2½ years' imprisonment with "obligatory induction to work".[8] Although Skulme's sentence was made conditional, he was required to perform unfamiliar work under the direct supervision of the authorities in another town where he was required to live in dormitory conditions with other convicted prisoners.

In the cases under Article 70 and Article 190-1 known to Amnesty International a wide range of literature has been officially treated as "anti-Soviet" and "slanderous" activity. For the most part such literature has included criticism of some government practice or information about such practices, but this has not always been the case. Authorities have confiscated copies of the United Nations Universal Declaration of Human Rights from dissenters, and in at least one case—that of the worker Mikhail Kukobaka in the Byelorussian SSR in 1976—have described it as "anti-Soviet literature". In a number of cases material of literary or academic character which did not include criticism of Soviet practices has figured in charges of anti-Soviet agitation and propaganda or slander.

A number of Soviet human rights advocates have called for publication of an official legal act listing works officially regarded as anti-Soviet and subject to criminal prosecution. Occasionally, usually in *samizdat*, there appears the text of an official regulation calling for the removal of particular books from all book shops, libraries, etc. However, such documents do not constitute an "index" of forbidden literature.

The publication of such an official list, iniquitous as it might be, would help eliminate one vicious aspect of the law against "anti-Soviet agitation and propaganda": its vagueness, which lends itself to arbitrary application. It has been argued that even Soviet citizens who are well versed in their country's law cannot know what type of document, or what level of distribution of it, will entail criminal prosecution. Mikhail Kheifets, a Leningrad writer sentenced in 1974 to 6 years' imprisonment and exile for "anti-Soviet agitation and propaganda", stated after his trial that among other charges he had been accused of "disseminating" among a few friends "several brochures by various authors, among which were some sharply criticizing our country's present system and others hotly defending it, as well as some commonplace literary and publicistic essays of neutral content."

It is probable, however, that most Soviet citizens who possess or distribute (to however small a group of people) literature critical of official practices, or who utter such criticism to others, are aware that such actions may entail criminal prosecution. The lack of public guidelines for what constitutes prohibited literature does not in itself make imprisonment for expression of opinion possible; it merely enhances that possibility which is inherent in the laws against "anti-Soviet agitation and propaganda" and "anti-Soviet slander".

## Freedom of Association

Article 51 of the USSR Constitution (1977) states:

> In accordance with the aims of building communism, citizens of the USSR have the right to associate in public organizations that promote their political activity and initiative and satisfaction of their various interests.
>
> Public organizations are guaranteed conditions for successfully performing the functions defined in their rules.

Nonetheless it has happened consistently that citizens who have associated together for the advancement of aims which are at odds with official policy have not obtained official recognition but have been subjected to repressive measures including imprisonment. This has happened to a succession of groups established since the mid-1960s to publicize human rights violations within the country, other groups trying to advance the national and cultural rights of national minorities and various "new left" groups which have persistently sprung up in cities around the country since the mid-1950s. Autonomous groups which have tried—even on ostensibly non-controversial subjects—to work outside the officially-established network of public organizations have been subjected to the same treatment. A telling example of the severity with which the authorities treat such groups is the history of a group of invalids that set out in 1977 to lobby publicly for improved benefits and facilities for physically handicapped people in the USSR and for the creation of an officially-recognized public association for the protection of such people. The organizers of the group have been repeatedly harassed by the authorities and in December 1978 one of them, Valery Fefelov, a 29-year-old paraplegic, was warned by officials of possible criminal prosecution if the group continued its activity.

One article of criminal law which explicitly circumscribes freedom of association is Article 72 of the RSFSR Criminal Code, which states:

*Organizational Activity Directed toward Commission of Especially Dangerous Crimes Against the State and Also Participation in Anti-Soviet Organizations*

Organizational activity directed toward the preparation or commission of especially dangerous crimes against the state, or toward the creation of an organization which has as its purpose the commission of such crimes, or participation in an anti-Soviet organization, shall be punished in accordance with Articles 64-71 of the present code.

This charge has been brought against a number of dissenters over the years. In July 1978, for example, Viktoras Petkus, a member of the unofficial Helsinki monitoring group in Lithuania (see below), was tried on this and other charges and sentenced to 10 years' imprisonment and 5 years' internal exile. However, as far as is known to Amnesty International, the authorities have much more frequently charged members of disapproved-of groups under other articles of criminal law.

The following is a selection of examples from recent years of imprisonment of members of unauthorized groups.

Beginning in May 1976, five unofficial Helsinki monitoring groups were established in the USSR with the express purpose of monitoring Soviet implementation of the human rights provisions of the Final Act (1975) of the Conference on Security and Cooperation in Europe. Groups were established in Moscow and in the Ukrainian, Lithuanian, Georgian and Armenian republics. By 1978 a total of about 50 people had become members of these groups, of whom no less than 17 were arrested and tried in 1977 and 1978. Eight of them were sentenced to terms of imprisonment and exile of 10 years or more. The others were sentenced to lesser terms of imprisonment or, in two cases, to terms of exile. In 1979, six more members of the Helsinki monitoring groups were arrested: Victor Striltsev, Oles Berdnyk, Petro Sichko and his son Vasyl and Yury Litvin of the Ukrainian group and Edward Arutyunian of the Armenian group.

In January 1977 a small group of Soviet citizens established an unofficial "working commission" for the investigation of political abuses of psychiatry in the USSR. During the ensuing two years the group, employing the services of consultants with psychiatric and legal expertise, made public a large body of information on individual cases and common practices of wrongful confinement to psychiatric hospitals. During the same period two of its members, Felix Serebrov and Alexander Podrabinek, were sentenced to imprisonment or exile, while Alexander Podrabinek's brother Kirill Podrabinek, who was not a member of the group, was also sentenced to imprisonment—officials had told the Podrabinek brothers and their father that Kirill would be imprisoned if Alexander did not emigrate.

In Moscow in 1974 a group of Russian Orthodox believers, mostly young people, established a seminar to discuss religious and philosophical questions. Officials subsequently told participants that the seminar was "anti-Soviet". In July 1976 a member of the seminar, 25-year-old Alexander Argentov, was forcibly confined to a Moscow psychiatric hospital. In September 1976 another member, Edward Fedotov, was also confined to a psychiatric hospital. Both men were detained in this way for approximately two months. Some members persisted with the seminar. It eventually took on the title "Christian Seminar on Problems of Religious Rebirth" and in 1978 its members began to produce a *samizdat* journal called *The Community* (*Obshchina*). In late 1978 seminar participants Alexander Kuzkin and Sergei Yermolayev were detained. Kuzkin was confined to a psychiatric hospital, while Yermolayev and a friend of his, Igor Polyakov, who was not a member of the religious seminar, were charged with "hooliganism". After two months in detention Yermolayev was sent by a court to the Serbsky Institute of Forensic Psychiatry for examination while Polyakov remained in prison custody. In November 1978 Alexander Ogorodnikov, the principle spokesman for the group, was tried and sentenced to one year's imprisonment for "parasitism". Another member, Alexander Pushkin, was reported to have been confined to a psychiatric hospital in Abramtsevo, near Moscow, in the spring of 1979. Yet another participant in the seminar was reported to have been arrested in November 1977 in Ufa and sentenced to 6 months' imprisonment on charges of using improper identity papers.

In October 1975 in Estonia four Estonians and a Russian (Matti Kiirend, Kalju Mattik, Arvo Varato, Artem Yuskevich and Sergei Soldatov) were tried for "anti-Soviet agitation and propaganda" for participation in a group called the "Estonian Democratic Movement". No charges relating to violence were brought against them and the charges related only to literature discovered in their possession. The indictment accused the five men among other things of "soliciting the interference of the United Nations in Soviet affairs" in a memorandum to the United Nations General Assembly and a letter to the United Nations Secretary General. Four of them were sentenced to 5 and 6 years' imprisonment and the fifth to 3 years' imprisonment, suspended for 5 years.[9]

In November 1977 a group of unemployed workers told foreign correspondents in Moscow that they were establishing an independent trade union, which soon came to be called the "Association of Free Trade Unions of Workers in the USSR". Within a few months the group issued a number of lengthy documents, signed by up to 153 people, and the origins of the group became known in considerable detail. The declared object of the group's members was to protest against violations of their labour rights and to obtain recognition as a trade union independent of the country's established trade unions.

From the documentation issued by the group it is evident that its members had been acting collectively since May 1976 at the latest. They had met while waiting to submit individual complaints and petitions at various central governmental and party offices in Moscow. After they associated together they continued to submit their complaints only to Soviet authorities and did not, as far as is known, make public statements or approach the foreign press or established human rights groups. Nonetheless, even before they finally went public in late 1977, at least five of the group's members (Valentin Poplavsky, Vladimir Klebanov, Varvara Kucherenko, Yevgeny Nikolayev and Gennady Tsvyrkov) were detained by the authorities in separate incidents. Most of these were either sentenced to jail terms of 10 or 15 days or confined for relatively short periods in psychiatric hospitals, although Vladimir Klebanov, who later became known as the group's leader, was confined to a psychiatric hospital for two months after being detained in February 1977.

In the three months after the group made itself known publicly in November 1977 at least 10 of its members were detained. At least four people, Vladimir Klebanov, Yevgeny Nikolayev, Gavriil Yankov and Varvara Kucherenko, were confined to psychiatric hospitals. Klebanov was confined to psychiatric hospital from 19 to 28 December 1977 and then confined again on 7 February 1978, after which he was sent to Donetsk in the Ukrainian SSR where in June 1978 a court ordered that he be confined to a special psychiatric hospital. Yevgeny Nikolayev was confined to a Moscow psychiatric hospital from 15 February 1978 to 12 September 1978. Gavriil Yankov was confined to a Moscow psychiatric hospital from 2 January 1978 to 16 January 1978. He was detained again in March 1978 while he was visiting Nikolayev in his hospital and held in a psychiatric hospital until 11 October 1978.

Valentyn Poplavsky, who was arrested on 6 February 1978, was tried in May 1978 and sentenced to one year's imprisonment for "parasitism". Others in the group were held by the police, usually for a check of their identity papers, and, apparently released after being expelled from Moscow.

In October 1978 eight people issued a statement announcing the establishment of another independent trade union body, the Free Inter-Professional Union of Workers. The signatories stated that their goal was "the defence of its members in cases of violation of their rights in various spheres of their lives", and that the group intended "to examine the judicial basis of workers' complaints, bring these complaints to the attention of Soviet organizations, promote their speedy resolution and, in the event of a negative outcome, to give them wide publicity before the Soviet and international public". The founders of the group indicated that it had about 100 members.

On 13 October Vladimir Skvirsky, one of the eight signatories to the group's founding statement, was arrested and charged with "stealing books from a library". He was tried in May 1979 and sentenced to 5 years' exile. On 1 November 1978 Mark Morozov, a member of the group though not a signatory to the above-mentioned statement, was arrested and charged with "anti-Soviet agitation and propaganda". He was sentenced in June 1979 to 5 years' exile. On 4 November 1978 Valeriya Novodvorskaya, another signatory, was detained and confined to a psychiatric hospital. She was released in early February 1979. On 20 March 1978 Lev Volokhonsky, also a signatory, was arrested in Leningrad and charged with "anti-Soviet slander". He was sentenced in June 1979 to 2 years' imprisonment.

Armenian Helsinki monitor
Paruir Airikian

Crimean Tatar spokesman
Mustafa Dzhemilev

Lithuanian prisoners of conscience
Balys Gayauskas and wife

Sergei Kovalyov

Levko Lukyanenko with wife and child, after his release from 15 years' imprisonment in 1976.

Baptist pastor Peter Peters

Seventh Day Adventist leader Vladimir Shelkov.

Lev Volokhonsky

German would-be emigrant Lily
Furman

Jewish would-be emigrant Amner
Zavurov while in a camp

Mikhail Kheifets

Germans from Estonia demonstrating
outside the FRG Embassy in early 1974

Baptist conscientious objector
Anatoly Koplik

Ukrainian prisoners of conscience
Irina Stasiv-Kalynets and Ihor Kalynets

Ukrainian prisoners of conscience
Vasyl Stus (l.) and Ivan Svetlichny

Alexander (left) and Kirill Podrabinek

The arrest of Alexander Podrabinek in Moscow in April 1977. He was sentenced to 15 days' administrative detention. In 1978 he was arrested again, tried and sentenced to five years' exile

Alexander Bolonkin in camp
uniform

Jewish would-be emigrant Joseph
Begun

Baptist prisoners of conscience Ludmilla (left) and Larissa Zaitseva

Released Helsinki monitor Pyotr Vins (l.) with his father, Baptist leader Georgy Vins, who was serving 10 years' imprisonment and exile

Ukrainian Helsinki monitor Oles Berdnyk

Alexander Ginzburg with his children before his arrest in 1977

*Freedom of Religion*

All religious groups in the USSR live under important restrictions imposed by the state, which is committed to the withering away of religion.

Throughout the 1960s and 1970s a very considerable proportion of known prisoners of conscience in the USSR have been religious believers. Although Soviet law closely restricts organized religious activity and provides for the imprisonment of religious believers explicitly for their religious activity, in recent years members of only several denominations are known to have been imprisoned under criminal laws dealing specifically with religion. Prisoners of conscience from most religious denominations have been prosecuted under broader provisions of those laws described elsewhere in this chapter and punished with psychiatric measures.

Thus, a number of members of the movement for human rights in the USSR are Russian Orthodox believers, and may have been motivated in their activities partly by their religious convictions, but they have been imprisoned for "anti-Soviet agitation and propaganda" or "anti-Soviet slander", as in the cases of Victor Khaustov, Gavriil Superfin, Andrei Tverdokhlebov and Alexander Ginzburg.

Some religious believers have been imprisoned for activities in which their religious belief was associated with broader protests within their national group. Father Vasyl Romanyuk, a Ukrainian priest of the Orthodox Church, was among scores of Ukrainian intellectuals imprisoned in 1972 in an official crackdown on Ukrainian dissent on cultural and human rights issues. He was sentenced to 10 years' imprisonment and exile for "anti-Soviet agitation and propaganda". Among Lithuanian Roman Catholic prisoners of conscience have been people sentenced to imprisonment since the mid-1970s for their involvement with a *samizdat* journal called the *Chronicle of the Lithuanian Roman Catholic Church*, which catalogues official harassment and disruption of clergy and believers of that faith. Among these were Petras Plumpa-Pluira, Povilas Petronis, Niole Sadunaite, Vladas Lapienis, Jonas Matulionis and Ona Pranskunaite. Vladimir Osipov, a "Slavophile" advocate of revival of the Russian Orthodox Church and of Russian national traditions, was sentenced in September 1975 to 8 years' imprisonment for "anti-Soviet agitation and propaganda" in the form of a journal he published in *samizdat*. Mustafa Dzhemilev, Reshat Dzhemilev and other Crimean Tartar prisoners of conscience are known to be adherents of Islam. Some of the imprisoned members of the Armenian and Georgian Helsinki monitoring groups such as Deacon Robert Nazaryan and Zviad Gamsakhurdia are active members of the Armenian Apostolic Church and Georgian Orthodox Church.

It is common for Russian Orthodox religious believers to be confined to psychiatric hospitals and to be told by government officials and psychiatrists that religious belief is a symptom of mental illness. Of six members of an Orthodox religious seminar mentioned above who were arrested between 1976 and 1979, four were confined to psychiatric hospitals. Other Orthodox believers who have in recent years been confined to psychiatric hospitals in connection with their religious beliefs and behaviour include Ivan Akinkin, Father Lev Konin, Valeriya Makeyeva, Valery Timokhin, Vladimir Veretennikov and Father Mikhail

Vorozhbit.

The True Orthodox Christians and the True Orthodox Church are two groups of religious believers whose members have been imprisoned directly for their religious beliefs but under articles of criminal law which do not deal exclusively with religion. Both are fundamentalist offshoots of the Russian Orthodox Church. Members of these churches do not recognize the secular authority of the Soviet state and are officially regarded as violating the law. According to both official and unofficial sources, the True Orthodox Christians and the True Orthodox Church were severely repressed during the Stalin period, but in recent years up until 1977 only fleeting references were made in *samizdat* and other sources to remaining individual prisoners from these groups, including Mikhail Yershov (born in 1911), a leading monk in the True Orthodox Christian Church who had spent more than 40 years in imprisonment for his religious activities by the time of his reported death in a Mordovian camp in 1974; Vasyly Kalinin, another monk who has spent decades in imprisonment; and Gregory Sekach, reported by a Soviet newspaper to have been sentenced in Georgia in 1976 to 4 years' imprisonment for leading a network of "underground" True Orthodox Church monasteries which had been active for 18 years and had used religion to "struggle with Soviet reality".

*Samizdat* reports and appeals from 1974 until 1977 brought to light the largest known group of imprisoned members of the True Orthodox Church. This consisted of 11 women, mostly elderly and mainly from Vladimir region (to the east of Moscow) who were serving sentences for "anti-Soviet agitation and propaganda". Most had been previously sentenced for the same offence and were serving sentences of more than 10 years' imprisonment and exile. According to the available information, their offence consisted of actions such as leaving notes in Orthodox churches calling on believers not to cooperate with the authorities, sending similar notes through the mail and living without passports or registration of residence (see below "Freedom of Movement"). One of the 11 women, Raisa Ivanovna, is reported to have died in the Kazan Special Psychiatric Hospital in or before 1977.

Over the years, imprisonment of members of the Uniate Catholic Church in the Ukraine and of Jehovah's Witnesses (both of which are officially regarded as illegal), has continued. In 1979 at least 25 Uniate believers and about 10 Jehovah's Witnesses were believed to be imprisoned for their religious activities, although these figures seem to be incomplete because of the general lack of information circulating in *samizdat* about these groups.

In recent years articles of criminal law dealing explicitly with religious activity have been applied for the most part to members of several Protestant denominations, in particular the Baptists, Pentecostalists and Seventh Day Adventists, as far as is known to Amnesty International. More than 1,000 members of the dissenting wing of the Evangelical Christians and Baptists, referred to in this report as "Baptists", are known to have been prisoners of conscience during the 1960s and 1970s. Fewer Pentecostalists and Seventh Day Adventists are known to have been prisoners of conscience during the same period.

Because the criminal laws dealing explicitly with religion are applied most directly to adherents of these denominations, it is useful to examine the Soviet law on religion with particular reference to these categories of prisoners of conscience.

The USSR Constitution (1977) states in Article 52:

Citizens of the USSR are guaranteed *freedom of conscience*, that is, the right to profess or not to profess any religion, and *to conduct religious worship or atheistic propaganda*. (Emphasis added by Amnesty International.)

This article supplies the broad framework for the country's other laws and official regulations regarding religious believers. It proclaims the right to conduct atheist propaganda but does not proclaim the right to conduct "religious propaganda", or what believers would regard as preaching and teaching religious beliefs—a central requirement of many religions and a form of exercise of freedom of expression.

Within this restrictive constitutional context religious behaviour in the USSR is governed by other laws and government pronouncements referred to broadly as the "legislation on cults". The basic published laws on religion are the decree "On the Separation of Church and State and of School and Church" (23 January 1918) and the decree "On Religious Associations" (8 April 1929, reissued in amended form on 23 June 1975). Both of these laws are still in force.[10]

The 1918 decree "On the Separation of Church and State and of School and Church" (signed by Lenin) ended previously existing special relationships between the Orthodox Church and the state and removed many previous rights of churches, most notably the right of a church to own property. At the same time, it proclaimed an end to restrictions on the rights of conscience of any religious group. Article 2 states that:

It shall be prohibited to issue any local by-laws or regulations restricting or limiting freedom of conscience, or establishing privileges or preferential rights of any kind based on the religious creed of citizens.

Article 3 states:

Every citizen may profess any religious belief, or profess no belief at all. All restrictions of rights incurred by professing one or another religious belief, or by professing no belief at all, are cancelled and void.

These proclamations of believers' and non-believers' rights were further strengthened by the decree's injunction: "All reference to professing or non-professing of religious creeds by citizens shall be expunged from all official documents." (Lenin's draft text of this decree was prefaced by the words: "Religion is the private affair of each citizen of the Russian Republic".) Numerous other statements by him, which are regularly quoted in official Soviet media, denied that religion was a private matter and called for "struggle" with it.)

Members of the Baptist, Pentecostalist and Seventh Day Adventist religious communities in the USSR frequently cite these passages of the 1918 decree in defence of their religious rights. However, other laws were published after 1928 which nullified the apparently liberal intentions of the above-quoted passages from the 1918 decree. Most prominent among these is the 1929 RSFSR decree "On Religious Associations". This decree was amended in 1975 by the Presidium of the RSFSR Supreme Soviet. Religious believers assert that the 1975 amendments place more restrictions upon their rights than did the original decree of 1929.

The decree "On Religious Associations" restricts in many ways Soviet believers' freedom of conscience. The following are some of its salient points:

- Article 2 states that all religious congregations must be registered with the Council for Religious Affairs, a state agency attached to the USSR Council of Ministers. Article 4 stipulates that no congregation of believers may begin its activity until the Council for Religious Affairs at federal level has decided whether to register the congregation.

- The congregation must obtain permission from the local Soviet for use of a prayer building and for general meetings of the congregation, although according to Article 12 specific permission is not needed for holding "prayer meetings".

- Each congregation must elect a representative committee or person to manage its affairs and represent it externally. According to Article 13, elections of these representatives must be "by open voting". Article 14 adds that the government's Council For Religious Affairs has the right to remove any person from among the congregation's elected representatives.

- Congregations are forbidden to create mutual credit societies and to give financial support to members of the congregation. Furthermore, congregations are forbidden "to organize special gatherings of children, young people or women for prayer or other purposes, to organize Bible meetings, literature meetings, handicraft meetings, work meetings or meetings for religious study, to organize groups, circles or departments, to organize excursions or children's facilities, to open libraries or reading rooms or to organize sanatoria or medical assistance".

- According to Article 16, "only books necessary for the conduct of the particular cult may be kept in the prayer building or premises".

- A clergyman of a particular congregation may carry out religious work only in the locality of the congregation and its prayer house.

- Other articles regulate congregations' obligations regarding property. In this connection Article 29 states that local representatives of the Council for Religious Affairs and the local Soviet must be given "unhindered" access to the prayer house for inspection purposes. Such access must be given to these government officials at any time except when religious rites are being conducted.

- The Council for Religious Affairs, may, at the request of local government authorities, order the closing of a congregations's prayer house, if the premises are needed for other state or public uses.

- A congregation may have its registration cancelled if it violates "the legislation on cults".

- Article 58 states that no religious rites may be conducted in state, public or cooperative institutions and enterprises. Exceptions are made with regard to seriously ill people who are in hospitals or places of imprisonment, for "especially isolated places" and for cemetaries and crematoria. In Amnesty International's experience clergy are never permitted to visit ill prisoners.

According to Article 59 religious processions and religious rites may be conducted in the open air or in private homes only with the special permission of the local government authorities, which must be obtained on each occasion. A congregation which wishes to obtain such permission for a procession or ceremony in the open air or in a private home must apply for permission two weeks in advance.

The decree "On Religious Associations" impinges deeply on the activity of religious congregations and on believers' freedom of conscience and provides many ways for the state authorities to interfere in or stop altogether the activity of any congregation. Most of the Baptist prisoners of conscience for whom Amnesty International has worked, and many of the Pentecostalists and Adventists, are members of congregations which have refused to register under the conditions laid down by this decree or have had their applications for registration refused by the authorities.

The Soviet authorities have stated publicly that religious communities which are not registered are illegal and may not exercise their rights of freedom of conscience. The following is the text of a letter written in 1976 by a representative of the government's Council for Religious Affairs to a Baptist congregation in Azerbaidzhan which had complained of arrests of members of the congregation, disruption of the congregation's religious services, including funerals and marriages, and denial of electricity and water supplies to believers' homes:

*In answer to the complaints you sent to the relevant authorities, we hereby inform you:*

*In accordance with Soviet law, religious communities and groups of believers are permitted to conduct their activities only after registration of the community or group of believers with Soviet organs on the basis of recognition and fulfilment of all the requirements of the law concerning religion. Your community is not registered and has not complied with the laws on religion but has ignored their requirements, and therefore the local bodies have been correct in demanding that the members of the community observe the law which forbids the conduct of religious meetings by an unregistered community.*

*Your community has never asked to be registered on the basis of recognition of Soviet legislation concerning religious cults. It has done just the opposite: it has always supported and continues to support malicious lawbreakers and extremist elements of the so-called "Council of Churches" and by virtue of this behaviour it has deprived itself of the right to function officially. As regards the bringing of criminal charges against and imposition of fines on individuals, we would like to point out that these persons are held criminally responsible not for their faith, as you incorrectly stated, but for gross violation of the Soviet law concerning religious cults.*

*We consider that your complaints are unfounded, since in order to function officially your community must first of all register with the Soviet organs on the basis of agreement to fulfil the Soviet laws on religious cults.*

*We regard as correct the actions of comrade Nikitin, who ordered that a meeting should not be held without the community being registered with Soviet organs, and we are grateful to him for his control over the observance of the law on cults.*

(signed)
Delegate for the Council for
Religious Affairs
A. Akhov

Other official statements make clear what is meant by "violation of the Soviet law concerning religious cults". In *Znaniye*, an official newspaper in the Kirghiz SSR, a local party official wrote on 29 November 1977 with regard to local Baptist congregations:

Some of them would like to have freedom to make religious propaganda in public places without restriction, to have an end to atheist education in the schools and to be able freely to teach religion to children. But the legislation allows the teaching of religion only in a private manner, that is, when it is conducted within a family of believers by the parents. And no more. Some of the followers of the Council of Churches of Evangelical Christians and Baptists would even like to have their own printing presses. In other words, the sectarians would like to put themselves outside the control of the state. It is perfectly clear that these illegal claims conflict with the law, and indeed have nothing in common with the satisfaction of religious needs.

The author said that local Baptists had been warned to stop their "illegal activities".

However there continue to take place illegal gatherings in private homes, to which minors are drawn. Gatherings are organized in unauthorized places. For example, in June this year a prayer meeting was conducted in a forest near the village of Nikol-Pol with the presence of young people from all congregations in the district.

The criminal sanctions most directly applicable to such "illegal" exercise of freedom of expression and association are provided by Articles 142 and 227 of the RSFSR Criminal Code. Similar articles are included in the criminal codes of the country's 14 other Union Republics. The majority of Baptist prisoners of conscience known to Amnesty International and many of the known prisoners of conscience from among the Pentecostalist and Adventists have been imprisoned under these articles of criminal law.

Article 142 states:

The violation of laws on the separation of church and state and of school and church shall be punished by corrective tasks for a term not exceeding one year or by a fine not exceeding 50 rubles.

The same acts committed by a person previously convicted of violation of laws on the separation of church and state and of school and church, as well as organizational activity directed to the commission of such acts, shall be punished by deprivation of freedom for a term not exceeding three years.

In 1966 the Presidium of the RSFSR Supreme Soviet (and similarly every other Union Republic's Supreme Soviet) issued a decree (which was still in force in 1979) listing the actions which constitute a crime under Article 142. These are:

1. Compulsory exaction of contributions and taxes for the benefit of religious organizations or ministers of the cult.

2. Mass dissemination, or preparing for the purpose of mass dissemination, of appeals, letters, tracts or other documents that urge non-observance of legislation on religious cults. (The official Commentary to Article 142 of the RSFSR Criminal Code explains that circulating such documents from hand to hand, through the post, by pasting them up "and so on" constitutes a criminal offence under this article.)[11]

3. Commission of deceptive actions for the purpose of arousing religious superstitions among the masses of the population. (The official Commentary adds that by "deceptive actions" is meant "staging of miracles", "circulating various rumours with the purpose of arousing superstitions among the populace", etc.)

4. Organization or conduct of religious meetings, processions and other religious ceremonies that violate the social order. (According to the official Commentary, the acts thus made criminal are "as a rule, the organization or conduct of religious ceremonies which take place in public places and are connected with violation of the rules of conduct established for such places; for example, the conduct of prayer meetings in parks, squares and other places of mass leisure of the workers, in open spaces and streets of cities, workers' settlements and villages, and in state, public or cooperative institutions or enterprises". Group singing in public places is prohibited, as are processions which disturb traffic or "cause citizens' indignation". The Commentary also explains that religious ceremonies conducted outside a prayer house can constitute a criminal violation of public order even when they are conducted with official permission.)

5. Organization or systematic conduct of studies of religion for the instruction of minors in violation of rules established by legislation. (This charge has most frequently been brought against Baptist believers. The official Commentary explains that the only religious instruction permitted for children is that carried on in religious classes opened "in the established order" and that given by parents to their own children. Although the Commentary refers the reader to Article 9 of the 1918 decree "On the

Separation of the Church and State and of the School and Church" and Article 18 of the 1929 (amended in 1975) decree "On Religious Associations", neither of those documents indicates what might be "the established order" for the opening of religious classes. Given the total absence of religious schools for children, and the legal prohibition (in Article 4 of the Fundamentals of Legislation of the USSR and the Union Republics on Education, 1973) of religious instruction in the country's public schools, religious believers are left to their own devices in the religious upbringing of their children. Since, as the Commentary says, the only permissible teaching of religion to children is that by parents to their own children, it is a criminal act for anyone to give religious lessons to a group of children which includes the children of other believers.)

6. Denial of work to a citizen or refusal to accept him in an educational institution, discharge from work or exclusion from an educational institution, deprivation of citizens' privileges and immunities established by law, or other material limitations of the rights of citizens on the basis of their attitude toward religion. (The Commentary specifies that an official can be held criminally responsible for dismissing a believer only if it is proved beyond a doubt that the dismissal was on account of the believer's religious convictions and not for any other reason. Religious believers have reported numerous cases of employment and educational discrimination against believers with no criminal prosecution of the culprits.)

Article 227 of the RSFSR Criminal Code states:

The organizing or directing of a group, the activity of which, carried on under the appearance of preaching religious beliefs and performing religious ceremonies, is connected with the causing of harm to citizens' health or with any other infringements of the person and rights of citizens, or with the inducing of citizens to refuse social activity or performance of civic duties, or with the drawing of minors into such a group, shall be punished by deprivation of freedom for a term not exceeding five years or by exile for a similar term with or without confiscation of property.

   The active participation in the activity of a group specified in paragraph one of the present article, or the systematic propaganda directed at the commission of acts specified therein, shall be punished by deprivation of freedom for a term not exceeding three years, or by exile for the same term, or by corrective tasks for a term not exceeding one year.

The official Commentary to this article [12] opens by saying that when applying this article judicial officials must first establish whether the given religious group is officially registered or not. It specifies that the sects usually involved in prosecution are "Pentecostalists and Jehovah's Witnesses". The Commentary also states that the phrase "under the appearance of performing religious ceremonies" does not mean that the only people who are envisaged by this article are those who merely pretend to be acting from religious motivations; on the contrary, it says, the crime does not cease to be a crime simply because the person guilty of it was doing what was essential to his or her religious beliefs.

The Commentary lists some of the forms of "infringement of the person and rights of citizens" which are envisaged by Article 227: among them are physical or mental damage as a consequence of religious hysteria or self-mortification, slander, insults, illegal imprisonment, threats, perverted actions or rape and prevention of citizens from exercising their rights to work, study or to be elected as a deputy of a Soviet.

The Commentary also states that inciting citizens not to take part in public organizations or to serve in the armed forces constitutes a violation of this provision. The "incitement" may take the form of "appeals, persuasion, promises of any sort of reward, threats, application of church penalties or any other methods of influence, including physical ones". The mere act of incitement is a crime, regardless of whether the subject of the incitement actually refused to take part in the social activity referred to, the Commentary states.

Although some of the actions mentioned in the Commentary to Article 227 might well cover violations of individuals' rights and well-being, the article has a much broader application and extends to ordinary religious activity. For example, a clergyman or ordinary believer who advises religious believers that their children should not enter the "Pioneers" or the Communist Youth League (*Komsomol*)—youth organizations sponsored by the Communist Party of the Soviet Union and whose members are taught militant atheism—is liable to imprisonment under Article 227. Similarly, any clergyman or believer who advocates conscientious objection to military service to a member of his congregation who is of age to be called up to the armed forces is liable to prosecution under this article.

It is notable that neither the article itself nor the official Commentary to it requires any complaints from the supposedly injured people in order to bring a prosecution under this article. It is the state authorities who take the initiative to decide that the believers have had their "person and rights" violated. In many cases known to Amnesty International congregation members have vigorously appealed against the imprisonment of their clergyman under Article 227, but to no avail.

According to Soviet law, it is the function of the Council for Religious Affairs to ensure that all laws on religion are observed by officials and believers alike and that believers' rights are respected. The Council for Religious Affairs is attached to the USSR Council of Ministers and has representatives at Union Republic level and below, down to the district level. Among its other functions is to decide on the registration or closure of religious congregations.

The Council for Religious Affairs, which is headed by Vladimir Kuroyedev, consistently denies that religious believers' freedom of conscience is violated and asserts that imprisoned religious believers have been imprisoned not for their beliefs but because of criminal actions on their part.

Members of registered congregations of Evangelical Christians and Baptists and members of registered Pentecostalist congregations are enrolled in an officially-recognized religious body called the All-Union Council of Evangelical Christians and Baptists. This union was created in 1944 by the merger of the Evangelical Christians and the Baptists, and was subsequently enlarged when some Pentecostalists and then some Mennonites joined it. Adventists who are in registered congregations also enjoy a measure of official tolerance so long as they abide by official regulations regarding religious practice.

Many Evangelical Christians and Baptists, Pentecostalists and Adventists, however, belong to congregations which do not have official registration. In numerous cases their congregations have sought registration but have been denied it because the authorities decided that the members or leaders of the congregation would not adhere to the official restrictions on their religious activity, particularly on their freedom to choose their own church leaders, bring their children up according to their own religious convictions and openly preach their beliefs. In other cases members of these denominations have for the same reason not sought registration. Within each of these religious communities there is then a "schism" between those prepared to accept official restrictions and involvement in their religious affairs and those who are not prepared to do so. Indicative of this was a report in January 1978 from a group of Seventh Day Adventists in Kharkov. They stated that they had left a local registered Adventist congregation because it was dominated by state influence, and that subsequently the local representative of the Council for Religious Affairs had told the pastor of the registered congregation: "Give us a list of the names of the believers who left, otherwise we'll close your prayer house".

The "dissenting" wing of the Evangelical Christians and Baptists is led by the Council of Churches of Evangelical Christians and Baptists. This body, set up in the mid-1960s, is not officially recognized and many of its leaders have been imprisoned. One of these, Georgy Vins, the elected Secretary of the Council of Churches, was arrested in 1974 after a period in hiding. He was sentenced in 1975 to 5 years' imprisonment and 5 years in exile for "violating the laws on separation of church and state and of school and church", "infringement of person and rights of citizens under the appearance of performing religious ceremonies" and "anti-Soviet slander". He was among five prisoners released in April 1979 before the expiry of their sentences and sent to the United States of America in exchange for the release of two Soviet citizens serving prison sentences there after being convicted of espionage.

The Adventist dissenters adhere to the All-Union Church of True and Independent Seventh Day Adventists, which was formed during the 1920s. Its leaders during the Stalin period died while imprisoned. The present leader, 84-year-old Vladimir Shelkov, spent 23 years in imprisonment prior to 1967, when he went into hiding. He was arrested again in March 1978 and subsequently sentenced to 5 years' imprisonment. Four other Seventh Day Adventists were sentenced to imprisonment at the same trial, the sentence of one of them being suspended. At least six other Adventists were arrested in connection with Shelkov's arrest. All either had been tried and sentenced to imprisonment or were awaiting trial by the time of writing (mid-1979).

In the absence of official statistics it is not possible to know the number of members of unregistered congregations, but it is estimated that at least several hundred thousand Baptists, Pentecostalists and Adventists are members of unregistered congregations.

All members of unregistered congregations are in an "illegal" situation. According to the decree "On Religious Associations" unregistered congregations do not have the right to exist. They have no right to buy or rent prayer houses. Many congregations have built their own prayer houses with their own funds and labour, and in hundreds of known cases these have been demolished or confiscated by the authorities, often amid scenes of violence. In the absence of prayer houses, unregistered congregations frequently hold their prayer meetings in open places (particularly forests) or in private homes. Such meetings are constantly being broken up by the authorities, again often by violent and humiliating methods.

The form of official repression most condemned by dissenting religious believers in the USSR is deprivation of parental rights. Article 19 of the Fundamentals of Legislation of the USSR and the Union Republics on Marriage and the Family allows the country's courts, "following an appropriate statement made by governmental or non-governmental organizations", to deprive parents of their parental rights if it is established that they have "neglected their duties" in bringing up their children. Among the duties which, according to the same law, parents have towards their children is to "educate them in the spirit of the moral code of the builder of communism". Religious believers, being at odds with the Communist Party's atheist program and in many cases with the country's legislation on religious cults, are vulnerable to application of this provision of the law. Numerous cases have been reported over the years in which Baptists, Pentecostalists and Adventists have been deprived of their parental rights and have had some or all of their children taken into care of the state. (In some cases children are known to have gone into hiding to avoid being taken away from their parents.) In a number of cases this law has been applied against believers who were already charged with "violation of the laws on separation of church and state and of school and church" or other offences, so that the believers have been sentenced both to imprisonment and removal of their children.

Apart from imprisonment under criminal law and deprivation of parental rights, believers who "violate the legislation on religious cults" have routinely been subjected to administrative penalties in the form of fines under a decree "Responsibility for Violation of the Legislation on Religious Cults", issued by the Supreme Soviet Presidium of each Union Republic in 1966.

More is known about the recent history of imprisonment of Baptists than about imprisonment of either Pentecostalists or Seventh Day Adventists. This is mainly because the dissenting Baptists have produced and distributed a great deal of *samizdat* literature about their conditions. Particularly significant in this respect was the formation in 1964 of a body called the Council of Relatives of Imprisoned Evangelical Christians and Baptists, which reports cases of imprisonment of Baptists for exercising their freedom of conscience. The Council of Relatives regularly produces lists of Baptist prisoners of conscience as well as a periodic *Bulletin* containing detailed background information on individual cases. More than 60 issues of this publication, usually running to 35 or 40 pages each, had been produced by 1979.

Only since the mid-1970s has detailed information begun to emerge from the

USSR about the imprisonment of Pentecostalists. The Pentecostalists have begun to produce and distribute such information in connection with two developments in particular: the development of a major emigration movement since the mid-1970s involving thousands of members of the denomination, and the creation of working contacts with the Moscow Helsinki monitoring group, which was formed in 1976 and which has collected information about violations of Pentecostalists' rights and made such information public. Nonetheless information on imprisonment of Pentecostalists remains scant and diffuse. This is generally true of the dissenting Seventh Day Adventists as well.

The difficulty in knowing comprehensively about cases of imprisonment of Pentecostalists and Adventists is highlighted by a report which appeared in issue 41 (3 August 1976) of *A Chronicle of Current Events*. The report listed 17 Pentecostalists who were imprisoned in a corrective labour colony in Vinnitsa region in the Ukraine. No other information on these prisoners has been forthcoming from any source, except one statement by a Ukrainian Pentecostalist who said that all 17 were imprisoned for exercising their religious rights.

Between June 1975 and June 1979 at least 68 dissenting Baptists, Pentecostalists and Seventh Day Adventists were sentenced to imprisonment as a direct result of their religious activity. This figure does not include people imprisoned for up to several months and then released without being tried, people arrested and still awaiting trial at the time of writing (mid-1979), the numerous cases of people sentenced administratively to jail terms of 10 to 15 days or those confined forcibly to psychiatric hospitals.

Most Baptist prisoners of conscience have been convicted under Articles 142 and 227 of the RSFSR Criminal Code (see above). Frequently Baptists—whether pastors or laity, and often including young people—have been convicted specifically of organizing local Sunday school classes for children, or for having permitted children to attend religious services. Those sentenced to imprisonment for exactly such behaviour during the past four years include Yekaterina Barin, Raisa Goncharova, Yakov Jantsen, Ivan Pauls and Ivan Schlecht.

Pentecostalists and Seventh Day Adventists have also been imprisoned under these articles for such behaviour. A representative case is that of Stepan Salamakha, Alexei Zhiltsov and Vasyly Pererva, three members of an unregistered Pentecostalist congregation in Voroshilovgrad region in the Ukraine. All were arrested under the Ukrainian Criminal Code articles equivalent to Articles 142 and 227 of the RSFSR Criminal Code. Salamakha was charged with the equivalent of Article 227 and with another offence: "Infliction of injury on another person". According to the text of the court judgment in their case, they were convicted of the following "criminal acts":

— The conducting of systematic organizational activity in the leadership of the "illegal Pentecostalist religious sect". They had done this "under the pretext of conducting religious ceremonies", through which they had harmed believers' health and incited them to refuse to carry out their social obligations. Salamakha was the leader of the congregation (the senior "presbyter"), and he had organized it with the help of Zhiltsov (the "presbyter") and Pererva (a "preacher"). They had held numerous prayer meetings, "no less than once a week", in the homes of members of the congregation.

In the prayer meetings believers had been brought by prayer "to an extremely excited emotional state". This had a bad effect on the health of the worshippers, the court said.

At the prayer meetings Salamakha systematically incited believers to avoid their "social obligations": he called on them not to marry non-believers, not to visit clubs and theatres, not to watch television and "in case of illness to turn for help first to the presbyter and then to a medical worker". He called on them not to take part in the Young Communist League, not to serve in the armed forces, not to take up weapons and not to take the military oath.

"In November 1973 . . . Salamakha categorically stated that he would not allow his daughter Valentina to enter the Young Communist League . . ."

"In the winter of 1972 the defendant V.T. Zhiltsov illegally organized a prayer meeting in the home of the believer E.I. Ridkokasha . . . where he conducted the meeting, read the sermon and called the believers to common prayer." He also enlisted new members. "Thus in the summer of 1971 he proposed to citizen N.Kh. Remez to become a member of their congregation in order to be allowed to marry his (Zhiltsov's) daughter."

Zhiltsov and Pererva conducted religious ceremonies which violated public order. Thus in June 1972 Zhiltsov organized his daughter's wedding in another believer's home. "This mass religious ceremony of the cult, at which 56 believers were present, included loud choral singing of religious songs accompanied by musical instruments, recitation of religious verses and reading of sermons. The singing of religious songs was audible far beyond the limits of the home, as a result of which public order was violated and other citizens expressed legitimate anger and indignation."

In June 1972 Pererva conducted a similar "mass religious ceremony" for the wedding of his son, which violated public order in the same way.

All three refused to admit that they were guilty of harming other people's health and defended their activity as the exercise of their religious beliefs. All three were found guilty and sentenced to 5 years' imprisonment plus terms in exile.

The following is an account of the circumstances in which Peter Peters, a Baptist pastor in Rostov-on-Don, was arrested in August 1977. The account is taken from issue 47 (30 November 1977) of *A Chronicle of Current Events*:

The Rostov congregation of Evangelical Christians and Baptists has more than 300 members. The congregation submitted an application for registration, stipulating that they did not want the government's commissioner for religious affairs and the KGB to take the place of Jesus Christ in the church. The local authorities refused to register the congregation.

The believers used to gather in the home of two elderly women, Terkhova and Khmara. In January 1977 this home was confiscated. The members of the congregation began to gather in other places. Their gatherings were dispersed.

Thus, on 8 February 1977 the police and People's Guards refused to allow the Baptists to enter the home of the Zakharova family. Many of the believers were beaten. Then for some time they left the believers in peace.

The believers constructed a 7 meter x 9 meter "tent" in the garden plot of the Zakharova family and conducted their prayer meetings in it. The executive committee of the district Soviet ordered that this tent be taken down. The Baptists refused to comply.

On 8 August 1977 the police took down the tent. They took away from the yard the building materials from which the tent was made and also seven cubic meters of firewood, a welding apparatus, two tanks of gas, electric lamps, a table and benches.

The Baptists continued to gather in the Zakharovas' yard and quickly put up a new tent there.

Late in the evening of 23 August 1977 police and workers acting on the orders of the district executive committee again took down the tent and removed the building materials.

On 26 August 1977 a prayer meeting was conducted in the Zakharovas' yard. Detachments of police, KGB officers and People's Guards filled the nearby street. When the service began, they turned on a powerful electric noise-maker. They began to disperse the believers, shoving them and twisting their arms. They took the church minister P. Peters away. Then the members of the congregation gathered outside the police station and demanded that he be released. Some of them were taken into the police station, others were packed into a bus and taken to distant parts of the city. During this, too, physical force was applied.

On 27-28 August the congregation called a "youth meeting". This time they gathered in a forest. The believers had scarcely arrived there when there appeared police, People's Guards and busloads of workers who had been especially brought away from the place of work. They used loud-speakers and a crush ensued. The service was cut short. Several persons were taken to the police station. After discussions the believers were permitted to go to the Zakharovas' yard.

However on 2 and 4 September prayer meetings at the Zakharovas' were again broken up.

On 14 September massive searches of members of the Rostov congregation were carried out.

Rumours circulated in the city that the Baptists had carried out child sacrifices and killed a policeman.

The Pervomaisky Soviet executive committee ordered that the home of the Zakharova family be confiscated. They deprived Nina Zakharova of her guardianship over her younger sister Lena. (The Zakharovas are the children of a Baptist minister. There are three sisters, aged 24, 19 and 11 years and a brother aged 22 years. Their parents died in 1971. The oldest sister, Nina, has raised the children.)

A criminal case has been started against P. Peters. He is 34 years old and has already served three terms of imprisonment as a Baptist-*initsiativnik*. In 1969 an attempt was made with the aid of threats to persuade him to collaborate with the KGB.

Peter Peters was evidently released after these events but was arrested again in January 1978. He was tried in March 1978 and on 9 March 1978 sentenced to 2½ years' imprisonment for "organizing group actions which violated public order" (Article 190-3 of the RSFSR Criminal Code).

Religious believers have also been imprisoned in connection with their efforts to overcome the non-availability of religious literature. All publishing in the USSR is done either by state agencies or with official permission, and religious groups are allowed to publish very little. Religious groups of all denominations complain of chronic shortages of copies of the Bible, and the authorities frequently confiscate the religious literature they do have. The shortage is especially severe for members of unregistered congregations. Baptist believers have attempted to take steps of their own to satisfy the believers' demands for religious literature. Throughout the 1970s such literature has been produced in large quantities on private printing presses, most notably through a *samizdat* publishing house called "The Christian", established by the "dissenting" Baptists in 1971. People caught assisting in these efforts have been arrested and sentenced to imprisonment, frequently under Article 162 of the RSFSR Criminal Code, "Engaging in a Prohibited Trade". There are regular reports of police searches of private homes in various parts of the USSR during which large quantities of such unofficially-produced literature have been confiscated. Sometimes such searches are followed by the arrest of those believed responsible for producing or distributing the religious literature.

During one such search in October 1974 at a farm in Estonia the police confiscated 15,000 Bibles. Nine Baptists were arrested in connection with this search. All nine were subsequently tried for "engaging in a prohibited trade" and sentenced to imprisonment. (Five of those sentenced were women and were released in May 1975 under an amnesty to mark International Women's Year.)

After a similar police search in Ivangorod, a town in the Leningrad region, in March 1977 nine tons of paper, printing equipment and religious literature were confiscated and four Baptists arrested: David Koop, Ivan Leven and the sisters Larissa and Lyudmilla Zaitseva. All were tried in November 1977 and sentenced to from 3 to 5 years' imprisonment.

Others recently arrested and sentenced to imprisonment after the police found religious literature in their possession are Boris Bergen, Yakov Fot and Pyotr Panafidin (all of Dzhambul, Kazakhstan) who were convicted in 1978 both of "anti-Soviet slander" and "engaging in a prohibited trade" and sentenced to from 2 to 3 years' imprisonment.

A number of Seventh Day Adventists have likewise been imprisoned, after being found to be in possession of religious literature produced by "The True Witness Publishing House", which was founded by Vladimir Shelkov. Detailed reports have circulated in *samizdat* regarding the detention of the Adventist

Yakov Dolgotyor on 29 January 1978 in Stavropol territory in the south of the Russian Federation. Dolgotyor, born in 1959, was questioned by KGB officers about where he had obtained publications of "The True Witness Publishing House". Dolgotyor subsequently alleged that his interrogators beat him and applied "some sort of chemical preparation" to his hand, causing it to become inflamed and swollen. According to Dolgotyor's account, he was subsequently moved to a psychiatric hospital where he was again questioned about the religious literature. He was held there for around three weeks before being transferred to a jail and then released on 1 March 1978. Dolgotyor was arrested again in August 1978, subsequently tried and sentenced to 4 years' imprisonment.

Twenty-two Baptists, Pentecostalists and Seventh Day Adventists are known to have been sentenced to imprisonment between June 1975 and May 1979 for refusing on grounds of their beliefs to meet the legal obligations for military service (see pages 51-56).

In the past several years more than 20,000 Pentecostalists and Baptists have applied to emigrate from the USSR. Pentecostalists form the majority of those who have applied to emigrate; their applications are often signed by whole families and congregations. The number of known Baptist would-be emigrants is considerably smaller and in some cases is related to the German ethnic background of the applicants, who like many other Soviet citizens of German origin seek to emigrate to the Federal Republic of Germany. In December 1977 two Baptists of German origin, Alwin Klassen and Yakov Wolf, were sentenced to imprisonment on charges of "malicious violation of the passport regulations" and "violation of the laws on separation of church and state and of school and church". Two Pentecostalists arrested in 1977 for "malicious violation of the passport regulations" are A.P. Makarenko and P.S. Smykhalov, both from Krasnoyarsk territory. Amnesty International does not know their subsequent fate.

Another Pentecostalist arrested in connection with his efforts to emigrate from the USSR is M. Yurkiv of Uzhgorod, in the western Ukraine. He was arrested in December 1977 after a police search of his home which at the time officials said was connected with his intention to leave the USSR. Yurkiv was subsequently charged with "stealing state property". He was still imprisoned awaiting trial in June 1978.

## Freedom of Movement

According to Article 13(2) of the Universal Declaration of Human Rights "everyone has the right to leave any country, including his own, and to return to his own country." The same right is proclaimed in Article 12(2) of the United Nations International Covenant on Civil and Political Rights and in other international instruments to which the USSR is party.

Soviet citizens may leave the country only with the express permission of the authorities. During recent years many thousands of Soviet citizens have applied for permission to leave the country. The most widely known movements for emigration involve Soviet Jews (of whom approximately 130,000 were permitted to emigrate during the years 1972-1977) and Soviet Germans (of whom approximately 40,000 were permitted to emigrate during that period). Less widely known is the emigration movement among religious believers, particularly Baptists and Pentecostalists. According to unofficial figures as many as 20,000 Pentecostalists applied to emigrate in 1977 alone. Furthermore, a great many individual applicants are known of who are not associated with any emigration movement by a population group.

These figures indicate that the Soviet authorities have made significant concessions in allowing Jewish and German-origin citizens to emigrate. However, the authorities have placed many difficult obstacles in the way of would-be emigrants in these categories, and this is even more so in the case of would-be emigrants from other population groups. The application procedure is difficult, applicants being required to provide invitations from close relatives abroad as well as other documentation which may be difficult or impossible to obtain. Many applicants are required to wait long periods for official permission to emigrate, while many are refused permission on a great variety of grounds.

Soviet Jews, Germans, religious believers and others have in many cases been imprisoned for persisting in their application for permission to emigrate. The same has happened to people who have been active in public campaigning for official respect for the right to leave the country.

Among Soviet Jews who during the four years preceding the writing of this report have been sentenced to imprisonment or exile for trying to emigrate through legal means are: Joseph Begun, Grigory Goldstein, Boris Kalandarov, Anatoly Malkin, Ida Nudel, Lev Roitburd, Anatoly Shcharansky, Simon Shnirman, Alexander Silnitsky, Maria Slepak, Vladimir Slepak, Alexander Vilik, Yakov Vinarov and Amner Zavurov. At least two Jews were confined briefly to psychiatric hospitals after submitting applications to emigrate: Lazar Brusilovsky (Rostov, 1977) and Yefim Pargammanik (Kiev, 1977).

Most of these prisoners have been sentenced either under non-political articles of the criminal law or for refusing to obey call-up to obligatory service in the armed forces.

Among citizens of German origin sentenced to imprisonment during the same four-year period for trying to emigrate legally are: Anton Bleile, Lily Furman, Albert Harlemann, Alwin Klassen, Artur Klink, Valentin Klink, Victor Klink, Helmut Martens, Otto Netzel, Ivan Peters, Yakov Peters, Heinrich Redikop, Ivan Redikop, Heinrich Reimer, Ivan Schultz, Ivan Teurer, Valentin Vins (or "Wins" in German transliteration), Ivan Wagner, Anton Windschuh and L. Windschuh. Several other would-be emigrants of German origin have been tried and sentenced to conditional terms of imprisonment or to corrective work without imprisonment.

Most of these would-be emigrants have been tried and sentenced either for "anti-Soviet slander" (Article 190-1 of the RSFSR Criminal Code) allegedly committed by them in applying to emigrate or in campaigning in support of their applications, or for "malicious violation of the passport regulations" (Article 198 of the RSFSR Criminal Code). In several cases, for example that of Alwin Klassen in Issyk, Kazakhstan in December 1977, Soviet Germans have been charged both with breaking the passport rules and with religious offences.

The regulations regarding internal passports are laid down in two regulations issued by the Council of Ministers of the USSR in 1974: "The Passport System of the USSR" and "Certain Instructions Concerning Registration".[13] According to these regulations, all citizens over the age of 16 are issued with a passport, which is their basic personal identity document. All citizens of the USSR must be registered with the authorities at their place of residence, and if they change their place of residence they must register this change with the authorities at the place they are leaving and obtain registration at the place to which they move. Such registration may be refused by the authorities on various grounds. Presentation of one's passport is necessary for obtaining registration of residence.

According to the same regulations, people applying for permission to leave the country must submit their passport to the authorities along with other documentation. However, according to the same regulations, "citizens obliged to have passports" may be subjected to administrative sanctions for residence without a passport. Citizens who violate these regulations more than twice may be treated as having "maliciously violated the passport regulations" and may be prosecuted under Article 198 of the RSFSR Criminal Code.

For example, Soviet would-be emigrants of German origin have been required to submit their passports together with their applications for emigration, and have subsequently been sentenced to imprisonment for being without their passport. Under Article 198 "malicious violation of the passport rules" is punishable only if it is committed in parts of the country where, in addition to the general passport regulations, "special" rules of registration are in effect. Most of the cases known to Amnesty International where would-be emigrants of German origin have been prosecuted for this offence have been in Kazakhstan.

Soviet would-be emigrants of German origin, like other applicants for emigration, are frequently put under considerable pressure to withdraw their applications. For example, in Kazakhstan in the summer of 1977 several German applicants for emigration were sentenced to imprisonment and then released when they agreed to take back their passports. Ivan Teurer, Helmut Martens and Valentin Klink, who were sentenced to imprisonment in 1977 for "violating the passport regulations" in connection with their efforts to emigrate, were offered conditional release before the expiry of their sentences if they agreed to take back their passports, but refused and served their sentences in full.

Non-Jewish and non-German applicants for emigration have similarly been imprisoned for trying by legal means to exercise their right to leave their country. Reference has been made above to the Nikolai Shatalov family, three members of which were imprisoned between 1976 and 1978 in connection with their efforts to emigrate. During the same period Vadim Konovalikhin, from Kaliningrad, several times tried to submit an application for emigration. The authorities did not accept his application and on 4 October 1977 he informed the authorities that he was going on hunger strike. The next day he was put in a psychiatric hospital. He was released a day later, but he was confined to a psychiatric hospital again on 25 March 1978. He was released on 23 May 1978 but arrested again on 26 May 1978 and charged with "anti-Soviet slander" under Article 190-1. He was tried in August 1978 and sentenced to 4 years' internal exile.

Other people have been confined to psychiatric hospitals after seeking permission to emigrate. Among recent such cases known to Amnesty International are those of Anatoly Uvarov, who was detained in April 1976 outside the Swedish Embassy in Moscow where he was carrying placards asking for asylum; Valentin Ivanov, who was detained on 14 June 1977 outside the Bolshoi Ballet in Moscow where he was carrying a placard protesting against official persecution of him on account of his efforts to emigrate; Lidiya Valendo (Minsk, 1978); Victor Borovsky (Kharkov, 1977); Anatoly Glukhov (Chelyabinsk, 1972, 1974, 1978); Yury Tarakanov (Leningrad, 1976).

Over the years a number of Soviet citizens have tried to leave the country by fleeing across the border, or by failing to return to the USSR when abroad. Such actions are liable to punishment under Article 64 of the RSFSR Criminal Code, which states:

*Treason*

(a) Treason, that is, an act intentionally committed by a citizen of the USSR to the detriment of the independence of the state, the territorial inviolability, or the military might of the USSR: going over to the side of the enemy, espionage, transmission of a state or military secret to a foreign state, flight abroad or refusal to return from abroad to the USSR, rendering aid to a foreign state in carrying on hostile activity against the USSR, or a conspiracy for the purpose of seizing power, shall be punished by deprivation of freedom for a term of 10 to 15 years with confiscation of property with or without additional exile for a term of 2 to 5 years, or by death with confiscation of property.

(b) A citizen of the USSR recruited by a foreign intelligence service for carrying on hostile activity against the USSR shall not be subject to criminal responsibility if he has committed no actions in execution of the criminal assignment received by him and has voluntarily reported to agencies of authority his connection with the foreign intelligence service.

Attempting to leave the country without official permission is punishable under Article 83 of the RSFSR Criminal Code as well:

*Illegal Exit Abroad and Illegal Entry into the USSR*

Exit abroad, entry into the USSR, or crossing the border without the requisite passport or the permission of the proper authorities, shall be punished by deprivation of freedom for a term of one to 3 years.

Operation of the present article shall not extend to instances of arrival in the USSR of foreign citizens, without the requisite passport or permit, for exercise of the right of asylum granted by the Constitution of the USSR.

Amnesty International knows little of cases where Article 83 has been applied to people who had tried to leave the country without official permission. However Amnesty International has always had under adoption a number of people who were imprisoned for "treason" under Article 64 in the form of "flight abroad or refusal to return from abroad to the USSR". Application of Article 64 is particularly serious because of the heavy penalties involved: in the cases known to Amnesty International of treason in the form of "flight abroad or refusal to return from abroad to the USSR" the sentence passed has usually been in excess of 10 years' imprisonment.

According to the text of Article 64, an act can be judged to be treason in this or any other form only if it was committed "intentionally . . . to the detriment of the independence of the state, the territorial inviolability or the military might of the USSR". Although Amnesty International has had access to only a handful of indictments, court judgments and similar documents in cases of this sort, it is evident that the prosecution and court authorities have often disregarded this qualification and have sentenced people to long terms of imprisonment under this article solely for trying to leave the country without official permission without any "treasonous" intention.

Vladimir Balakhonov was working in Geneva as a translator and editor in the Secretariat of the World Meteorological Organization when in September 1972 his wife and daughter were told by Soviet officials to return to Moscow. The family went into hiding and Balakhonov asked for political asylum for all of them. However, his wife and daughter returned to the USSR and Balakhonov followed them on 1 December 1972. According to a later statement by Balakhonov, before returning to the USSR he was assured by Soviet diplomats in Switzerland that he would not be prosecuted on his return. Nonetheless in January 1973 he was arrested and charged with treason. He was subsequently tried and sentenced to 12 years' imprisonment.

Maigonis Ravinsh, a Latvian, was charged with treason in 1975 or 1976 after being apprehended trying to flee the USSR across the border with Finland. He was approximately 20 years of age at the time. He was sentenced to 5 years' imprisonment.

In a number of cases people who have tried to leave the USSR without official permission have been confined to special psychiatric hospitals. The brothers Alexander and Mikhail Shatravka were arrested sometime in the mid-1970s while trying to cross the Soviet border into Finland. Both were subsequently ordered confined to the Dnepropetrovsk Special Psychiatric Hospital in the Ukrainian SSR. Testimony from a former inmate of that institution who knew of their case while there, together with the fact that not one but both brothers were officially ruled to be dangerously mentally ill, gives further cause to believe that they were so confined because of their effort to leave the country rather than for authentic medical reasons. Both brothers were still in psychiatric hospitals in 1978.

Article 13(1) of the Universal Declaration of Human Rights proclaims that "everyone has the right to freedom of movement and residence within the borders of each state". This right is also proclaimed in Article 12(1) of the International Covenant on Civil and Political Rights.

Reference has been made above to the system of passport regulations in the USSR and the requirement that everyone have official registration for their residence anywhere in the country. In recent years there have been numerous arrests and trials of Crimean Tartars who have been seeking permission to reside in the Crimea, their ancestral homeland.

The Crimean Tartars were deported from the Crimea to Central Asia and the Ural mountains area in 1944, accused *en masse* of "collaboration" with the invading German forces. The Crimean Tartars were "rehabilitated" by a government decree in 1967, but the authorities have systematically refused to allow large numbers of them to resettle in the Crimea.

Spokesmen for the Crimean Tartars have expressed fear that the approximately 500,000 remaining Crimean Tartars will become assimilated with other population groups in Central Asia since they do not have their own national-territorial administration and have very few cultural and language institutions. Many thousands of Crimean Tartars have signed appeals and petitions for permission to resettle in the Crimea, and many have tried to take up residence there. However, between 1967 and 1976 only about 5,000 Crimean Tartars succeeded in obtaining registration to reside in the Crimea. Many others have been refused registration and have been forced to leave the Crimea, while according to unofficial sources several thousand Crimean Tartars (around 700 families) were residing there without registration in 1978.

According to numerous, detailed reports, local authorities in the Crimea have applied severe measures to Crimean Tartars whom they have refused to register for residence: refusal to authorize purchase of homes, cutting off essential services to their homes, denial of jobs and refusal to admit their children to schools. In numerous documented cases the local authorities have simply demolished the homes of unregistered Crimean Tartars. There have been frequent reports of incidents in which unregistered Crimean Tartars were physically attacked and then forcibly dispatched from the Crimea to neighbouring regions or to Central Asia.

Between 1975 and 1979 more than 100 Crimean Tartars have been put on trial on charges of "violation of the passport regulations". Most of them have been sentenced either to banishment from the Crimea for up to five years, to a term of imprisonment suspended but with a requirement that the defendant take a job assigned by the authorities, or to corrective work without imprisonment. In the latter two types of sentence the authorities invariably assign convicted Crimean Tartars to jobs outside the Crimea, so that the outcome is similar to banishment.

Between 1975 and 1979 a number of Crimean Tartars were sentenced to terms of imprisonment for "malicious violations of the passport regulations", for example, Enver Reshatov, Zubeit Kalafatov and Musa Mamut. After being released from serving this sentence, Musa Mamut subsequently took his life by self-immolation in protest at official treatment of Crimean Tartars.

In a number of cases Crimean Tartars seeking to establish residence in the Crimea have been sentenced to imprisonment on charges of ordinary criminal offences. In February 1978 a group of about 100 Crimean Tartars were stopped by police in Simferopol while on their way to try to see the Chairman of the Executive Committee of the Crimea Regional Soviet of People's Deputies. According to subsequent reports, a group of police and army officers used violence on the group. A number of people were detained and soon released. Riza Muslyadinov, however, was charged with "resisting a representative of authority" (the Ukrainian SSR Criminal Code equivalent of Article 191 of the RSFSR Criminal Code). According to *A Chronicle of Current Events*: "He was charged with resisting the police and beating up six policemen. In fact, he had come to the defence of a woman who was being beaten up by the policemen, but did not resist his own detention". Muslyadinov was subsequently sentenced to 3 years' imprisonment.

Similar sentences have also been meted out to Crimean Tartars who had managed to obtain registration for residence in the Crimea. In February 1979 Lyufti Bekirov, Yakub Baitullayev, Sefran Khyrkhara and Izek Usta were arrested and charged under the Ukrainian equivalent to Article 191-1 of the RSFSR Criminal Code with "resisting the police". The arrest occurred when Bekirov and his friends were present while police were evicting the family of Izek Usta's brother. Amnesty International does not yet know the full details of what happened, but it appears likely that the charges against the four were similar to those against Riza Muslyadinov, described above. Bekirov was sentenced to 4 years' imprisonment and each of his companions to 3 years'.

Of the Crimean Tartars who have been imprisoned in recent years probably the best known are Mustafa Dzhemilev and his relative Reshat Dzhemilev. Mustafa Dzhemilev was first imprisoned in 1966, when he was sentenced to 18 months' imprisonment for refusing to respond to call-up to obligatory military service. His refusal was based on the grounds that he was "deprived of his rights as a citizen", a reference to official discrimination against the Crimean Tartars with regard to their right to live in the Crimea. In 1970 he was sentenced to 3 years' imprisonment for "anti-Soviet slander". In 1974 he was jailed for 15 days and then almost immediately called up again for military service. He again refused and was sentenced to one year's imprisonment. In 1975, when he was nearing the end of this sentence, new charges of "anti-Soviet slander" were brought against him with regard to writings found in his possession in his place of imprisonment and opinions he had expressed to fellow prisoners. This time he was sentenced to 3 years' imprisonment. After his release in 1978 he was placed under administrative surveillance (see below). In March 1979 he was sentenced to 4 years' internal exile for "malicious violation of the rules of administrative surveillance".

Reshat Dzhemilev was imprisoned from 1972 to 1975 for taking part in a demonstration which "violated public order" and for "anti-Soviet slander". He was arrested again in April 1979 in Tashkent, charged with "anti-Soviet slander" and held for trial.

## *Imprisonment of Conscientious Objectors to Military Service*

The obligation of Soviet citizens to do military service is laid down in the country's Constitution. Article 62 of the USSR Constitution (1977) states in part:

> Defence of the Socialist Motherland is the sacred duty of every citizen of the USSR.

Article 63 of the Constitution states:

> Military service in the ranks of the Armed Forces of the USSR is an honourable duty of Soviet citizens.

The details of compulsory military service in the USSR are laid down in a law passed by the USSR Supreme Soviet on 12 October 1967, entitled "On

Universal Military Obligation". Article 3 of this law states:

All male citizens of the USSR, regardless of their race or nationality, their religious creed, education, place of residence or their social or proprietary position, are obliged to do military service in the ranks of the Armed Forces of the USSR.

Article 10 of the same law specifies that male citizens over the age of 18 are liable to military call-up for a term of active service which, according to Article 11, varies in duration from one to three years according to the branch of the services in which the person is serving and according to his educational qualification. According to Article 26, the only men who are not subject to this obligation are those under criminal conviction or investigation.

The only legally-approved ground for release from the obligation to do active military service is physical unfitness. People whose illness renders them temporarily unfit for military service can be allowed a deferment of their call-up, as can certain categories of students. Those whose military service is deferred so that they can continue their studies may be recalled to active service until they reach 27 years of age.

Penalties for failure or refusal to fulfil the obligation to do active military service are laid down in the criminal code of each of the Union Republics of the USSR.

The RSFSR Criminal Code contains four articles (Articles 80, 81, 198-1 and 249) proscribing evasion of military service under various circumstances.

Articles 81 ("Evasion of Call-Up by Mobilization") and 249 ("Evasion of Military Service by Maiming or Any Other Method") carry a possible death penalty if committed in wartime or in a combat situation.

Article 80 ("Evasion of Regular Call to Active Military Service") applies to Soviet civilians who refuse to respond to call-up for active military duty in peacetime. People charged with this crime are tried in civilian courts. If they are convicted of evading call-up by means of forgery or deception or by some form of self-mutilation or "malingering", they are liable to imprisonment for from one to 5 years. If they are proved to have evaded call-up without recourse to such methods, they may be sentenced to imprisonment for from 1 to 3 years. A second conviction for this offence may be punished by up to 5 years' imprisonment.

The official Commentary to the RSFSR Criminal Code states with regard to Article 80: [14]

The motives for evasion (unwillingness to serve in the army, particularly under the pretext of religious convictions, etc) are not relevant to the designation of the crime.

One category of people imprisoned for refusal to serve in the Soviet armed forces consists of young Jewish applicants for emigration. Between June 1975 and May 1979 Boris Kalendarov, Anatoly Malkin, Simon Shnirman, Alexander Silnitsky, Alexander Vilik and Yakov Vinarov were all sentenced to imprisonment for this offence. In each case the subject had applied unsuccessfully for permission to leave the country and had been called up for military duty only after applying to emigrate. In each case the subject had a double motive for refusing military service. In the first place, each was a Jew who regarded himself as a citizen of Israel, a state which for many years had had hostile relations with the USSR. Second, each would have been aware that in many cases the authorities have refused would-be emigrants permission to leave the country on the formal grounds that, as a result of having served a period in the armed forces, they had access to sensitive information. On such grounds the authorities have refused Jews permission to emigrate for five years or longer, even where the person's armed service did not involve any sensitive work or information. Soviet dissenters estimated in the mid-1970s that 40 per cent of known refusals to permit Jews to emigrate were officially based on the fact that the applicant or his relatives had performed military service.

Representative of these cases is that of Anatoly Malkin, from Moscow. In July 1974 he submitted an application for permission to emigrate to Israel. At the time, he was a third-year student in an institute of higher education and although he had recently completed his examinations and been passed into the next year of his course, he was dismissed from the institute less than five weeks after applying to emigrate. He subsequently received Israeli citizenship and in August 1974 he submitted to the Soviet authorities a statement in which he renounced his Soviet citizenship. Having been dismissed from the institute where he was studying, he had lost his deferment from military service and was called up in September 1974. On several occasions after that he submitted statements saying that he could not serve in the armed forces or take the military oath, but in May 1975 he was arrested and charged with evasion of call-up to the armed forces. He was tried in August 1975 and sentenced to 3 years' imprisonment. At his trial he said in his defence: "Knowing that I was already a citizen of the state of Israel, I considered that not only was I not obliged, but did not even have the right to serve in the Soviet army . . . I do not, therefore, consider myself guilty."

Between June 1975 and May 1979, 22 Baptists, Pentecostalists and Seventh Day Adventists are known to have been sentenced to imprisonment as conscientious objectors. All were objectors on account of their pacifist convictions. In the case of Pentecostalists and Adventists, the total number of imprisoned conscientious objectors is likely to be considerably higher than the number of reported cases.

Some of the imprisoned religious conscientious objectors known to Amnesty International have refused outright to serve in the armed forces. In such cases they have been sentenced under Article 80 of the RSFSR Criminal Code ("Evasion of Regular Call-Up to Active Military Service"). Apparently, however, in most cases pacifist conscientious objectors from among the Baptists, Pentecostalists and Seventh Day Adventists have expressed willingness to serve in the armed forces in a capacity which does not involve the bearing of arms or the taking of the military oath. In such cases either Article 80 or Article 249 ("Evasion of Military Service by Maiming or Any Other Method") may be applied. The latter charge is the more common among cases known to Amnesty International.

The best documented case of a Pentecostalist conscientious objector is that of Daniil Grigorevich Vashchenko, a member of the Pentecostalist community in Nakhodka, in the Maritime Territory in the Soviet Far East. The documentation available to Amnesty International on this case includes the indictment against Vashchenko (12 July 1974), his father's statement at his trial (6 August 1974), the trial verdict in the case (8 August 1974), his father's appeal against the verdict (17 August 1974), the finding of the appeal court (12 September 1974) and a number of related materials.

The official documents and the appeals made by Vashchenko's father do not conflict with regard to the basic facts of the case. Daniil Vashchenko was born in 1955 and employed as a driver. In May 1974, after he was called up to active military service in Nakhodka, he reported to the local call-up commission and for a medical examination as required by law. He was pronounced medically fit and the call-up commission stated that there were no grounds for deferment. However, when Vashchenko reported for departure to his designated military unit, he stated, orally and in writing, that because of his religious convictions he would neither bear arms nor take the military oath.

He offered to serve in an unarmed unit without taking the military oath and to fulfil his military obligation by some form of "socially useful labour". Soviet law makes no reference to any form of service alternative to regular military service, and Vashchenko was arrested and brought to trial under Article 80 of the RSFSR Criminal Code ("Evasion of Regular Call-up to Active Military Service").

At his trial in August 1974 Vashchenko's father argued that his son could not bear arms because of his pacifist religious views. He argued further that compulsory military service represented a restriction of "freedom of conscience", guaranteed in Article 124 of the USSR Constitution (1936), and that Lenin had, in a 1919 decree, recognized the right of individuals to refuse military service on religious grounds.

Vashchenko was sentenced to 3 years' imprisonment.

One interesting sidelight in this case appeared in an appeal against the verdict by Vashchenko's father. In this appeal, he stated that a criminal case had been opened against his son in 1973 on the same charge: evasion of military service. He cited official documents from the earlier case which revealed some official readiness at that time to allow his son to fulfil his military obligations by means of civilian labour, without having to take the military oath. These efforts were, he said, motivated by recognition of Vashchenko's claims of conscience. According to Vashchenko's father, this official attitude facilitated the termination of the criminal case against Vashchenko in 1973. This information indicates that unpublished official instructions or policy norms may exist in the USSR which allow for some form of non-military alternative service within the armed forces. Similarly, in a number of cases believers have appealed to be allowed to work in "construction" batallions—another indication that the authorities have provided some means for enabling pacifist conscientious objectors to serve in the armed forces without violating their convictions. Such provisions do not exist in any published law and obviously are applied only selectively.

In a number of cases, conscripted religious believers have joined military units after telling the military authorities that they would not take the military oath or bear arms. In the training program of the Soviet armed forces conscripts need not bear arms or take the military oath until completion of several months of basic training, and so a number of conscientious objectors have been prosecuted only after spending several months with a military unit.

The military oath to which all personnel in the Soviet armed forces must swear and give their signature, and to which pacifist conscripts have objected, is as follows:

I, a citizen of the Union of Soviet Socialist Republics, entering the ranks of the Armed Forces, take oath and solemnly swear to be a conscientious, brave, disciplined and watchful soldier, to keep strictly military and state secrets, to fulfil without question all the military regulations and the orders of commanders and officials.

I swear to be conscientious in my military studies, to protect in every possible way military and public property and to be loyal to my last breath to my People, my Soviet Motherland and the Soviet Government.

I am prepared always to go on the order of the Soviet Government to the defence of my Motherland—the Union of Soviet Socialist Republics— and as a soldier in the Armed Forces I swear to defend it manfully and capably, with dignity and honour, not sparing my blood or my life to win complete victory over the enemy.

If I violate this my sacred oath let me suffer the rigorous punishment of the Soviet law, universal repugnance and the contempt of the workers.

Religious conscientious objectors who join military units are reported to be subjected to continuous pressure to renounce their convictions and take the military oath. A case well-documented in Baptist *samizdat* literature is that of the conscript Nikolai Kravchenko who was beaten by a sergeant on 3 February 1977 in his military unit in Kursk region, to the extent that he suffered fractures to both jaws. Kravchenko was subsequently sent home from the army with his jaw injuries still unhealed. Less drastic forms of pressure include frequent verbal efforts at persuasion, conspicuous surveillance and singling out for extra work assignments.

The grounds for conscientious objection of conscripts in this category are illustrated by those expressed by Vladimir Minyakov, a Baptist from Estonia, in the following deposition to his military commander in April 1977:

To: Commander of Military Unit 17646
From: Private Minyakov, V.D.

*I, Minyakov, V.D., born in 1958, was called up in 1976 by the Valgask District Military Command for service in the ranks of the Soviet Army. Prior to my call-up I had informed Colonel Frosh, the Military Commissar of the Valgask District Military Command, that I am a believer and that from my purely religious convictions I cannot take the military oath or bear arms. When I was summoned to the military unit, I at once told the commander the same thing. And now throughout the past five months they have conducted conversations with me in which they propose that I take the oath and promise that otherwise I will be imprisoned. But I cannot do so, since from my conviction and religious faith I cannot take a weapon*

*in my hands, and on these grounds I also cannot take the oath, because
what is in it amounts to weapons. I do not refuse to serve in the ranks of
the Soviet Army and I am prepared to fulfil conscientiously all that my
service demands of me. But with regard to the oath, as a religious believer,
I cannot alter my thoughts and convictions.*

4 April 1977
Private Minyakov

Although Minyakov was threatened with prosecution, as far as Amnesty
International knows he was not subsequently sentenced to imprisonment.

Conscripts who persist in refusing to take the military oath or bear arms are
liable to be charged with "refusal to perform military duties", which is listed
under Article 249 of the RSFSR Criminal Code as a form of "evasion of military
service". In the cases of Baptists, Pentecostalists, Adventists and conscientious
objectors known to Amnesty International to have been convicted of this offence
the sentence has invariably been 3 or 4 years' imprisonment.

Between June 1975 and May 1979 at least one Pentecostalist conscientious
objector, Victor Korneyev, was sentenced to 5 years' imprisonment for refusing
to meet the requirements of military service after having served a previous term
of imprisonment for the same offence.

## Application of Non-Political Articles of Criminal Law to Dissenters

It is common for the authorities to imprison dissenters under articles of criminal
law for alleged offences which have no ostensible relationship to the dissenting
activities of those convicted. Unlike those charged under articles of criminal law
which explicitly restrict exercise of human rights, dissenters who have been
charged with ordinary criminal offences have normally denied the charges. In
many cases it has been evident that the authorities have brought false criminal
charges against dissenters or misapplied the law to obtain their imprisonment.

One charge which has been used in this manner is "hooliganism" (Article 206
of the RSFSR Criminal Code), which is punishable by up to 5 years' imprisonment or up to 7 years' if any sort of weapon is used in the commission of the
offence. This article of law has frequently been criticized for its extraordinary
lack of precision in defining the offence concerned. The elasticity of Article 206
has over the years facilitated the trial and imprisonment of dissenters for
"hooliganism".

Article 206 states:

Hooliganism, that is, intentional actions violating public order in a coarse
manner and expressing a clear disrespect toward society, and, likewise,
petty hooliganism committed by a person to whom a measure of
administrative pressure for petty hooliganism has been applied within a year,
shall be punished by deprivation of freedom for a term of 6 months to one
year, or by corrective tasks for the same term, or by a fine of 30 to 50 rubles.

Malicious hooliganism, that is, the same actions distinguished in their
content by exceptional cynicism or special impudence, or connected with
resisting a representative of authority or representative of the public

fulfilling duties for protection of public order or other citizens who are restraining hooliganistic actions and, likewise, actions which are committed by a person previously convicted of hooliganism, shall be punished by deprivation of freedom for a term of one to 5 years.

Actions provided for by paragraphs 1 or 2 of the present article, if committed with the use or attempted use of a firearm, a knife, brass knuckles, other sidearms, or any other objects especially adapted to the infliction of bodily injuries, shall be punished by deprivation of freedom for a term of 3 to 7 years.

Illustrative of the application of this article to dissenters are the cases of Vladimir and Maria Slepak who were tried for "hooliganism" in Moscow on 21 June and 26 July 1978 respectively. Vladimir Slepak, a 52-year-old Jewish electronics engineer, had been applying unsuccessfully since 1970 for permission to emigrate from the USSR, and was a member of the Moscow Helsinki monitoring group.

The following passage from the indictment against Maria Slepak describes the charges against both:

Maria Isaakovna Slepak committed malicious hooliganism, that is, premeditated actions rudely disrupting public order and showing open disregard for the public, of a particularly impertinent nature, namely: On 1 June 1978 at about 4 pm she and Vladimir Semyonovich Slepak, motivated by hooliganism, hung out on the balcony of their flat, No. 77 at No. 15 Gorky Street, overlooking a street in the centre of Moscow— Gorky Street—several sheets with the inscription "Let us go to our son in Israel" and, notwithstanding repeated requests by policemen and officials of the Housing Allocation Bureau to cease her activities, she continued to demonstrate, holding in her hands a sheet with the inscription "Let us go to our son in Israel", accompanying her actions of a prolonged and persistent nature with threatening gestures, shouts of anti-Soviet content and spitting, and by these actions attracted a large crowd on both sides of Gorky Street, as well as in the street itself, causing a temporary interruption of the normal functioning of public transport, serious disruption of order in the street and disturbance of citizens; i.e. she committed the crime stipulated in Article 206, part 2 of the Russian Criminal Code.

Vladimir Slepak was sentenced to 5 years' exile and his wife to 3 years' imprisonment suspended for five years. In Moscow in June 1978 Ida Nudel, another Jewish would-be emigrant and a prominent campaigner for prisoners of conscience in the USSR, was sentenced to 4 years' exile for an identical offence, also under Article 206 of the RSFSR Criminal Code.

In these cases the authorities did not disguise the fact that the charge of "malicious hooliganism" was brought for the holding of a non-violent demonstration. In other cases there is every reason to believe that the authorities have deliberately fabricated incidents to lend some credibility to such charges. Vadim Smogitel, a Ukrainian musician who applied to emigrate after being harassed by the authorities since the early 1960s, apparently because of his efforts to popularize Ukrainian national music, was arrested and charged with this offence in December 1977 after an incident which was described as follows in the Moscow *samizdat* journal *A Chronicle of Current Events*:

On 12 December 1977 Smogitel said in a telephone conversation to Canada. "Get me out of here somehow."

The next day, when Smogitel was walking alone down the street in the evening, a man fell under his feet—and immediately police and volunteer militia appeared at his side.

According to the indictment against him, Smogitel "attacked the man in the street and struck him, causing him to fall and receive serious injury". He was sentenced to 3 years' imprisonment.

Other Criminal Code articles sometimes applied in the same manner are "resisting a representative of authority or a representative of the public fulfilling duties of protection of public order" and "resisting a policeman or people's guard" (Articles 191 and 191-1 of the RSFSR Criminal Code). The imprisonment of five Crimean Tartars in 1978 and 1979 under these articles has been described above (pages 50-51). Others convicted under these articles in recent years and adopted by Amnesty International include Lev Roitburd (Odessa, 1975), Pyotr Naritsa (Latvia, 1976), Joseph Bondarenko (Krasnodar, 1978) and Vasyl Ovsienko (Zhitomir region, Ukraine, 1979).

A criminal charge to which dissenters are particularly vulnerable is "parasitism" (Article 209 of the RSFSR Criminal Code). Soviet dissenters have frequently argued that official practice in applying this article of law is in contravention of international conventions against forced labour.

Article 209 (as amended in 1975) states:

*Systematically engaging in vagrancy or begging*

Systematically engaging in vagrancy or begging and also leading any other parasitic way of life over a protracted period of time shall be punished by deprivation of freedom for a term of up to one year or by corrective labour for the same term. These acts, if committed by a person previously convicted under the first paragraph of this article, shall be punished by deprivation of freedom for a term of up to 2 years.

In 1975 the Presidium of the RSFSR Supreme Soviet adopted a resolution explaining in detail how Article 209 was to be applied. As with numerous other government decrees which closely affect the legal position of Soviet citizens, the government did not publish this resolution, but its text has become available abroad.[15] According to the resolution a person is leading "a parasitic way of life" if, as an adult fit for work, that person lives "on unearned income with avoidance of socially useful work for more than four months in succession or for periods adding up to one year". Local authorities are obliged to formally warn anyone in this position and give them one month in which to take employment at "socially useful work". If the subject does not respond to this admonition he or she is to be warned again and given another month in which to find paid employment, after which he or she is liable to prosecution for "parasitism". The resolution also requires local authorities to help anyone who requests assistance in finding a job by ensuring that they are placed in jobs, and in doing this the local authorities are to take into account the particular skills of the person.

What makes this legislation particularly dangerous for dissenters is that it is common for Soviet citizens to be dismissed from their jobs directly because of their nonconformist behaviour. This applies not only to people in professional posts but also to ordinary workers and to released prisoners of conscience, who often have difficulty finding any employment. In numerous cases dismissed scientists and other professional employees have been unable to find even low-paid, menial work, since the authorities not only have not helped them to find work suited to their particular skills but have put obstacles in the way of their finding any work at all. Thus the threat of being charged with "parasitism" has hung over people who have seriously tried to find employment. Furthermore, the authorities—including the courts—have, in known cases, disregarded such matters as whether the person had resources in the form of personal savings or was actually earning a living in some way outside the state employment system. The authorities and courts have also been arbitrary in adjudging what constitutes "socially useful labour". For example, in two separate cases in late 1977 and early 1978 two Baptist pastors, Grigory Kostyuchenko (in Krasnodar) and Ivan Antonov (in Kirovgrad) were sentenced to imprisonment for "parasitism" even though their congregations had notified the authorities that they were employing the men as pastors and would pay their living expenses. The decisive factor in the authorities' decision to prosecute the two men was not whether they were "living on unearned income", but the fact that both of the congregations were "unregistered" congregations—that is, congregations of Baptists who did not accept official restrictions on religious practice. In other cases too, the authorities have used the law on "parasitism" as a means of repressing dissenters rather than for the purposes suggested by the law itself.

One recent case is that of Joseph Begun. Begun, born in 1932, is a highly qualified mathematician. Beginning in 1951 he was gainfully employed for 20 years without interruption and by 1971 he was employed as a senior scientific worker in the USSR State Planning Commission in Moscow. He was dismissed from his post in that year after applying to emigrate to Israel. During 1971 and 1972 he worked as a watchman, first at a telephone exchange and then for a local government authority. However, as he said later, "I was not allowed to work peacefully even in such unqualified and low-paid work since I was illegally detained in prison three times in 1972 and my absence from work was counted as truancy since they did not give me any documents attesting to the fact that I had been detained." (Begun was among many Jews who have been sentenced to 10 or 15 days in jail for their part in the campaign for emigration rights.) After 1972 Begun earned income by giving private Hebrew lessons. In late 1976 and early 1977 he was particularly active in the Jewish emigration rights campaign and he was issued a warning for "parasitism". Twice Begun wrote to responsible local authorities, the first time to explain the reasons for which he did not have regular paid employment, the second time to ask for help in finding a job. However, he was arrested on 3 March 1977 and charged with "parasitism". He was tried in June of that year and sentenced to 2 years' exile. Begun's sentence expired in February 1978 on account of the length of time he had spent in pre-trial detention. When he returned from exile he was refused registration for residence in Moscow, even though his home was there. He remained in Moscow while pursuing registration for residence in Moscow and on 17 May 1978 he was present outside the courtroom where Yury Orlov, the founder of the Moscow Helsinki monitoring group, was on trial for "anti-Soviet agitation and propaganda". On the same day Begun was arrested and charged with "violation of the passport regulations" under Article 198 of the RSFSR Criminal Code. He was subsequently sentenced to another 3 years' exile.

Other dissenters who have been imprisoned for "parasitism" in the period from June 1975 to May 1979 include Grigory Goldstein, Alexander Ogorodnikov, Valentin Poplavsky, Pyotr Vins, Ivan Wagner and Amner Zavurov.

Among other charges which have in recent years been brought against dissenters on account of their exercise of their human rights rather than for criminal activity are "insulting a policeman" (the German would-be emigrants Arthur and Victor Klink, in 1976); "forging a document" (Felix Serebrov, in 1977, when he was active in publicizing political abuses of psychiatry); "theft of state property" (Alexander Bolonkin, who was convicted on this charge in 1978 when he was nearing the end of a 6-year sentence imposed for "anti-Soviet agitation and propaganda"); "treason" (on which charge the Jewish activist and Helsinki monitor Anatoly Shcharansky was sentenced to 13 years' imprisonment in 1978).

## Administrative Surveillance of Released Prisoners of Conscience

Virtually all prisoners of conscience are subjected after their release to intense discrimination by local authorities. Many prisoners of conscience may not return to their home towns, since under an unpublished section of the 1974 USSR Council of Ministers decree "Certain Instructions Concerning Registration" certain categories of released prisoners, including those convicted of "anti-Soviet agitation and propaganda" or "anti-Soviet slander" may not after their release reside in those cities barred to them by another unpublished decree. Moscow and Leningrad, for example, are on the forbidden list for many released prisoners. The record of conviction of released prisoners is marked in their personal documents and many have great difficulty in finding even menial employment. They are thus often exposed to possible charges of "parasitism". Former prisoners who try to take up contacts with dissenters are subjected to searches, police questioning and the risk of fresh criminal charges.

For some released prisoners, post-release restrictions are formalized as "administrative surveillance", which may virtually amount to an administratively-imposed extension of deprivation of liberty. Administrative surveillance is dealt with in this chapter because under Soviet criminal law it offers the authorities additional grounds for arresting and trying former prisoners of conscience.

The provisions for administrative surveillance are laid down in a statute issued by the Presidium of the USSR Supreme Soviet on 26 July 1966 and entitled "On Administrative Surveillance by the Militia Organs of People Released from Places of Imprisonment". Administrative surveillance is also dealt with in the Corrective Labour Code of each Union Republic (Chapter 20 of the RSFSR

Corrective Labour Code).

According to these laws, only prisoners in certain categories may be subjected to administrative surveillance after release. Any person who has been imprisoned for "anti-Soviet agitation and propaganda" or another "grave crime", and likewise anyone who has been imprisoned more than twice for premeditated crimes, may be subjected to administrative surveillance if the administration of the camp or prison where he or she was imprisoned declares that he or she showed "stubborn unwillingness to go on the path of correction", or if the militia at his or her place of residence rules that he or she has continued to "lead an antisocial way of life".

In either of these cases a procurator's agreement is required for the measure to be applied. However, the law's provisions on this are so loosely phrased as to enable this measure to be applied to many released prisoners simply if they continue to manifest views disapproved of by the authorities. In Amnesty International's experience, administrative surveillance is applied routinely to anyone released from imprisonment for "anti-Soviet agitation and propaganda" or another "especially dangerous crime against the state" and similarly to people who have been prisoners of conscience more than twice.

Administrative surveillance is carried out by the militia at the subject's place of residence after his or her release from imprisonment.

According to the 1966 statute, the purpose of administrative surveillance is "observation of the behaviour of people released from places of imprisonment, prevention of crimes by them and showing them necessary educational influence".

Individuals who are under administrative surveillance must report to the militia up to four times a month and also whenever summoned, comply with militia requests for information about their behaviour, inform the militia whenever they wish to make a trip from the district where they reside, and register with the militia at the place of their temporary sojourn and inform the militia of any change in their home address or place of work. The militia may without previous warning enter the subject's home at any time of the day or night. As well, the militia may require that the subject not leave his or her home during specified times of the day, prohibit his or her entry into specified places in the district of residence and prohibit departure from the district for any personal reasons.

Still according to the 1966 statute, these restrictions do not have as a goal "the humiliation of the subject's human dignity and compromising him at his place of work and domicile". However, these restrictions are regularly imposed so as to subject the released prisoner to restrictions little different from those of a court-imposed sentence of exile (see Chapter 2) and former prisoners of conscience regularly describe administrative surveillance as a form of imprisonment. Typical is the complaint to the USSR Supreme Court by Levko Lukyanenko, a lawyer who was subjected to administrative surveillance in 1976 after his release at the end of 15 years of imprisonment for trying to establish a group to work for constitutional reform in the Ukraine.

Being under surveillance, I do not have the right to leave the city without the permission of the militia. From evening to morning I can't leave my flat. I do not have the right to visit the hotels, cafes, bars and restaurants of the city and I am obliged to appear at the militia headquarters for registration every Friday from 5.00 am to 6.00 pm. They check up on me at work. All this is the official surveillance. But where is the limit to the unofficial surveillance as a result of which the authorities know my every step? It takes the privacy from my whole life.

Lukyanenko went on to describe how the authorities also tampered with his mail and telephone and used administrative surveillance as a means of isolating him and preventing any public activity on his part and as a constant threat of renewed imprisonment. Like most former prisoners of conscience, Lukyanenko was also denied any possibility of working in his own profession. In 1977 Lukyanenko was arrested, charged with "anti-Soviet agitation and propaganda" for his activities in the Ukrainian Helsinki monitoring group and sentenced to another 15 years' imprisonment.

According to the law, administrative surveillance may be imposed for from six months to one year, and thereafter it may be re-imposed for repeated periods of six months up until the date of expiry of the released prisoner's "record of conviction" (*sudimost*), the duration of which depends on the length of the sentence of imprisonment served by the subject. In this way, administrative surveillance may be continued for up to eight years, and in cases of people who have served more than 10 years' imprisonment it may be continued indefinitely, since their record of conviction may remain in force indefinitely unless lifted by a court decision (Article 57 of the RSFSR Criminal Code).

The law does not specify the grounds on which an order of administrative surveillance may be renewed. It says only that it may be renewed "in case of necessity", and thus leaves complete discretion to the local authorities to continue administrative surveillance (and restricted residence) on the grounds that the subject is still liable to commit a fresh criminal offence (such as "anti-Soviet agitation and propaganda") or is still pursuing an "anti-social way of life". Local authorities often make clear to former prisoners of conscience that administrative surveillance over them will continue as long as they maintain contact with dissenters, or continue to behave as dissenters.

On the initiative of the local militia, the courts may impose administrative penalties such as fines and warnings, etc. on individuals who violate the rules of administrative surveillance. Penalties can be imposed in cases such as those in which individuals visit places forbidden to them, leave the district on personal business, fail to answer militia queries about their behaviour or fail to report as scheduled to the militia.

An individual who is subjected to such a penalty twice within a year is then liable to arrest and conviction in a court of law under Article 198-2 of the RSFSR Criminal Code for a third violation of the rules of administrative surveillance. Article 198-2 states:

Malicious violation of the rules provided for by the Statute on
Administrative Supervision by Agencies of the Police Over People
Released from Places of Deprivation of Freedom in order to evade

supervision, if committed by a person who has been subjected to administrative pressure for the same violations twice within a year, shall be punished by deprivation of freedom for a term of six months to two years or by correctional tasks for a term of six months to one year.

It should be noted that this article of criminal law specifies that the offence must be deliberate and carried out "in order to evade supervision". In cases known to Amnesty International where former prisoners of conscience have been tried under this article such intent has not been proved by the authorities.

Prisoners of conscience sentenced in recent years to imprisonment or exile for this offence include Mustafa Dzhemilev, Yury Fyodorov, Anatoly Marchenko and Victor Chamovskikh.

64

*Notes*

1. Report submitted by the USSR to the Third Session of the Human Rights Committee (CCPR/C/1/Add. 22, 31 January 1978).
2. See "Introduction" to the 1975 edition of the Amnesty International report, *Prisoners of Conscience in the USSR: Their Treatment and Conditions*.
3. R. Kulikov, "Genuine and Purported Defenders of Human Rights", *Partiinaya Zhizn*, Number 3, (February 1974), page 69.
4. *Commentary to the RSFSR Criminal Code*, Moscow, 1971, pages 167-169.
5. *Ibid*, pages 403-404.
6. In this report, this offence is frequently referred to by an abbreviation of its title: "anti-Soviet slander".
7. See *The Case of Kovalyov*, Khronika Press, New York, 1976, for a 68-page unofficial transcript of the trial of Kovalyov. The excerpts are quoted from a translation of this transcript commissioned by Khronika Press.
8. See below, Chapter 2.
9. The group's documents have been published in English in Viktor Haynes and Olga Semyonova, *Workers Against the Gulag*, Pluto Press, London, 1979.
10. The Decree "On the Separation of Church and State and of School and Church" is available in English in Mervyn Matthews (editor), *Soviet Government: A Selection of Official Documents on Internal Policy*, Jonathan Cape, London, 1974. The Decree "On Religious Associations", as amended in 1975, is available in English in *Review of Socialist Law*, Leyden, Volume 1, Issue 3, September 1975.
11. This and the following references to the official Commentary to Article 142 are from *Commentary to the RSFSR Criminal Code*, Moscow, 1971, pages 306-309.
12. *Ibid*, pages 475-478.
13. The most complete available texts in English of these regulations appear in Leon Lipson and Valery Chalidze (editors), *Papers on Soviet Law*, The Institute of Socialist Law, New York, 1977.
14. *Commentary to the RSFSR Criminal Code*, Moscow, 1971, pages 181-182.
15. Complete texts in English of the current legislation on "parasitism" appears in Lipson and Chalidze, *Papers on Soviet Law*.

# CHAPTER 2

# Arrest, Trial and Sentencing

It is characteristic of political imprisonment in the USSR that virtually all political prisoners are arrested, tried and sentenced under criminal law, and released at the end of their court-imposed sentence. A broad category of exceptions to this rule are people confined to psychiatric hospitals (see Chapter 7).

In no case known to Amnesty International has a Soviet court acquitted a defendant brought to trial either specifically or in disguised form for his political or religious activity. Trials in such cases more closely resembly "show trials" than serious attempts to determine guilt or innocence, the correct application of the law or the proper degree of punishment. Furthermore, only in rare cases is there any evidence to suggest that the courts or other judicial agencies with a supervisory capacity have attempted to effect remedies of manifest illegalities in political cases.

## Arrest and Pre-trial Confinement

The actual arrest and indictment of religious, political or other dissenters in the USSR often comes as a culmination of official efforts to intimidate them through other means, in an effort to persuade them to give up their activities or to obtain information from them. By the time a prisoner of conscience is arrested, he or she is likely to have already been subjected to measures such as police surveillance, house searches, sessions of questioning by police or other authorities, confiscation of literature, typewriters, and other possessions, hostile newspaper articles about them in official media or dismissal from employment.

In many cases, KGB (Committee of State Security) officials have issued dissenters with a formal administrative warning that if they persist in their activity they may face criminal charges. This procedure is authorized under an unpublished decree issued by the Presidium of the USSR Supreme Soviet on 25 December 1972. Under it, the KGB can without any recourse to the courts label a person's behaviour as "anti-social" and harmful to state security and include this warning in any future criminal case against the subject and stimulate "educative measures" toward the subject at his or her place of work.[1]

It is also common for dissenters to be arrested and sentenced to up to 15 days in jail under administrative procedures. Such "administrative detention" may be imposed by decision of a local judge for such offences as "wilfully disobeying a police officer" and "petty hooliganism". The procedures are simple. Normally no defence counsel is present and the judge simply considers the police complaint and the defendant's response before making a decision. The simplicity of the procedures involved, and the vagueness of the charges for which the penalty may be imposed, makes it convenient for the authorities to apply it repeatedly to individual dissenters or to whole groups of dissenters.

People sentenced to administrative detention serve their sentences in jails attached to militia institutions, in cells in investigation prisons or in "sobering-up stations" for drunkards. Conditions in such places of detention are harsh. Prisoners under administrative detention receive warm meals only on alternate days and are given bread and water otherwise. They are not given bedding, are not permitted to smoke nor to write or receive letters. Besides these legalized deprivations, prisoners commonly complain about the unhygenic conditions and absence of medical attention in places of administrative detention.[2]

Apart from being held in administrative detention, many dissenters have been arrested and held for one or two days "on suspicion" under legal provisions allowing suspects to be detained for up to three days without charges being brought.

However, Amnesty International's most important concern remains people who are arrested, charged with an offence under criminal law and brought for trial and sentencing under criminal law.

According to Article 89 of the RSFSR Code of Criminal Procedure, people who are accused of criminal offences may be arrested and taken into custody for the period of pre-trial investigation only under certain circumstances: if there is a danger that otherwise they will flee, engage in criminal activity or hinder the investigation of their case. The law provides that even if these risks exist, measures of restraint other than arrest and confinement may be applied such as a signed promise not to depart; personal surety by a trustworthy person or by a public organization; or deposit of bail in the form of money or valuables.

Almost all prisoners of conscience known to Amnesty International have been taken into custody for the duration of the investigation and trial of their case.

By law, within one day of a person's being taken into custody the investigating authority must inform the Procurator's Office of the grounds and reason for detention, and the Procurator's Office must rule on the legality of the arrest within 24 hours after that.

According to the offence with which the accused person is charged, the investigation agency may be the Procuracy, the MVD or the KGB. The KGB is limited to dealing only with certain specified types of crime and mostly investigates "especially dangerous crimes against the state" (Articles 64 to 73 of the RSFSR Criminal Code, including "treason" and "anti-Soviet agitation and propaganda"). However, in practice this restriction on the role of the state security police does not exclude their involvement in the preparation of cases against prisoners of conscience charged under other articles of criminal law, since the KGB plays the main role in the surveillance and monitoring of dissenters and, evidently, in the decision to prosecute them.

According to Article 97 of the RSFSR Code of Criminal Procedure, an accused person may be held in custody for nine months at most for investigation before trial. Nowhere does Soviet law recognize any grounds for extension of the nine-month limit on pre-trial custody. However it is quite common for prisoners of conscience to be held in custody for a year or more before coming to trial.

Soviet authorities have occasionally justified this violation of criminal law on the grounds that the USSR Supreme Soviet, as the highest legislative authority, has the authority to issue edicts making exceptions to the law as it stands. Nevertheless, even this dubious procedure to legitimize excessively long custody of prisoners of conscience is known to have been followed only in a few cases (for example, that of Leonid Plyushch in 1973 and that of Anatoly Shcharansky in 1978).

People in custody for investigation of their cases are held in "investigation-isolation prisons" of the MVD or, if their cases fall within the jurisdiction of the KGB, in investigation-isolation prisons of the KGB. Their conditions of confinement are laid down in the Statute "On Preliminary Confinement", issued by the Presidium of the USSR Supreme Soviet in July 1969.

According to available accounts, there is chronic overcrowding in many investigation prisons of the MVD, where the great majority of arrested criminal suspects are held. Accounts of the MVD central investigation prison in Riga (Latvia SSR) in the mid-1970s indicated that it held around 5,000 inmates at any one time and although it had recently been enlarged to cope with the overflow it was still so overcrowded that there were not enough sleeping places for all the inmates who, as a consequence, were often required to sleep on the floor. It appears that KGB investigation prisons are not so overcrowded, a reflection of the restrictions on the KGB's formal jurisdiction.

People in custody on charges connected with political dissent are usually held in a cell with one or two other people or, less commonly, in solitary confinement. While some prisoners have expressed their content at being thus free of the overcrowded conditions to which most arrested people are subjected, others have complained that prolonged semi-isolation is a severe hardship, especially when, for many months, the prisoner is denied any visits from his or her family, friends or lawyer (see below). Furthermore, prisoners frequently have reported that the cell-mate assigned them was an *agent provocateur* or informer, which only added to the psychological pressure on them.

Arrested suspects are permitted one hour's exercise every day. They are required to observe a strict order of the day regulating reveille, lights out, meal times, exercise times, etc. Prisoners are required to rise and remain standing whenever anyone enters the cell. Prisoners under investigation have also complained about the quantity and quality of their meals, which they take in their cells, although they are better fed while in pre-trial custody than after they are convicted. They are permitted by law to receive a parcel weighing up to five kilograms each month and to spend up to 10 rubles each month on supplementary food and basic necessities. Prisoners under investigation in some prisons have a flush toilet in their cells, but most must make do with a slop bucket (*parasha*).

Conditions in investigation prisons are strongly determined by security considerations. There is a peep-hole in the door of each cell and, at least where political prisoners are concerned, guards peer into the cells every few minutes. A light shines in each cell 24 hours a day, and the cell windows are painted over or otherwise blocked so as to prevent the prisoners from seeing out and daylight from coming in. Inmates are required to sleep facing the cell door and with their hands outside the bedcovers. They are not permitted to talk when being taken through the corridors for exercise, to the toilets or for interrogations and must walk in front of their guards with their hands behind their backs. To prevent prisoners meeting one another in the corridors, the guards accompanying them make noises by clicking their tongues or fingers or jangling their keys and force the escorted prisoner to face the wall or stand in a closet-like facility known as a "box" whenever they hear another guard approaching with a prisoner. Prisoners who violate prison discipline in pre-trial custody may be put in a punishment cell for up to 10 days, with reduced rations and other deprivations.

Interrogation of prisoners takes place in the offices of the investigators in the prison. As indicated in Chapter 1, people charged under the purely political articles of criminal law normally do not deny the actions with which they have been charged (for example circulating *samizdat* or teaching religion to children) but deny that their actions were criminal. From numerous available accounts, it appears that the questioning of dissenters focuses on trying to persuade them to recant their views or confess that their dissident activity was "criminal" and on trying to get information about other dissenters.

In a number of trials prisoners of conscience (and similarly trial witnesses) have retracted testimony given by them during the pre-trial investigation, stating that it was extracted from them by coercion in the form of threats of a heavy sentence or psychiatric confinement or of reprisals against relatives.

There is also considerable evidence that physical ill-treatment during inter-rogation has frequently been inflicted on prisoners, particularly on ordinary criminal prisoners but also on some prisoners of conscience.

In 1975 comprehensive documentation arrived outside the USSR regarding systematic and brutal ill-treatment of suspects in custody in the main MVD investigation prison in Tbilisi, capital of the Georgian republic. The central document was an unofficial transcript of the April 1975 trial of two inmates of the prison on charges of beating a fellow inmate to death. One of the defendants, Yury Tsirekidze, testified that he had beaten the victim on instructions from prison authorities, and that he had undertaken this sort of task many times over a period of years to help obtain "confessions" from prisoners charged with criminal offences.

The trial transcript and other materials indicate that investigative officials of the prison, abetted by certain local officials, had regularly employed convicted prisoners in this way. Among the methods allegedly used were beatings, burning victims with cigarettes and subjecting them to homosexual rape. The material further indicated that over the years several prisoners had died as a result of such treatment.

When this situation came to light in connection with the Tsirekidze case several officials were transferred from their positions, and the judge in the Tsirekidze trial said that some implicated officials should be brought to criminal responsibility. Issue number 38 of *A Chronicle of Current Events* (dated 31 December 1975) reported that criminal charges had been brought against two members of the prison's staff.

Similar ill-treatment of arrested suspects in order to extract "confessions" from them has been reported regarding a number of other prisons.

Beatings of prisoners of conscience, or at least those whose cases are known to human rights groups within the country and abroad, are far from inevitable, but a number of instances of this have been recorded. For example, Alexander Bolonkin, a Moscow engineer, was nearing the end of 6 years' imprisonment and exile on charges of "anti-Soviet agitation and propaganda" when, in 1978, charges of "stealing state property" were brought against him. He was taken to an investigation prison in Ulan-Ude (in the Buryat ASSR) where, he subsequently said in a complaint to Soviet judicial authorities, a criminal cell-mate beat him, threatened him with a knife and with rape and demanded that he "confess" to the charges against him. According to Bolonkin's detailed account, his cell-mate made clear that he was acting with the compliance of the prison authorities. Bolonkin was subsequently sentenced to 3 years' imprisonment.

The USSR Statute on Preliminary Confinement states that people held in custody during the investigation of their case may meet relatives or other individuals only with the express consent of the investigation officials. If visits are permitted, they may be of up to two hours' duration and no more than once a month, and must take place in the presence of a guard. No more than two adults and, in addition, children under the age of 16 may visit the prisoner at any one time. It is exceptional for arrested dissenters to be permitted any visits from the time of their arrest until after their trial, even when the pre-trial detention is a year or more in duration.

An accused person (unless he or she is a minor or dumb, deaf or blind) in custody has the right to meet a lawyer only when the investigator formally announces to him that the preliminary investigation is complete and that he has the right to study the documents of the case against him with the help of a defence lawyer.[3] Legally, this may occur as long as nine months after the arrest; in practice it has often been even longer. Prisoners of conscience have normally had access to a lawyer only in the few days, or at best weeks, before their trial.

From the moment when the investigator announces to the prisoner that the preliminary investigation is complete the proceedings are set in motion for formulating the indictment and bringing the case for trial. According to Article 202 of the RSFSR Code of Criminal Procedure, the accused and his or her lawyer may meet alone together to study the materials of the case, although in cases of "especially dangerous crimes against the state" the lawyer is not permitted to take the case materials away for study, as is normal in non-political cases. Both the accused and his or her lawyer have the right to petition for additional investigation to be undertaken, for additional materials to be added to the case file and for additional witnesses to be listed for testifying at the forthcoming trial. However, the investigator is not obliged to accede to these petitions and in political cases they have systematically been rejected.

After the accused and the defence lawyer have studied the file, the investigator draws up a document known as the "conclusion to indict" (*obvinitelnoye zaklyuchenniye*), which consists of an account of the substance of the case, the evidence against the accused and a formal accusation. The investigator submits the conclusion to indict to the procurator. It is the procurator's task to establish among other things whether the preliminary investigation "has been conducted thoroughly, completely and objectively", whether there is a *corpus delicti* and whether the accusation is based on the evidence accumulated.[4] Within five days of receiving the conclusion to indict, the procurator must act on it, either by submitting it to the court in whose jurisdiction it falls (if he confirms the indictment), by returning it to the investigator for supplementary investigation or reformulation of the accusation, by re-writing the indictment, or by terminating the case.

When, as almost invariably happens in cases involving dissenters, the procurator submits the conclusion to indict to the court, the court assigns the case to one of its judges. The judge to whom the case is assigned must decide within 14 days whether to bring the case to trial. In certain circumstances, for example if the judge disagrees with the indictment, he or she may convene what is known as an "administrative session" of the court to decide the issue. Participation of the procurator in an administrative session of the court is obligatory, but the pertinent articles of the RSFSR Code of Criminal Procedure do not mention possible participation of the accused or his or her defence counsel in this proceeding.[5] The court may decide to bring the accused to trial, or it may decide to terminate the case, return it for supplementary investigation or alter the indictment in various ways, for example by reducing the charges to less serious articles of the criminal code. Once the court has decided to bring the case to trial, it must also decide such matters as whether to accept as defence counsel the lawyer selected by the accused person, whether to appoint defence counsel on the accused person's behalf, whether to hold the trial in open or closed session and which witnesses to summon to the trial. Under Article 239 of the RSFSR Code of Criminal Procedure, the trial must begin within 14 days of the court's decision to bring the case to trial.

Throughout these pre-trial proceedings there are numerous points at which decisions could be taken to benefit the accused. Indeed, given that Soviet courts invariably convict people brought to trial on account of their political or religious behaviour, it is only during the preliminary proceedings that a decision might be made which would have the effect of preventing the accused from being sentenced. In most cases of prisoners of conscience either the investigator (in conducting the preliminary investigation and drawing up the conclusion to indict) or the procurator (in approving the conclusion to indict) or the judge (in deciding whether to bring the case to trial) would have strong grounds for deciding that no criminal offence had been committed. This is so, for example, if there is no reason to believe that a person's utterances were made with "anti-Soviet intent" in a case of "anti-Soviet agitation and propaganda", or if there is no likelihood that "hooliganism" or "parasitism" had taken place as charged. During these preliminary proceedings decisions could also be made which would facilitate a thorough and objective examination of the facts of the case, which in cases of prisoners of conscience would almost inevitably be to the benefit of the accused even when they were charged under articles of criminal law aimed specifically at the exercise of freedom of conscience. This is often so, for example, when the accused asks for witnesses or experts to be called who could cast light on his or her intentions in carrying out the allegedly criminal behaviour or actions, or who could testify as to the truthfulness of the statements he or she was accused of circulating as "anti-Soviet slander".

However, in Amnesty International's experience people who are faced with criminal charges on account of their behaviour as dissenters are as unlikely to benefit from exacting application of the law during preliminary proceedings as during their trials. Defence petitions for supplementary examination of the case or listing of supplementary witnesses have been refused as a matter of course if they would upset the prosecution's case or if they would lead to an embarrassing confrontation at the trial. Dissenters have been regularly indicted and brought to trial for actions which do not constitute a criminal offence even under the overtly political articles of the criminal code and often dissenters have been brought to trial on conspicuously fabricated charges. Soviet dissenters have persistently complained that the main hope prisoners of conscience have of having the charges against them dropped during the preliminary proceedings is if some political aspect of the case favours this, especially if they cooperate in some way with the authorities or if there is sufficient scandal (internationally, given the complete official censorship of the Soviet media) to make it expedient for the authorities to release them rather than procede with the case.

## Defence Counsel

An accused person in custody is permitted to consult a lawyer only at the end of the preliminary investigation of his or her case. Thus the accused is left without benefit of counsel throughout most of the pre-trial proceedings in the case.

According to Article 48 of the RSFSR Code of Criminal Procedure, an accused person has the right to choose his or her own defence counsel. The court may assign a defence lawyer if the accused person so requests, but if this happens the accused has the right to reject the lawyer selected by the court (Articles 48 and 50, RSFSR Code of Criminal Procedure).

The legal position and professional organization of lawyers are laid down in the Statute on the Advocates of the RSFSR (1962) and similar statutes in other Union Republics. The legal profession is supervised by the USSR Ministry of Justice and its local administrations. All practising lawyers are members of the College of Advocates of their region or territory, a body roughly equivalent to Bar associations in other countries. There is a College of Advocates for each intermediate level territorial unit in the USSR, that is to say for each region, territory, Autonomous Soviet Socialist Republic and National Area, as well as for Moscow and Leningrad, and for each Union Republic which is not subdivided into such intermediate levels (Armenia, Estonia, Latvia, Lithuania and Moldavia). Each College of Advocates is led by a Presidium (headed by a chairman), which, among other things, decides on the admission of a lawyer into the College and likewise the expulsion of a lawyer for misconduct or incompetence.

In their day-to-day activity lawyers work out of Legal Advice Centres, which have offices in lower territorial units, such as districts and smaller cities. A person wishing to engage a lawyer normally approaches one of these Legal Advice Centres.

In practice prisoners of conscience facing trial very often experience considerable difficulty in obtaining a defence lawyer of their own choice. This is only partly because they are held *incommunicado* and are not permitted to consult with their family or friends who might assist them in the task of finding a lawyer.

An important restriction on the right to choose a lawyer is that in cases of crimes such as "treason" and "anti-Soviet agitation and propaganda", the investigation of which is in the jurisdiction of the KGB, lawyers may act as defence counsel only if their names are on a list giving them a clearance (*dopusk*) to defend in such cases. According to lawyers who have left the USSR and other sources, the list is drawn up by the KGB and is unpublished; it is filed with the Chairman of the Presidium of each College of Advocates. By all accounts, only a minority of lawyers are listed as having a clearance for such cases.

Lawyers who are known to have made an energetic defence in a political case are likely to have their names struck off the list. Among lawyers in Moscow to whom this has happened are Dina Kaminskaya, Sofiya Kallistratova, Yury Pozdeyev and Vladimir Shveisky.

Colleges of Advocates may also use other pretexts to bar lawyers from defending in political cases. For example, the Moscow College of Advocates has repeatedly refused to allow members to act as defence counsel in trials of dissenters which were held outside the Moscow area, although there are no grounds for this in law. This happened in the case of Victor Nekipelov in 1974, Vyacheslav Igrunov in 1975, and Pavel Bashkirov in 1976.

Many lawyers who do have a clearance to act as defence counsel in political cases are reluctant to appear for the defence in such cases. Evidently some lawyers fear being made to choose between their obligations to the client and their sworn commitment to the official ideology. The possibility of conflict between these positions is compounded by the role assumed by the Communist Party of the Soviet Union in determining what constitutes the interests of society. Most lawyers are members or candidate members of the Communist Party of the Soviet Union. This means that they have a dual allegiance: to the law and to the party, the latter institution requiring uncompromising obedience to its rules and policies.

According to one lawyer who has left the USSR, some defence lawyers refuse to defend in political cases on moral grounds, believing that they have no hope of influencing the outcome of the case and that their participation would help give a false impression that the case was conducted with proper respect for the rights of the accused.

Another very real deterrent is simple fear of reprisals. There have been well known cases of outright persecution of lawyers who refused to compromise in their defence of political clients. The best known such case was that of B.A. Zolotukhin, a leading Moscow lawyer who defended Alexander Ginzburg in Moscow in 1968. Zolotukhin's defence was greatly admired by friends of Ginzburg. However, within five months of the trial Zolotukhin was expelled from the party, from the Presidium of the College of Advocates, from his post as head of a legal consultative office and finally from the College of Advocates itself. The reason given was Zolotukhin's "adopting a non-party, non-Soviet line in his defence" of Ginzburg. The consequence was that he was deprived of the right to work as a defence lawyer.

Another lawyer who has suffered a similar fate is I.S. Yezhov, who in 1973 in the Ukraine defended Alexander Feldman, a Jewish would-be emigrant convicted on fabricated charges of hooliganism. Yezhov was subsequently struck off the register of the Kiev College of Advocates and subjected to other forms of pressure.

The difficulties political defendants may have in appointing defence lawyers of their own choice are illustrated by the case of Anatoly Shcharansky. Shcharansky, facing charges of "treason" which carried a possible death penalty, was held totally *incommunicado* for almost 16 months before being brought to trial in July 1978. His family was at no point permitted to see him to learn his wishes regarding choice of defending counsel. In June 1978 Anatoly Shcharansky's mother asked the Moscow lawyer Dina Kaminskaya to defend her son. Mrs Kaminskaya was well known for her work as defence counsel in a number of cases of prisoners of conscience. She had in 1970 been struck off the list of lawyers with clearance to act as defence counsel in cases investigated by the KGB after she defended in the Tashkent trial of two prisoners of conscience, Ilya Gabai and Mustafa Dzhemilev. Subsequently she was refused permission to act as defence counsel in several political cases, including that of Andrei Tverdokhlebov, who was charged with "dissemination of fabrications known to be false which defame the Soviet state and social system", an offence which is not legally within the competence of the KGB to investigate. When approached by Shcharansky's mother, Mrs Kaminskaya agreed to take the case, and Shcharansky's mother submitted her name to the College of Advocates as the lawyer chosen by her to defend in the case. Eleven days later, in Mrs Kaminskaya's absence, the Presidium of the Moscow College of Advocates expelled her from the College. Mrs Kaminskaya, who had been a practising lawyer for 17 years, was thus barred from further practice. Over the next six months she was persecuted in various ways: steps were taken under civil law to have her evicted from her flat; her husband was summoned for questioning and then dismissed from his job; their flat was searched by police; and finally they were told that if they did not leave the USSR her husband would be imprisoned for "anti-Soviet agitation and propaganda". Mrs Kaminskaya and her husband left the USSR six months after she was prevented from taking on the Shcharansky case.

Shcharansky's mother then asked 20 other lawyers to take her son's case. Some turned out not to have the necessary clearance, others said they would take the case only if Shcharansky pleaded guilty and others refused outright. In the end, the court appointed a lawyer to defend Shcharansky. At his trial Shcharansky refused the services of this lawyer and conducted his own defence.

According to the law a defendant can refuse the services of a court-appointed lawyer and, if no acceptable replacement is found, conduct his or her own defence in court. While in some cases, like that of Shcharansky, the court has permitted the officially selected lawyer to withdraw from the case, in other cases courts have defied the wishes of the defendant in this matter and insisted that the court-appointed lawyer conduct the defence. This happened in June and July 1977 when Mykola Rudenko and Oles Tikhy, two members of the Ukrainian Helsinki monitoring group, were tried for "anti-Soviet agitation and propaganda". At their trial, the court-appointed defence counsel defied the defendants' own views by acknowledging them as guilty, conducted only a formal defence and pleaded only for mitigation of the sentence.

Occasionally the courts do not even pretend to ensure the right of legal defence. In March 1979 the Crimean Tartar Mustafa Dzhemilev was tried and sentenced to 4 years' exile without his defence counsel or him being present. A few of his relatives were in the courtroom and walked out when they heard the judge begin to hear the case in these circumstances.

In some political trials defence lawyers have tried to present the strongest defence case possible and to have their client recognized as not guilty, in defiance of all the presssures put upon them by official agencies and their own College of Advocates. However, defence lawyers in political trials face overwhelming disadvantages in trying to defend their clients. Soviet courts are strongly biased against political and religious defendants. When hearing such cases the courts almost invariably refuse to allow the defence lawyer to develop any promising line of defence and obstruct the defence when it tries to call defence witnesses, cross-examine prosecution witnesses or undertake serious examination of controversial elements of the charges or the evidence. The courts are liable to interpret any defence of the actions or motivations of a political defendant as endorsement of the defendant's actions. This was made plain by one of the country's most eminent legal scholars, Professor M.S. Strogovich:

> The most important and pressing concern is that a Soviet lawyer is not
> allowed to use nor will he support any line of defence which smacks of
> being anti-Soviet in its essential thrust.[6]

Thus, lawyers are virtually prohibited from offering the most logical and legally meaningful defence of defendants charged explicitly for their political or religious activity: that such activity is not criminal even under Soviet law but is rather legitimate exercise of human rights.

For these reasons, the work of defence counsel in political trials in the Soviet Union has little influence on the outcome either in the pre-trial or trial stages. Even the most honest, forthright and competent lawyers often place their main hope on trying to persuade the court to reduce the charges against the defendant or pass a more lenient sentence. However, all information available to Amnesty International indicates that such issues are not resolved in the courtroom but are decided according to decisions taken elsewhere by the political and state security organs.

## Trial

Amnesty International is not aware of any case in which a Soviet court has acquitted a defendant who was brought to trial either directly or indirectly because of his or her political or religious activity. Although Soviet authorities frequently state publicly that the principle of "presumption of innocence" is respected in Soviet judicial practice, prisoners of conscience and their relatives and friends regard a guilty verdict as inevitable once a case is brought to trial. That such cases once begun always end in a conviction indicates that criteria other than criminal culpability are decisive. The counter-argument might be that the investigative organs do their job so thoroughly that there is no chance of a mistake. However, if the investigators are always correct, then the courts' decisions as to guilt or innocence are irrelevant. The question of guilt having been pre-decided by the simple decision to bring the case to trial, the only question not known to the defendant before the trial begins is the severity of sentence to be handed down.

The Soviet authorities do not make available official transcripts of political trials. Most trials of concern to Amnesty International have gone unreported in the Soviet news media. When accounts have been published in the official Soviet media they have usually been brief, have apparently been published mainly because of foreign public interest in the case in question and have invariably been totally hostile to the defendant. Indeed, the Soviet news media appear not to be bound in political and religious cases by the principle of "presumption of innocence" and, on a number of occasions in recent years, the Soviet news media have acted as "public accusers" of dissenters, printing stories directly accusing them of crimes even before they had been arrested or charged.

Although the authorities take strong measures to minimize public attendance at trials and disrupt efforts by private individuals to take notes on the proceedings, there exist numerous detailed accounts, often verbatim, of political trials by friends and relatives of defendants, as well as retrospective accounts by convicted people themselves. Furthermore, the law requires that a copy of the judgment of the court against a defendant must be given to him or her. Although in many cases prisoners of conscience have not been given a copy of the judgment, this requirement is respected sufficiently often that a number of such documents have found their way into *samizdat* circulation, as in many cases have copies of "the conclusion to indict". From these and other sources observers have been able to learn a great deal about the nature of political trials in the USSR.

Soviet courts exist at three levels. The highest level consists of the Supreme Court of the USSR. Below it are the Supreme Courts of each Union Republic. The intermediate level consists of the court for each region, territory, autonomous republic or national area, as well as the city courts of Moscow and Leningrad. The lowest level consists of the People's Courts of each district and of the smaller cities and towns. Five Union Republics (Armenia, Estonia, Latvia, Lithuania and Moldavia) do not have intermediate territorial subdivisions, and so in these republics the Union Republic Supreme Court takes over the jurisdiction of the intermediate level courts.

The Code of Criminal Procedure spells out which types of case fall within the jurisdiction of each of the different levels of the courts. Cases of "especially dangerous crimes against the state" (such as "treason" and "anti-Soviet agitation and propaganda") are within the jurisdiction of the intermediate level courts and are normally tried in the first instance by courts at that level. In the five Union Republics which do not have intermediate level courts, the Union Republic Supreme Court tries such cases at the first instance. Most crimes, and most cases of concern to Amnesty International, are tried in the first instance at the lowest level, the level of the People's Courts. Thus, most cases of "dissemination of fabrications known to be false which defame the Soviet state and social system", most cases involving charges of "hooliganism" or "parasitism" and most religious cases are tried at district level People's Courts. Any higher level court can take over a case from a lower level court within its jurisdiction and try it as the court of first instance, but generally the pattern of jurisdiction described above is maintained in practice.

Most trials of political and religious dissenters are held in the normal seat of the court. Those present in the courtroom normally include at least the following: a bench of three (including a professional judge, who presides over the court, and two lay people known as "people's assessors"), the secretary to the court, the prosecutor (an official of the procuracy), the defence counsel, the defendant and the armed police escort guarding the defendant.

Both the judges and the people's assessors are elected officials, and may be recalled from office for misbehaviour. The people's assessors do not have legal training. Although their participation is intended in part to ensure some sort of public control over the workings of justice, in Amnesty International's experience the people's assessors play virtually no role in political trials, but instead sit silent throughout the proceedings.

In the trials known to Amnesty International the presiding judge has usually acted aggressively toward the defendant, treating him or her as guilty from the outset, systematically disrupting the defence and frequently making remarks hostile to the defendant's beliefs and associates.

The willingness of the court to participate in violations of procedural norms has almost always shown itself at the very outset of the trial, when the question arises as to the admission of the public to the trial. According to Article 18 of the RSFSR Code of Criminal Procedure, a trial must be open unless it involves state secrets, sexual crimes, a defendant who is less than 16 years of age or "intimate aspects of the lives of persons participating in the case". In virtually all the trials of political and religious dissenters known to Amnesty International the court has declared the trial open but has systematically barred the general public and friends and relatives of the accused from entering. In many trials groups and sometimes large crowds of people sympathetic to the defendant have gathered outside the courtroom. As a matter of routine they have been told they could not enter because of lack of space, or because "they had not been invited". It is normal for the authorities to pack the courtroom with specially invited spectators, often carrying specially-issued passes. Very often the invited audience consists largely of state security personnel. In other cases, groups of workers, law students or others have filled the courtroom. In some cases it is known that transportation and even hotel accommodation have been provided for the invited audience. Often the spectators have interrupted the proceedings with loud remarks hostile to the defendant, such as the cries of "traitor" and "spy" which rang out during the trial of Helsinki monitor Yury Orlov in 1978 in Moscow.

In some instances the authorities have justified the practice of inviting special audiences to such trials on the grounds that this serves to extend the "educative influence" of the trial. In fact, this is but one way in which such trials still retain the flavour and quality of show trials.

Friends and relatives of political and religious dissenters are regularly barred from entering the courtroom, even when there are free places left by the invited audience. Usually the authorities admit the one or two relatives closest to the defendant and sometimes a few friends. For example, at the first session of the trial of Vladimir Shelkov and four other Seventh Day Adventist defendants in January 1979 in Tashkent the judge admitted a total of three relatives of the five defendants, although a large crowd of sympathizers and relatives was gathered outside the court building.

One technique used to keep the trial closed is for the prosecution to summon a friend or even close relative of the defendant as a witness, and schedule their appearance relatively late in the proceedings. Since in law witnesses are not permitted to come into the courtroom until they are called to testify, people summoned in this way are barred from much of the trial and thus prevented from reporting to others what happened during the proceedings. Political and religious defendants have frequently refused to participate in their trials unless at least some of their relatives were admitted to the courtroom.

Other techniques are frequently used to keep the public away from political trials. Sometimes the court hears the case in some other locality or premises, for example the place of work or residence of the accused or some public building. The court has the right to do this in law, and may justify such a change of venue as necessary to maximize the "educational significance" of the trial. However, the main effect is not to make the case better known publicly (since political and religious trials are usually effectively barred to the public anyway) but to hinder the friends and relatives of the defendant from getting to the trial, since they are often not notified until the last moment, or not at all, of the time and place of the trial, or are given misleading information. In a number of trials large detachments of police have cordoned off the area of the courtroom to keep sympathizers away. It is not uncommon for sympathizers gathered outside a political trial to be picked up by police, detained for questioning, sentenced to up to 2 weeks' administrative detention or simply returned forcibly to their homes. In some cases the police have detained people about to leave home to attend a trial and forbidden them to leave their residence.

Trials of political and religious dissenters are usually brief, lasting a week or so at most. This too is indicative of the low quality of the trials, especially when one bears in mind the severity of the sentences liable to be passed and the complexity of any serious proof of such charges as "anti-Soviet agitation and propaganda" or "anti-Soviet slander". Much of the time is taken up by purely formal aspects of the case: the reading of the indictment; the final summing up by the defence and prosecution; the "last word" of the defendant; and the reading of the court's judgment. Only a relatively small proportion of the limited time available is devoted to actual examination of the evidence and the issues. As mentioned earlier, presiding judges systematically refuse defence petitions for calling supplementary witnesses or bringing in additional evidence, prevent defence counsel from conducting any serious cross-examination of witnesses and cut short statements by defence witnesses and the defendant. Even when the most flagrant breaches of the rules of evidence or other procedures on the part of the investigative organs are brought to the attention of the court, the presiding judge can be expected to stop any examination of such matters.

The three-person bench retires from the courtroom to formulate the verdict and to fix the sentence. One member of the bench, usually the presiding judge, reads out the judgment in the courtroom. According to Articles 314 and 315 of the RSFSR Code of Criminal Procedure, the court's judgment must summarize the accusation and the evidence, declare the court's judgment as to the guilt of the defendant and state the sentence of punishment decided on by the court. The numerous court judgments seen by Amnesty International are all at least several pages in length, and sometimes considerably longer. The court judgment normally simply recites at length the contents of the "conclusion to indict", omitting reference to disputation raised by the defence counsel or defendant. While in political cases the courts occasionally drop or alter some of the specific charges contained in the indictment, they invariably uphold the important substance of the indictment both as regards the evidence and as regards the conclusion of guilt.

## Sentencing

The Criminal Code specifies minimum and maximum sentences for each offence contained in it. For some offences sentences may be imposed which do not involve any form of imprisonment: for example, the imposition of a fine, deprivation of the right to hold a particular type of job or confiscation of property. Five types of punishment involve or may involve, depending on the manner of execution of the sentence, imprisonment or restriction of physical liberty: these are imprisonment, exile, banishment, corrective work without imprisonment and obligatory "induction to labour" of people sentenced conditionally to imprisonment. (See Chapter 3 for a description of these punishments.)

Apart from the death penalty, the most severe type of punishment is *imprisonment*, which is known in Soviet law as "deprivation of liberty". The maximum sentence of imprisonment which may be imposed for any offence or combination of offences is 15 years. In passing a sentence of imprisonment the court indicates not only the duration of the imprisonment but also the type of corrective labour institution in which the sentence is to be served.

According to the law the most severe type of institution in which imprisonment may be served is a *prison*. It is fairly rare for prisoners of conscience to be sentenced at their trial to a term in a prison, and when such a sentence is passed it is usually for the person to serve the first part of his sentence (usually around five years) in a prison and the remainder of the term of imprisonment in a corrective labour colony. Most prisoners of conscience sentenced to a term in prison had been convicted a second time of an "especially dangerous crime against the state", such as "anti-Soviet agitation and propaganda". However, the law does not limit this type of sentence to second offenders and occasionally, as in the case of Anatoly Shcharansky in 1978, a court has sentenced a first offender in a political case to a term of confinement in a prison.

The second most severe type of institution in which a term of imprisonment may be served is a *corrective labour colony with special regime*. This type of imprisonment may in law be applied to "especially dangerous recidivists" and people for whom the death penalty has been commuted through pardon or amnesty. Prisoners of conscience sentenced to this type of imprisonment are usually people convicted a second time of "anti-Soviet agitation and propaganda". Women may not be sentenced to imprisonment in a special regime corrective labour colony.

The third most severe type of institution in which a term of imprisonment may be served is a *corrective labour colony with strict regime*. According to the law, those convicted for the first time of "especially dangerous crimes against the state" and some categories of second offenders convicted of other crimes are to be sentenced to this type of imprisonment. Most prisoners of conscience who are convicted of "treason" or "anti-Soviet agitation and propaganda" serve their sentences in this type of imprisonment.

*Reinforced regime colonies* and *ordinary regime colonies* are in law the least severe types of corrective labour institution and are reserved mainly for first offenders convicted of crimes considered less serious.

Most prisoners of conscience known to Amnesty International have been sentenced to imprisonment in strict or ordinary regime corrective labour colonies.

Although 15 years is the maximum length of imprisonment a court may impose in convicting a defendant, people who are convicted of a crime committed while serving a term of imprisonment may be required to serve their second sentence of imprisonment in addition to their first sentence. Furthermore, in sentencing someone to imprisonment a court may require that he or she serve out any remaining part of a previous sentence from which he or she was released early by way of pardon or amnesty.

It is also important to note that there are still a considerable number of prisoners in the USSR who are serving 25-year sentences of imprisonment. Prior to 1958, when the present criminal law entered into force with its maximum sentence of 15 years' imprisonment, the maximum term was 25 years. Shortly after enacting the new criminal legislation in 1958, the Presidium of the USSR Supreme Soviet issued a decree saying that those who had been sentenced under the previous legislation for "especially dangerous crimes against the state" could not benefit from reduction of their sentences to the new limit on the length of imprisonment. Despite constant protests, people in this category (including a number of Ukrainians and members of the Baltic nationalities who during and after the Second World War participated in a nationalist resistance to Soviet rule) have been required to serve their sentences in full. Some are not due for release until the early 1980s, while others have had fresh sentences added while serving imprisonment.

Another frequently imposed punishment is *exile* to a specified locality within the USSR. The maximum permitted sentence of exile is five years. A sentence of exile may be imposed either as the basic punishment or as a supplementary punishment to be served after a term of imprisonment. It is quite common for prisoners of conscience to be sentenced to a combination of imprisonment and exile, especially prisoners convicted of "anti-Soviet agitation and propaganda".

Another type of punishment is *banishment* of the convicted person from his or her place of residence with possible prohibition against living in other specified localities as well. The maximum term of banishment is five years. In Amnesty International's experience, the dissenters most commonly sentenced to this type of punishment are Crimean Tartars put on trial for attempting to take up residence in the Crimea.

Baptist pastor Pyotr Siemens being led from his trial in 1975. He is being taken to a "Raven" (*Voronok*), a truck for carrying prisoners

Lithuanian prisoner of conscience Romaldes Ragaishis being taken from his trial in Vilnius, 10 July 1979

Ukrainian Helsinki monitor Mykola Rudenko

Lyubyanka KGB Headquarters and Investigation—Isolation Prison in Dzerzhinsky Square, Moscow

The maximum sentence of *corrective work without imprisonment* is one year. Imposition of this type of sentence has not been common in political and religious cases, although during recent years there may have been some tendency towards its becoming more common in cases involving charges under less serious articles of criminal law.

In passing sentence the court is required to take into account various aspects of the case and the defendant's personality which might mitigate his or her responsibility or aggravate it, and determine the sentences accordingly. In some cases the courts have said in their judgments that they assigned a lesser punishment because of the defendant's family circumstances, age, state of health or previous record of behaviour. In other cases courts have disregarded any mitigating circumstances and applied the maximum sentence even on ill or aged defendants. Certainly the most important "mitigating circumstances" in political and religious cases is the willingness of the defendant to express "sincere repentance" (Article 38, point 10 of the RSFSR Criminal Code), and court judgments frequently stress the refusal of political or religious defendants to express repentance or recognize guilt.

The court also has the option of making a sentence of imprisonment conditional. In doing so the court sets a probation period of up to five years during which the convicted person is not required to serve the sentence unless he or she commits a fresh crime. Conditional sentences are rare in political or religious cases.

In certain types of cases the courts may impose a "conditional sentence of imprisonment with obligatory induction of the convicted person to labour".[7] This type of suspended sentence may be imposed only where the sentence of imprisonment is no more than three years, and may not be imposed in cases of "especially dangerous crimes against the state".

## Appeal, Review and Other Means of Relief from Sentence

According to law the convicted person must receive a copy of the court's judgment within three days of its being proclaimed. Within seven days of receiving a copy of the judgment the convicted person may *appeal* to a higher court against the verdict or sentence of the court of first instance. This is known as "appeal by way of cassation". If the convicted person does not lodge an appeal, the court judgment takes legal effect at the end of the seven-day period, and within the next 10 days he or she must be sent from the investigation prison to serve the sentence.

The lodging of an appeal suspends execution of the sentence, and after lodging an appeal the convicted person must, according to law, remain in the investigation prison until the appeal has been resolved. In some cases even this formality has not been respected. For example, Felix Serebrov, a member of a human rights group set up in Moscow to monitor political abuses of psychiatry, was sent off in 1977 to serve a sentence of imprisonment before his appeal had been heard. A court of appeal at the intermediate level must consider the appeal within 10 days of receiving it; a Union Republic Supreme Court when acting as an appeal court must consider the appeal within 20 days. Like trials, appeal hearings must be held in open session, except where state secrets, sexual crimes, defendants who are under 16 years of age or intimate details of participants' lives are involved. However, the appellant may attend the appeal hearing only if the appeal court so decides. In Amnesty International's experience, relatives and sympathizers of political defendants are usually barred from appeal hearings to the same extent as they are from trials, and the defendant is not normally permitted to attend the court hearing.

The court of appeal has the task of "verifying the legality and well-founded nature" of the judgment of the court of first instance. It may vacate the judgment, ask for a fresh trial or alter the judgment, although an appeal court may not increase the severity of the sentence passed at the trial.

In Amnesty International's experience appeal courts only very rarely alter the verdict or sentence of the court of first instance in favour of prisoners of conscience.

There is no possibility of appealing to the USSR Supreme Court. One effect of this is that in five Union Republics (Armenia, Estonia, Latvia, Lithuania and Moldavia) where, in the absence of intermediate level courts, defendants on charges of "especially dangerous crimes against the state" are tried by the Union Republic Supreme Courts, some people convicted of political offences have no possibility of appeal.

The convicted person's sentence comes into effect immediately after it has been considered on appeal. He or she must be sent from the investigation prison to the place where the sentence is to be served within 10 days.

A second possibility of altering the verdict or sentence is provided by the procedure of *judicial review* (known in Soviet law as "review by way of judicial supervision"). In contrast to appeals, which must be filed within seven days of the convicted person's receiving a copy of the judgment against him, judicial review may be undertaken by a higher court on receipt of a protest from an authorized person at any time after the trial judgment comes into effect. Such a protest may be brought only by a procurator or court chairman, whose degrees of competence in this procedure are laid down by the Code of Criminal Procedure.

A court reviewing a case "by way of judicial supervision" has broad authority to alter the verdict or sentence, order a fresh trial or reverse the judgment and terminate the case. The terms of reference for judicial review are similarly broad: the court may act on the grounds that the preliminary investigation or the trial was one-sided, on the grounds of incorrect application of criminal procedural law or criminal law, or on the grounds that the punishment assigned at the trial was too severe or too mild.

Because judicial review may be undertaken at any time, even years after the prisoner has begun serving his or her sentence, and because this procedure enables a thorough re-examination of any case, it is in principle a most important remedy in cases of unfair trial. Grounds for changing court verdicts and sentences exist in most or all cases of prisoners of conscience, and many prisoners have petitioned procurators and court chairmen to lodge a protest against the verdict or sentence passed against them. Almost invariably such petitions have been refused. The competent officials have only very rarely used their right to lodge protests in cases of political or religious dissenters, so that prisoners of conscience have very rarely benefited from the remedy of judicial review. During the period 1937-1973 Soviet legal journals published a total of 826 protests and similar representations to the country's courts. Of these not one dealt with cases under any of the articles of criminal law dealing explicitly with the exercise of human rights.[8]

Various mechanisms exist in law whereby a convicted person may, under specified circumstances, be relieved from serving out a sentence of imprisonment. None of these mechanisms entails any revision of the original guilty verdict, and all are dependent in whole or in part on "good behaviour" by the prisoner.

One method of early release is "pardon" (*pomiloyaniye*), an act of clemency. The right of pardon is exercised by the Presidium of the Supreme Soviet of each Union Republic, except in certain types of cases where the right is vested in the Presidium of the USSR Supreme Soviet.[9] (Article 121 of the 1977 USSR Constitution, Article 115 of the 1978 RSFSR Constitution and analogous articles of the other Union Republic Constitutions.) An act of pardon may entail a person's outright release from his or her sentence or a reduction of his or her sentence. In several known cases, prisoners have been released by way of pardon while still in custody under investigation, that is, before being tried and convicted.

Generally an act of pardon will be granted only if the prisoner petitions for it. In numerous cases the authorities have put pressure on convicted prisoners of conscience to induce them to apply for pardon and thus implicitly recognize their guilt. A few prisoners of conscience have been released in this way, but in most known cases they have consistently refused to cooperate with the authorities by petitioning for pardon.

Another method of early release is "amnesty" (*amnistiya*), an official act ordering the release or reduction of sentence of specified categories of convicted prisoners. According to Article 121 of the USSR Constitution, country-wide amnesties may be issued by the Presidium of the USSR Supreme Soviet. The constitutions of the Union Republics authorize the Presidia of the Union Republic Supreme Soviets to declare amnesties for prisoners convicted by courts within the Union Republic, but Amnesty International knows of no amnesties at the Union Republic level.

According to a recent official compilation of USSR legislation, 21 amnesties were decreed by the Presidium of the USSR Supreme Soviet between 1938 and 1975. One more amnesty has been declared since then, in 1977. During the 1970s there have been four amnesties, each on the occasion of a major public event (the 60th anniversary of the October Revolution, the 30th anniversary of Soviet victory in 1945, International Women's Year and the 50th anniversary of the establishment of the USSR in 1922).

Each of these amnesties ordered the release or reduction of sentence of fairly broad categories of convicted prisoners and prisoners awaiting trial. While there was some variation in the categories covered, each of the amnesties focused on prisoners serving short terms of impirsonment, war veterans, prisoners who had received medals and decorations of the Soviet Union, elderly prisoners, prisoners less than 18 years of age, invalids, pregnant women and women with young children.

Although each of these amnesties reportedly benefited a considerable number of prisoners, only a tiny proportion of known prisoners of conscience were released or had their sentences reduced. Each amnesty was applicable only to prisoners who had "gone on the path of correction" or had not "maliciously violated the regime" in their place of imprisonment. Besides thus leaving great discretion to the camp and prison administrations as to which prisoners would be released, the amnesties explicitly excluded certain categories of prisoners, notably prisoners convicted of "especially dangerous crimes against the state" and prisoners convicted more than once of deliberate crimes, which include many of the known prisoners of conscience.

Soviet criminal law also provides a procedure known as "conditional-early release from punishment" (*uslovno-dosrochnoye osvobozhdeniye ot nakasaiya*).[10] "Conditional-early release" resembles parole or remission of sentence in the penitentiary systems of other countries. It may be granted only after the prisoner has served one half, one-third or three-quarters of his or her sentence, depending on the nature of the offence. The released prisoner may be subjected to supervision at his or her place of residence after release, and may be compelled to return to serve out the remainder of the sentence if he or she commits a fresh crime during the unserved part of the sentence. It may be granted only if the prisoner "has proved his correction by exemplary conduct and an honest attitude to work" while serving the sentence. "Conditional-early release" is granted by a court, and such relief from serving sentence may be made only on the recommendation of the MVD, which operates the corrective labour system. The law (Article 44-1, Fundamentals of Criminal Legislation of the USSR and Union Republics, as amended on February 1977) excludes the application of this measure to those convicted of "especially dangerous crimes against the state".

Because of the dependence of "conditional-early release" on the recommendation of the MVD authorities who administer the camps and prisons, this form of early release from sentence has mainly been applied to prisoners who co-operated with the authorities in some way during their imprisonment. Very few prisoners of conscience are known to have been released under this procedure. An important exception occurred when, beginning in late 1974, the authorities began a program of releasing imprisoned dissenting Baptists from imprisonment before completion of their sentence. These releases, which evidently were not made conditional on repentence by the prisoners, had the effect of reducing by more than half the number of known Baptist prisoners of conscience.

A somewhat similar procedure for early release is known as "conditional release from places of imprisonment with obligatory induction of the convicted person to labour" (Article 44-2 of the USSR Fundamentals of Criminal Legislation as amended on 8 February 1977). This measure too is applied by a court and on the recommendation of the MVD administrations of the camps and prisons. It is applied only to people who have completed part of their sentence and shown "good behaviour". It may be applied to people convicted of "especially dangerous crimes against the state".

Although this procedure too allows the authorities complete discretion as to which prisoners should benefit from early release from imprisonment, there has been a significant (though still small) number of cases in which prisoners of conscience serving relatively short terms of imprisonment have been released under it from corrective labour colonies. The explanation for this evidently lies in the fact that the person's release is conditional on his or her going to work at a job assigned by the authorities and in a place designated by them and that at that place he or she will be housed in a communal dwelling with other convicted individuals conditionally released in this way, kept under police supervision and restricted in other ways. (Articles 78-1 to 78-6 of the RSFSR Corrective Labour Code, as amended in 1977.) Officials often refer to this labour as "work for the economy", and prisoners often refer to it as "going to work at chemistry (*na khimiyu*)"—a reference to the fact that prisoners released under this procedure have often been sent to work in construction projects for the country's chemicals industry. If the prisoner is returned to his or her place of imprisonment for evading work or leaving the district assigned for his or her residence, the time spent "working for the economy" does not count as part of the sentence served. This happened to the Jewish prisoner of conscience Amner Zavurov in 1978.

A final legal procedure for early release is "release from punishment on grounds of illness" (Article 362 of the RSFSR Code of Criminal Procedure, Article 100 of the RSFSR Corrective Labour Code). This procedure is dealt with in Chapter 4. Very few prisoners of conscience have been released under this procedure, although in well-known cases there appear to have been clear medical grounds for applying it.

In spite of the various procedures which exist for altering court judgments and sentences and for providing early release, the vast majority of prisoners of conscience have been released only at the very end of their sentence. The length of time spent in custody by the convicted person from the moment of his or her arrest is counted against the sentence. The time spent in custody—that is, confinement pending trial and in transport under guard to the place of imprisonment—counts triple against a sentence of exile.

## The Death Penalty

The Soviet Government has abolished the death penalty three times since coming to power in October 1917: in 1917, 1920 and 1947. Since the last time the death penalty was restored (1950), there has been an unbroken trend towards broadening the range of offences for which it may be imposed. This is in spite of the fact that the Soviet Government remains committed in principle to its ultimate abolition.

The death penalty may be imposed in peacetime for 18 different offences under criminal law. Among these are some crimes which may involve violence but need not involve the taking of life (for example "banditry" and "actions disrupting the work of corrective labour institutions") and some crimes not involving violence at all (such as counterfeiting money, stealing state property and taking bribes, all of which carry the death penalty when committed "on an especially large scale" or "with especially grave consequences").

The Soviet authorities do not publish comprehensive statistics on the use of the death penalty, so it is not possible to say precisely how many death sentences or executions occur in the USSR. Official Soviet media are known to have reported the passing of the death sentence on about 30 people each year during the mid- and late-1970s. This is known to be an incomplete figure, and it is highly probable that it is only a fraction of the annual number of death sentences passed. Each year some of those sentenced to death are officially reported to have been executed, but virtually all death penalty cases are shrouded in official secrecy, to such an extent that it is not possible to learn from official sources the nature of the proceedings or evidence against convicted people or their subsequent fates. During the late 1970s a number of Soviet dissenters spoke publicly about the need to abolish the death penalty and, as a minimum improvement, to open the workings of criminal justice to public scrutiny.

In recent years most of those known to have been sentenced to death had been convicted of violent crimes. A large proportion were convicted of war crimes committed during the Second World War. Each year some people have been sentenced to death (and some executed) for economic crimes not involving violence. A very small minority of those sentenced to death during the 1970s had been convicted of politically-motivated offences. In some such cases no violence or loss of life figured in the charges. For example Edward Kuznetsov and Mark Dymshits, both Jews, were sentenced to death in 1970 for conspiring to steal an aircraft as a means of getting out of the country. Their death sentences were subsequently commuted. In two known recent cases people were sentenced to death and executed after being convicted of acts of political terrorism: the Georgian Vladimir Zhvania in 1977 and the Armenians Stepan Zadikian, Zaven Bagdasarian and Akop Stepanian in 1979. In both of these cases it is impossible for observers outside government circles to assess the charges, the evidence or the proceedings because of the lack of publicly available information. In spite of government efforts to indicate the contrary, political dissent in the USSR has been almost uniformly non-violent. Some human rights activists there have expressed the view that some or all of the defendants in the Zadikian case were innocent of the charges against them.

The death penalty is carried out by shooting. Government sources do not reveal whether it is carried out by firing squad or by the traditional bullet in the back of the head. However, scattered references in *samizdat* writings suggest that the death penalty is carried out by a single executioner. According to one report, Stepan Zadikian was executed by "the KGB executioner Rafik Nikitich Gambarian".[11]

88

## Notes

1. On this decree see especially issues 30 and 32 of *A Chronicle of Current Events*, Amnesty International Publications, London.
2. On conditions in several places of administrative detention see Number 28 of *A Chronicle of Current Events*.
3. RSFSR Code of Criminal Procedure, Article 201.
4. RSFSR Code of Criminal Procedure, Article 213.
5. RSFSR Code of Criminal Procedure, Articles 221-239.
6. Cited by Fyodor Turovsky, a Soviet lawyer, after he emigrated from the USSR, in Irwin Cotler, *The Shcharansky Case*, Montreal, 1978, Appendix XXXVIII.
7. Article 23-2 of the Fundamentals of Criminal Legislation of the USSR and Union Republics, as amended on 8 February 1977.
8. For English translations of all procuracy protests from 1937 to 1973 see Leon Boim and Glenn G. Morgan, *The Soviet Procuracy Protests*, Sijthoff and Noordhoff, Alphen aan den Rijn, 1978.
9. Article 121 of the USSR Constitution (1977), Article 115 of the RSFSR Constitution (1978) and analogous articles of the constitutions of the other Union Republics.
10. Article 44 of the Fundamentals of Criminal Legislation of the USSR and Union Republics, as amended on 8 February 1977.
11. For a fuller account of the death penalty in the USSR, see the section on that country in *The Death Penalty*, Amnesty International Publications, London, 1979.

# CHAPTER 3

# Corrective Labour Legislation

Institutions where sentences of imprisonment are served are known in Soviet law as corrective labour institutions.

The principles on which corrective labour institutions operate are laid down in a law approved in July 1969 by the USSR Supreme Soviet, entitled Fundamentals of Corrective Labour Legislation of the USSR and the Union Republics.

This document contains 47 articles covering the main areas of concern in the operation of corrective labour institutions in the USSR.

After 1969 each of the constituent Union Republics passed a corrective labour code embodying the principles set down in the Fundamentals and prescribing in greater detail the manner of operation of corrective labour institutions. The codes of the different Union Republics are identical except in minor detail. For the sake of simplicity, the code which will be cited throughout this report is the Corrective Labour Code of the RSFSR (1970).

Like the criminal legislation instituted at the end of the 1950s, the current Soviet corrective labour legislation represents an effort to codify changes made in official policy since the death of Stalin. The drafting and promulgation of these laws were preceded in the mid-1960s by debate on the subject of penal institutions—a debate involving not only jurists and criminologists but some expression of public opinion as well. The legislation, when it was introduced, did not meet the hopes of some Soviet jurists for a sweeping reform of the Soviet penal system. The current corrective labour legislation retains most of the system of theory, regulations and practices laid down in official decrees in 1954, 1958 and 1961. The most significant changes embodied in the 1969-1970 corrective labour legislation were the ostensibly ironclad guarantees for the respect of legality and adherence to regulations—an apparent reaction to the anarchy which prevailed in the corrective labour system under Stalin. Unfortunately, the current legislation's invocation of the rule of the law is contradicted by many aspects of contemporary practice.

## *Theory*

Article 1 of the Fundamentals of Corrective Labour Legislation of the USSR and Union Republics states:

Purposes of Soviet Corrective Labour Legislation. The purpose of corrective labour legislation shall be to effect punishment of crime with a view not only to inflicting a penalty for a committed offence but also to correcting and reforming convicted offenders in the spirit of a conscientious attitude to labour and exact observance of the laws and respect for the rules of the socialist community, preventing the commission of fresh crimes both by convicted offenders and by other persons, and also promoting the eradication of crime.

The execution of a sentence shall not aim at inflicting physical suffering or degrading human dignity.

The fundamental question in the Soviet debate on prison legislation concerned the proper blend of two features of imprisonment: the negative feature of inflicting suffering (*prichineniye stradaniye*) and the positive feature of reforming and correcting the imprisoned individual (*ispravleniye i perevospitanye*). The USSR Fundamentals and the Union Republic Corrective Labour Codes represent the official solution to the dilemma of reconciling humanitarian values and socialist ideals with the exigencies of the "struggle against crime".

According to Soviet criminologists, Soviet corrective labour law has long since rejected the notion that criminal punishment is a means of gaining revenge on, and retribution from, criminals. For example, the late Professor M.D. Shargorodsky, one of the most eminent Soviet legal theoreticians, asserted that legislators in socialist societies have rejected the principle of retribution and regard it "as nothing other than a contemporary form of primitive revenge".[1]

Nonetheless, even the most recent Soviet corrective labour legislation deviates from this humanitarian principle. Rather than prohibiting or condemning the inflicting of suffering on prisoners or the degradation of their human dignity, Article 1 states merely that this is not the "aim" of the execution of punishment in the USSR. This statement of principle appears in the corrective labour code of every Union Republic. Nowhere in the Fundamentals or Union Republic codes of corrective labour law are such actions expressly prohibited. However, the article is frequently cited by Soviet commentators as indication of the "socialist humaneness" essential to Soviet penal legislation. Yet its curious phraseology points to a question of principle which is resolved only with difficulty in Soviet corrective labour theory.

The official explanation of this apparent anomaly is that punishment is by definition characterized by some degree of suffering, both physical and moral. The element of suffering in deprivation of liberty (and other forms of punishment) is a necessary deterrent, both for the individual prisoner and for "unstable" elements of the population who might be tempted by crime. Therefore, while Soviet literature on penal policy features frequent warnings against infliction of unnecessary suffering on prisoners, official policy is also characterized by prohibition of undue mildness in the treatment of prisoners.[2]

The intensity of the punitive element varies from regime to regime of corrective labour institution. As the official Commentary to the RSFSR Corrective Labour Code explains:

In defining the conditions of imprisonment of prisoners in the different types of corrective labour institutions the corrective labour legislation is guided by the principle: the more serious the crime committed and the greater the social danger of the criminal act and the personality of the convicted person, the more hard and severe must be the convicted person's conditions of imprisonment in the aim of strengthening the punitive influence exercised on him.[3]

That Soviet corrective labour legislation and theory have not rejected outright the regularized infliction of suffering on prisoners is not merely a matter of criminological principle, but is of central importance in evaluating Soviet prison conditions in terms of human rights considerations.

The most clear expression of the purely punitive aspect of the Soviet corrective labour system is that official policy makes it mandatory that prisoners should be kept in a state of permanent hunger. Article 56 of the RSFSR Corrective Labour Code legalizes the providing of prisoners with only that amount of food which is biologically necessary:

> Convicted persons shall receive food providing for the normal functioning (*zhiznedeyatelnost*) of the human organism.

A comparison of this legal norm with paragraph 20 of the United Nations Standard Minimum Rules for the Treatment of Prisoners is instructive:

> Every prisoner shall be provided by the administration at the usual hours with food of nutritional value adequate for health and strength, of wholesome quality and well prepared and served.

The punitive motivation for the Soviet legal norm that prisoners should receive only the biologically necessary minimum quantity of food is explained in the following remarkable passage which appears in a 1971 textbook approved by the MVD (Ministry of Internal Affairs), the ministry charged with administration of corrective labour institutions.

> Non-supply of the physiologically demanded minimum norms of food and material provisions . . . inflicts physical suffering and leads to the emaciation (*istoshcheniye*) of the organism, to illness and, finally, to the biological impoverishment of the person. The everyday material maintenance of convicted persons who observe the demands of the regime is carried out within the physiologically necessary limits . . . Proceeding from the punitive content of the punishment and the necessity of using it in order to obtain the goals of public deterrence and corrective education, Soviet corrective labour legislation to a certain extent utilizes the daily material maintenance of prisoners as a means of gaining the goals established in Article 20 of the Fundamentals of Corrective Labour Legislation of the USSR and Union Republics.[4]

Article 20 of the Fundamentals states that the "correction and re-education of prisoners is a goal of the corrective labour system." Thus, the prisoners "who observe the demands of the regime" are to receive just enough food to sustain them physically. Prisoners who are judged to have violated discipline, refused to work or deliberately not fulfilled their output norms at work receive less than the minimum necessary amount of food.

This policy of legally-prescribed hunger for all prisoners will be discussed at greater length below (Chapter 4). It is mentioned in the part of this report dealing with the Soviet corrective labour legislation because along with other purely punitive attributes of the Soviet prison system it puts into perspective the claim that the infliction of suffering "is not a goal" of the Soviet criminal and corrective labour law. Although it is officially claimed that Soviet corrective labour law and policy are so characterized by "humaneness" that, by comparison, non-socialist penitentiary systems are barbaric, the very legislation governing the Soviet corrective labour system includes provisions making the infliction of suffering mandatory. In this respect, Soviet corrective labour legislation today is not qualitatively different from the legislation which existed during the last 20 years of the Stalin era.

The current Soviet corrective labour legislation also abides by long-established Soviet tradition in asserting that a primary goal of the corrective labour system is the "correction and re-education" of convicted persons. This principle has been affirmed by Soviet criminal and penal legislation throughout the existence of the Soviet state. However the earlier corrective labour codes (1924 and 1933) recognized a distinction between members of the working class whose crimes did not fundamentally threaten the new state and members or adherents of the "enemy classes" who were imprisoned for actions having political significance. Under this system, only common law criminals were to be reformed: political prisoners were regarded as not being susceptible to reform.

The present corrective labour legislation does not formally recognize this distinction, and calls for the "reform and re-education" of all prisoners. However, by calling for more rigorous measures against "especially dangerous state criminals", who must always serve their sentences in the stricter regimes of camps and prisons, the current corrective labour legislation still implicitly singles out political prisoners for distinctive treatment.

The official Soviet viewpoint on the treatment of prisoners is influenced profoundly by the Marxist-materialist tenet that people's behaviour and attitudes are determined in large measure by the objective circumstances under which they are found and the subjective influences to which they are exposed. On the basis of this principle, it is maintained, Soviet corrective labour institutions are charged with the task of devising and implementing a scientifically sound programme for the "correction and re-education" of prisoners, the goal being that set down in Article 20 of the Fundamentals of Criminal Legislation of the USSR and Union Republics, which states in part:

> Punishment is not only chastisement for the crime committed but also has
> as a goal the correction and re-education of convicted persons in the spirit
> of an honest attitude toward work, exact compliance with the laws, respect
> for the rules of socialist public life . . .

This conviction brings to Soviet corrective labour legislation and theory a spirit of optimism and confidence that in the USSR imprisonment is of positive value to the prisoner rather than being mere punishment for violation of the law. However there exist among Soviet jurists and criminologists differences of opinion as to what can be expected from practical application of the principle that prisoners can and should be "corrected" and "re-educated". For example, A.Y. Natashev and N.A. Struchkov, writing in a monograph officially published in 1967, shared the opinion:

> that we can speak of correction and re-education of a convicted person
> only when he has become a useful member of society, that is, when he has

been corrected in a moral sense and not simply ceased to commit violations out of fear of being held to account.[5]

Natashev and Struchkov went still further:

In other words, correction and re-education must give one result: the person who has served his sentence must no longer be dangerous to society, and more, he must be able to be only of use to society.[6]

The jurist M.D. Shargorodsky rejected this fundamentalist approach as an "idealization" of the goals of punishment:

. . . the educational tasks of punishment are gained when the law-breaker, after completing his sentence, no longer commits crimes. The position of those authors who demand the changing of the guilty person's consciousness in a moral sense (so-called moral correction) goes beyond the limits of the narrow tasks which must stand before punishment in criminal law. The general task of educating a person to be a conscious citizen of a socialist society, of educating a person morally, is far from always achieved successfully even in the conditions of a normal family, school or collective; it is all the more Utopian to assign such a task to measures of criminal punishment . . . where conditions are considerably more difficult for education so broad in its moral aspect.[7]

The current corrective labour legislation reflects the more radical of the two views just described regarding the desirable and expected degree of "correction" of imprisoned persons. Article 30 of the Fundamentals of Corrective Labour Legislation of the USSR and the Union Republics sets as a goal "enhancing the consciousness, raising the cultural level and developing the positive initiative of the convicted persons".

According to the official Commentary to the Fundamentals of Corrective Labour Legislation of the USSR and the Union Republics, an intensive effort to reform persons convicted for violations of criminal law is required because of the character traits common to such persons:

Re-education of persons who have committed violations of the law is a most complicated and important task, inasmuch as exactly persons in this category as a rule have the most tenacious anti-social views and habits and a lower consciousness than other citizens.[8]

For the correct fulfilment of this task, it is necessary that all individual prisoners be subjected to the most intimate scrutiny by the administrations of corrective labour institutions. According to the same official source:

Workers of corrective labour institutions who are implementing individual educational work with condemned persons must strive to study better the personality of the convict, to find the negative qualities of his character, the weakness and gaps in his education which led him to commission of a crime, systematically to scrutinize his behaviour in the places of deprivation of freedom, to study his moral qualities, his attitude to work and to study, to the fulfilment of his social obligations, etc. All this is necessary so as to choose for the convicted person such means of individual education which will most effectively influence him and facilitate his correction and re-education.[9]

The means employed to "correct" and re-educate prisoners are labour and various forms of educational activity, although their physical conditions and discipline are also seen as part of the corrective influence. Labour and some forms of moral-political education are compulsory. Because the "program" for each prisoner varies according to such factors as the type of sentence he or she is serving, the "production profile" of the particular corrective labour institution and the institution's assessment of his or her character and need for correction, the administration of each corrective labour institution is given much latitude in deciding the nature of the effort required to reform each prisoner.

On the one hand, this threatens the officially-proclaimed principle that corrective labour institutions shall be highly regulated so as to prevent violations of "socialist legality" by administrators or prisoners alike. On the other hand, camp and prison administrations have been provided by law with a mechanism which, however well-intended, is used to "degrade the human dignity" of prisoners in contravention of Article 1 of the Fundamentals of Corrective Labour Legislation. This is particularly true with respect to prisoners whose "crimes" were motivated by the promptings of conscience.

The subjection of such prisoners to the demand that they change their views represents an effort not to eliminate any criminal tendencies, but to force them to recant their beliefs on intellectual and moral, political and religious questions. Since the "correction" and "re-education" of prisoners is in practice connected with a broad variety of punitive measures which can be applied both in corrective labour institutions and after release, prisoners of conscience are, in fact, faced with a degrading form of blackmail.

## Socialist Legality

The present Soviet corrective labour laws were drafted in response to the absence of such legislation prior to 1969. The last corrective labour code to have been approved in the USSR was the RSFSR Corrective Labour Code of 1933. It has been recognized by Soviet jurists and officials that by the end of the Stalin era this code (and other Union Republic corrective labour codes) no longer applied. The majority of its provisions had been made obsolete or superseded by new regulations. Most of these other regulations were in the form of departmental instructions issued by the NKVD (the People's Commissariat of Internal Affairs), after 1946 the MVD (the Ministry of Internal Affairs). In other words, the law had been superseded by a series of administrative decisions issued by various non-accountable security chiefs. This situation was characteristic of the anarchy which prevailed throughout the last 20 years of Stalin's life—anarchy which pervaded many areas of Soviet life but which was nowhere so endemic as in the relations between police organs and citizens, prison administrators and prisoners.

The years since 1953 have been marked by efforts to restore formal legality and order to the corrective labour system. The 1969 Fundamentals represented an attempt to re-establish the unchallengeable and binding authority of corrective labour legislation over the operation of the corrective labour system. The Union Republic Corrective Labour Codes were intended to strengthen the binding

A view of strict regime camp ZhKh 385/19 in Mordovia

A view of strict regime camp OS-34/1 near Syktyvkar in the Komi ASSR

character of the All-Union Fundamentals by providing "the fullest possible regulation of the corrective labour rules".[10]

According to Article 8 of the Fundamentals of Corrective Labour Legislation, all prisoners enjoy "the rights established by the law for the citizen of the USSR" except where these are limited for them by the legislation and by the terms of their sentences. Political prisoners, especially those imprisoned on charges involving the circulation of *samizdat* or participation in demonstrations, might well greet with derision the acknowledgement that prisoners cannot exercise such constitutional rights as the right to "freedom of speech" or the right to hold "meetings, street processions and demonstrations". In the Soviet literature on the subject, there appears to be no clarification of the right of prisoners to enjoy freedom of religious worship, a right guaranteed by Article 52 of the Soviet Constitution (1977). This right has been routinely denied to prisoners, including clergy and others imprisoned on account of their religious activities.

Nonetheless, the principle is established in Soviet law that prisoners are "subjects possessing defined rights and obligations" and that consequently the treatment of prisoners must be in accordance with legal definitions of their rights and obligations. Despite severe official restriction of publication of critical descriptions of the operation of corrective labour institutions, Soviet jurists and criminologists have on numerous occasions revealed their awareness of the potential which exists for arbitrariness and perpetration of abuses against prisoners within such institutions. This recognition is reflected in numerous statements in official Soviet literature on the subject condemning violations of "socialist legality" by prison administrations, of which the following is representative:

Instances of illegality and arbitrariness, intolerable in any conditions of our activity, are of even greater public danger in places of deprivation of liberty.[11]

This attitude is based in part on the perception that lawlessness by corrective labour officials is not conducive to development of respect for law on the part of convicted people.

Soviet corrective labour legislation has established mechanisms intended to ensure that legal norms are respected by officials and prisoners alike. Most important is the Procuracy, whose approval is required for many types of decisions made by the MVD and by the corrective labour administrations and which is "obliged to take measures in good time to prevent and eliminate any breaches of the law from whomsoever they emanate and to bring the guilty to account".

Yet for all the formal legislative guarantees of this sort, the operation of the Soviet corrective labour system is characterized by flagrant and regular violations of and deviations from the law. Allegations of lawlessness on the part of administrators appear constantly in the only accounts available to us of conditions in Soviet camps and prisons: *samizdat* appeals and statements by prisoners and former prisoners.

The hopes of many Soviet jurists that the current corrective labour legislation would provide ironclad guarantees of respect for the law have been betrayed, and on several levels.

Although they have accepted the principle that the corrective labour laws should provide strict and thorough regulation of the operations of places of imprisonment, Soviet legislators have retained the view that many decisions cannot be determined by legislation but must be made on the spot. Consequently, in many areas of decision-making the corrective labour laws provide only vague declarations of principle. Much is left to the discretion of those charged with operation of the corrective labour system.

The MVD, which administers the corrective labour system, has throughout the 1970s issued numerous directives determining the manner in which camps and prisons operate. None have been published, as far as is known to Amnesty International, and their texts are not made available to prisoners and their relatives. The most comprehensive of these directives, and the one referred to often in the corrective labour legislation and the official Commentaries to it, is known as the "Rules of Internal Order", which regulates many aspects of day-to-day life in the camps and prisons.

The currently applicable Rules of Internal Order (MVD Directive 37) came into effect in March 1978, replacing the Rules of Internal Order (Number 20) which had been applied since 1972.[12]

All available information on the Rules of Internal Order and other MVD directives regarding corrective labour institutions makes clear that in using the discretion permitted it by the law the MVD tends undeviatingly to make the treatment of prisoners tougher and their rights more restricted wherever the law, which itself provides for a tough regime of imprisonment, allows this. For example, although the published legislation makes 15 days the maximum term of punishment in a punishment cell or punishment-isolation cell, the 1978 Rules of Internal Order permit prisoners to be punished by successive 15-day terms without interval. Although the published law nowhere states that prisoners are required to meet any particular norms of output while doing compulsory labour, an MVD directive permits this. Although the published law says that prisoners have a right to periodic visits from "relatives and other people", the Rules of Internal Order stipulate that relatives must be "close relatives" and that "other persons" may visit prisoners only if the camp or prison administration approves of them. Many similar examples could be cited.

The general character of these unpublished MVD directives is to fill in the gaps of the legislation with numerous additional hardships for prisoners, some petty, some major. Because the law is itself vague, and because it explicitly leaves a great deal of discretion to the MVD to make its own rules, many regulations and practices of the MVD which make the regime of imprisonment considerably tougher than the law itself suggests are usually technically not illegal, even though they are extra-legal.

Corrective labour institutions are staffed by MVD personnel. Taking their lead from the harsher provisions of the corrective labour legislation and the directives issued by the MVD, camp and prison administrations frequently, though not always consistently, find ways of making the regime of imprisonment even stricter. They have a great deal of discretion in deciding when and how prisoners should be punished, when they should be let off work or hospitalized, how long their visits from relatives should be, whether their mail should be passed to them, whether they should be given extra rations because of the heaviness of their work, what type. of work they should be assigned and many other matters of the utmost importance to prisoners.

Prisoners of conscience have continually been victimized by deliberately harsh application of the law and of the MVD's decrees. Whether they are political or religious dissenters, such prisoners are frequently attacked either individually or collectively in the official press or even by the country's top leaders, and this affects the attitude of administrators and even guards toward them. They often incur the antagonism of the administrators by insisting on their rights under the law, by going on hunger strikes or taking other actions to protect themselves and each other from arbitrary treatment, and by trying to inform the outside world of the names and actions of the administrators. They are regarded as "ideologically hostile elements", and, as has very often been reported, are frequently singled out for ill-treatment.

While much of the ill-treatment of prisoners, including prisoners of conscience, is technically not illegal, there are numerous instances of prison and camp officials not only condoning but even participating in flagrant violations of criminal law, let alone corrective labour law. Prisoners have frequently been denied necessary medical treatment. Prisoners' mail, both incoming and outgoing, has been confiscated or delayed in straightforward violation of the provisions of the corrective labour legislation. There are numerous accounts of prisoners being beaten, in some cases to death, either by other prisoners acting with the connivance of the administration or by guards and officials.

The Procuracy is entrusted with ensuring the observance of legality in the camps. It is also responsible for ensuring that certain administrative regulations (including those of the MVD and the administrations of individual corrective labour institutions) conform to provisions in written law. The Procuracy, however, does not in practice have the degree of autonomy necessary for the proper execution of this task. Despite its great legal authority the Procuracy almost invariably seems incapable of challenging the decisions of the MVD or of the MVD officials in charge of prisons and colonies.

## Categories and Places of Imprisonment

The corrective labour legislation regulates the conditions of five types of punishments which are imposed by the courts on convicted adults: imprisonment, exile, banishment, corrective work without imprisonment and "obligatory induction to labour" of people sentenced conditionally fo imprisonment. All these punishments are administered by the MVD.

### (a)  Imprisonment in prisons and colonies

A small minority of known prisoners of conscience serve all or part of their sentence in a *prison*. Prisons are especially high security institutions, intended for people who have committed "grave crimes" and for "especially dangerous recidivists". Most of the known prisoners of conscience who have served sentence in a prison have been sent there not under the sentence passed at their trial but as a form of punishment for disciplinary offences committed while serving sentence in corrective labour colonies. (See Chapter 6.)

Soviet corrective labour law regards prisons as places with a regime more punitive than that in corrective labour colonies, and less suited to the reform of prisoners. A major difference between the two types of institution is that inmates of prisons live in cells rather than communal barracks. The regime is also stricter as to the amount of food given to prisoners and their rights to correspondence, visits, receipt of parcels and supplementary food purchases.

The prison best known to Amnesty International is Vladimir prison, in the ancient city of that name, 175 kilometers east of Moscow. Former inmates report that Vladimir prison holds about 1,200 inmates. For about two years after 1975 prisoners of conscience were successful in smuggling out a considerable amount of information about conditions in Vladimir prison, which had previously been even more secretive than other corrective labour institutions. From this and other sources Amnesty International was able to identify about 50 prisoners of conscience who were in that prison between 1975 and 1977. Accounts by inmates indicated that there were about 70 or 80 political prisoners there at that time.

In 1978 the authorities transferred a number of inmates of Vladimir prison, including all the known prisoners of conscience, to a prison in Chistopol, located in the Tartar Autonomous Soviet Socialist Republic some 700 kilometers further away from Moscow. There is no reason to doubt the assessment by prisoners that this move was intended as a means of making more difficult the flow of information from the prisoners involved. According to former prisoners, Chistopol prison is an old prison, smaller than Vladimir prison and has a tougher regime.

Amnesty International has over the years received occasional reports of prisoners of conscience being sent to prisons other than Vladimir or Chistopol; however, most known prison inmates convicted of explicitly political offences have been confined in those two prisons.

In the past, women prisoners have served sentences in Vladimir prison, but at present it is reserved for male prisoners. The only prison where female prisoners of conscience have served sentences in recent years is one in Byelorussia, the location of which is not precisely known to Amnesty International and which has been referred to in *samizdat* as the "Central Women's Prison". One prisoner of conscience, Nadezhda Usoyeva, a True Orthodox Christian serving a lengthy sentence for "anti-Soviet agitation and propaganda", is known to have been sent there as a punishment in 1975.

Most prisoners of conscience serve their sentences in "corrective labour colonies". In official terminology the word "colony" (*koloniya*) has completely replaced the word "camp" (*lager*). Nevertheless, prisoners almost always use the term "camp", signifying their attitude that the traditional character of these places remains unchanged.

Corrective labour colonies with different regimes are physically separate from one another, although there may be colonies with different regimes in one complex of colonies. Normally prisoners of conscience serve their entire term of imprisonment under the regime specified in their sentence, the only common exception being when prisoners are transferred to a prison as a punishment.

The four regimes of camps are, in increasing order of severity, ordinary, re-inforced, strict and special. Each entails a progressive reduction in prisoners' rights to visits, correspondence, receipt of parcels and supplementary food purchases. Prisoners in special regime colonies are kept in cells.

Since official penal statistics are classified as state secrets, it is difficult to say how many corrective labour colonies exist and where and how they are distributed in the USSR. Amnesty International has worked for the release of prisoners of conscience in several hundred colonies. Colonies known to Amnesty International exist in every Union Republic and at almost every intermediate level (region, territory, ASSR, national area) territorial unit in the country. The only exception is Moscow region: it is most unusual for people to serve sentences of imprisonment anywhere in the Moscow region (*oblast*).

While many corrective labour colonies are in rural areas, the existence of colonies in cities is not uncommon, and is partly explained by the use of convict labour on construction projects in urban areas. For example, a *samizdat* list of colonies in the Latvia SSR in 1975 identified four colonies in the republic's capital, Riga.

The Fundamentals of Corrective Labour Legislation (Article 6) provide that convicted people shall "as a rule" serve their sentence in the republic where they resided prior to arrest or conviction.

Exceptions to the rule are previous offenders, aliens, and persons convicted of "especially dangerous crimes against the state". Such people may be "sent to serve sentence in corrective labour institutions set aside for these categories of offenders, regardless of the Union Republic in which they resided prior to arrest or conviction."

The category "especially dangerous crimes against the state" (Articles 64-73 in the RSFSR Criminal Code) embraces a number of specifically political offences of which prisoners of conscience are frequently convicted: "treason", "anti-Soviet agitation and propaganda" and "anti-Soviet" organizational activity. Prisoners who are convicted a second time under other articles of law may be classified as "recidivists", and they too are liable to be sent to serve sentences in a republic other than their native one.

In practice, people in these categories are almost always sent to serve their sentences in corrective labour institutions in the RSFSR. For citizens of other than Russian nationality this imposes disadvantages and deprivations which were foreseen and warned about by Soviet jurists. One official source states:

It is fully understandable that the nearer a prisoner is located to the place of residence of his relatives the greater will be his possibility to utilize his right to meetings with them.[13]

The same authority recognizes that imprisonment in a distant place increases the punitive element of a sentence because the prisoner "must live and work in climatic conditions to which he is unaccustomed and face difficulties in the exercise of a number of rights".

In RSFSR colonies and prisons, Russian is *de facto* the language used in com-munications of all kinds between administrators and prisoners. There are provisions for the use of interpreters, but cases have been recorded of prisoners being reprimanded or even punished for speaking a language other than Russian in colonies in the Russian Republic. This is true of political prisoners from, for instance, the Ukraine and Lithuania. Many of them have been sentenced for expression of their nationalist views, which normally consist of the advocacy, on principle, of their national culture and language and resistance to what they regard as an official policy of Russification in their republic. Prisoners' correspondence in languages other than Russian is often confiscated for official translation, or they are asked to rewrite letters in Russian. Visits may be terminated if conversation is not in Russian. Some non-Russian prisoners of conscience (the Lithuanian Petras Plumpa-Pluira and the Uzbek Babur Shakirov, for example) have declared that they would no longer speak to camp and prison officials in Russian.

This practice of placing prisoners in institutions located in remote parts of the RSFSR makes it extremely difficult for many families to take advantage of the already highly restricted visiting rights. Cases have often been reported of families being unable to meet the costs of visiting imprisoned relatives.

The largest concentrations of known prisoners of conscience are in the complex of colonies in the Mordovian ASSR and in Perm region.

The Mordovian complex has the institutional acronym ZhKh 385. It contains a large number of colonies. In recent years known political prisoners have been held in colonies ZhKh 385/1, /3, /17 and /19. Colony 1 holds all the prisoners of conscience known to Amnesty International who are serving special regime. Women prisoners convicted of "especially dangerous crimes against the state" are held in colony 3 and men convicted of such offences are held in colony 19. In the late 1970s colony 17 and zone 5 in colony 3, where male prisoners in this category had been held, were closed down. In addition, colony ZhKh 385/5 holds foreigners convicted of crimes while in the USSR.

No report on imprisonment in the USSR could avoid singling out the special regime colony in Mordovia. This camp has the worst features of both prisons and camps. As will be indicated in the following chapters, the cramped and unhygenic conditions of the prisoners' cells, the unhealthy and exhausting nature of the compulsory labour, the meagre and miserable food rations and the lack of possibility for exercise combine with other deprivations to make it probably the most punitive known corrective labour institution. What makes it particularly dangerous for its inmates is that all are serving lengthy sentences of imprisonment— more than 10 years in virtually all cases. Furthermore, the prisoners of conscience there are all "recidivists", and must endure these appalling conditions after having served long terms of imprisonment previously.

The Perm complex (VS 389) holds men convicted of "especially dangerous crimes against the state" in three colonies: VS 389/35, /36 and /37.

## (b) *Exile, Banishment, Corrective Work Without Imprisonment and Assigned Labour*

Exile, banishment and corrective work without imprisonment are all intended in law as milder punishments than imprisonment. However each may be applied in such a way that the restrictions imposed approximate to imprisonment. Furthermore, people who attempt to leave their place of exile may be sentenced to imprisonment (Article 186, RSFSR Criminal Code); people who return to a place from which they are banished may be imprisoned for the unserved part of their sentence (Article 187, RSFSR Criminal Code); people who "maliciously evade" punishment in the form of corrective work without imprisonment or assigned labour may be imprisoned for the remainder of their sentence (Article 28, RSFSR Criminal Code).

The basic restriction imposed by a sentence of *exile* is strict confinement to a particular locality other than the convicted person's established place of residence. The Commentary to the RSFSR Corrective Labour Code [14] states that a goal of this punishment is to isolate convicted people from the environment where they committed their offence.

The area in which the convicted person may move about varies, but may be no larger than the administrative district (*raion*) to which he or she is assigned. According to the Commentary, the USSR Council of Ministers and Union Republic Council of Ministers establish and maintain an unpublished list of districts which may serve as places of exile. The Commentary states that "as a rule these localities are far from regional capitals and major industrial centres". The MVD, not the court passing sentence, decides in which listed locality a convicted person shall serve a sentence of exile. In Amnesty International's experience, dissenters sentenced to exile are almost invariably sent to remote parts of Siberia, the Far North or the Far East.

According to the law, people may be sent into exile either "in convoy" (that is, under guard and with other prisoners going into exile) or without guard. In practice, prisoners of conscience are normally sent into exile in convoy, and endure the conditions of transportation and transit prisons which are described in Chapter 4. According to the law, time spent by the exiled person in convoy on the way to the place of exile counts triple against his sentence, as does all time spent in custody from the moment of arrest.

People serving exile are kept under surveillance by the District Administration of Internal Affairs (specifically, the militia) in the place of exile. The person's internal passport is taken away for the duration of the sentence, and in its place he or she is given an identity card. He or she must register with the local MVD branch on arrival, and report to it in person once a month. The local MVD may— and in cases of prisoners of conscience usually does—"strengthen the surveillance" by requiring the person to report to it in person as often as four times each month. If the exiled person changes his or her place of residence or work he or she must report this to the local MVD. The MVD systematically observes the exiled person's whereabouts and his or her behaviour at work and at home, and can "if necessary" demand that he or she give an account of his or her behaviour.

According to the law, the local MVD may permit exiles to leave their place of exile temporarily under certain circumstances (for example, in the event of death or serious illness in their immediate family). This privilege has not been granted to most known prisoners of conscience, although there have been rare exceptions.

Exiles are required to perform "socially useful labour". Soviet corrective labour law treats such labour as a basic element in the "correction and re-education" of the exiled person. According to Article 83 of the RSFSR Corrective Labour Code, the Executive Committee of the local Soviet of People's Deputies is obliged to help the exiled person to find a job, and in this should take into consideration the person's work capabilities, training and experience. However, in the many cases known to Amnesty International few prisoners of conscience in exile have been given work compatible with their previous work experience or training. Most often they are required to perform manual labour, and in some cases they have had difficulty in obtaining any regular job at all. In some cases this may be explained by the limitations of the job market in remote areas. In other cases, it is a consequence of straightforward discrimination and obstruction by the local authorities.

A number of prisoners of conscience have arrived in exile after serving their term of imprisonment and found themselves penniless and unable to find work. Without money, prisoners in this situation have in a number of known cases been unable to find accommodation and have spent their first weeks in exile sleeping in militia stations or even out-of-doors, having to rely on meagre hand-outs from the militia as their only source of money with which to buy food. Among prisoners who have been treated this way after arriving in exile after imprisonment in camps are Pavel Kampov (Tomsk region, 1976) and Vladimir Gandzyuk (also Tomsk region, 1976). Although some exiles have been able to find accommodation in the form of a room or small dwelling, many have had to live in hostel type accommodation, sharing a small part of a room with others.

The local MVD must conduct "political education work" with the exiled person, with the assistance of public organizations at the person's places of work and residence. This public involvement sometimes takes the form of spying on exiled prisoners of conscience, and sometimes (as with Vyacheslav Chornovil in 1979) manifests itself when the management of local public organizations warn people to have nothing to do with the exiled person.

For violations of discipline (for example failure to report regularly to the internal affairs authorities) the local MVD may impose various punishments on the exiled person, including a further restriction of the permitted area of residence for up to six months.

According to the official Commentary to the RSFSR Corrective Labour Code, sentences of banishment (*vysylka*) are "relatively rare". In Amnesty International's experience, the only dissenters on whom they have often been imposed in recent years are Crimean Tartars put on trial for trying to take up residence in the Crimea. (See Chapter 1.)

The main element in a sentence of banishment is the expulsion of the convicted person from a particular locality and prohibition of return for the duration of sentence. In addition, the USSR Council of Ministers and the Union Republic Councils of Ministers establish and maintain lists of other localities from which persons serving this punishment are banned. Apart from these restrictions, the person serving banishment may, according to the law, choose any locality in the country for residence.

While serving the sentence the banished person does not have to report regularly to the local MVD, but must inform them that he or she has taken up residence in the particular locality, giving his or her address, place of work and any subsequent change in address or place of work. The banished person is obliged to engage in "socially useful labour" and the local MVD is obliged to keep watch over his or her behaviour. As well, "political education" work must be carried out with the banished person by social organizations at his or her places of work and residence.

According to the Commentary to the RSFSR Corrective Labour Code, as of 1973 "about 20 per cent of all convicted people" were sentenced to *corrective work without imprisonment*.[15] However this punishment has been applied only occasionally in the cases of dissenters known to Amnesty International.

Corrective work without imprisonment may be no more than one year in duration. The sentenced person may be permitted to continue in his or her own job, or may be forced to leave his or her job and be assigned work in a locality somewhere else sufficiently close in the same administrative district (*raion*) to enable him or her to commute daily to and from work and home. The sentenced person may not change jobs of his or her own free will while serving the sentence. He or she is not permitted annual holiday leave, and must pay between five per cent and 20 per cent of his or her salary over to the state, the amount of the monthly deductions being set by the court in passing sentence. The sentenced person must be subjected to "political education" and supervision of behaviour at his or her places of work and residence. All matters relating to this punishment are in the charge of the "inspectorates of corrective work", under the local MVD administration.

The RSFSR Corrective Labour Code was amended in 1977 so as to cover the execution of "conditional sentence of imprisonment with obligatory induction of the convicted person to labour".[16] People sentenced in this way are required to work at a job and in a place assigned them by the authorities. They may be required to move from their home district, and "as a rule" they are required to live in a communal residence with other convicted people. They are not free to leave their district of assigned residence, their family need not be permitted to join them and they are subject to police surveillance, "political education" measures and other restrictions. For evading work or leaving their district of assigned residence they may, by a court decision, be sent to serve their full sentence in a corrective labour camp.

# *Notes*

1. M.D. Shargorodsky, *Punishment, Its Goals and Effectiveness*, Moscow, 1973, page 26.
2. See for example the injunction to that effect by V. Bolysov, the RSFSR's chief inspector for corrective labour institutions, in his article "Utilize All Means of Procuracy Supervision", *Sotsialisticheskaya Zakonnost*, Moscow, March 1975.
3. *Commentary to the RSFSR Corrective Labour Code*, Moscow, 1973, page 59.
4. *Corrective Labour Laws*, Moscow, 1971, pages 323-324.
5. A.Ya. Natashev and N.A. Struchkov, *The Fundamental Principles of the Theory of Corrective Labour Law*, Moscow, 1967, page 25.
6. *Ibid*.
7. Shargorodsky, *ibid*, page 32.
8. *Commentary to the Fundamentals of Corrective Labour Legislation of the USSR and Union Republics*, Moscow, 1972, page 112.
9. *Ibid*, page 113.
10. *Ibid*, page 23.
11. Natashev and Struchkov, *ibid*, page 56.
12. Although the 1972 directive, like numerous MVD directives on more specific matters, has not been published, human rights activists in the USSR and foreign specialists have been able to ascertain much of what it says. The most thorough exposure of the contents of this directive from within the USSR appeared in Number 33 of *A Chronicle of Current Events*. Dr Friedrich Feldbrugge, a Dutch professor of Soviet law, was able to reconstruct much of its contents by analysis of the official *Commentary to the RSFSR Criminal Code*. See the "Appendix" to his article "Soviet Corrective Labour Law in Soviet Law After Stalin" Part I, Leyden, 1977. The most thorough available account of the contents of the 1978 Rules of Internal Order appeared in issue 12, 1979, of *News Brief*, Munich, edited by Cronid Lyubarsky.
13. *Commentary to the Fundamentals of Corrective Labour Legislation of the USSR and Union Republics*, Moscow, 1972, page 30.
14. *Commentary to the RSFSR Corrective Labour Code*, Moscow, 1973, pages 204-214.
15. *Ibid*, page 220.
16. Articles 78-1 to 78-6 of the RSFSR Corrective Labour Code, as amended in 1977.

# CHAPTER 4

# Maintenance of Prisoners

The physical conditions in which convicted people serve imprisonment in the USSR inflict greater physical suffering and degradation on them than is admitted or condoned in the law and official literature on the subject.

## Transport of Prisoners

Prisoners of conscience and their relatives and friends frequently regard transportation to and from places of imprisonment and exile as one of the most severe aspects of the entire process of imprisonment. Former Jewish prisoner of conscience Ilya Glezer's description of it as a "brutalizing nightmare" has been echoed in numerous other accounts by prisoners.

Prisoners are transported over relatively short distances (up to about 100 kilometers) in a van-type vehicle known as a *voronok* (or "raven"). According to accounts by former prisoners, prisoners travelling in a *voronok* sit on a bench running along three sides of the passenger compartment, each of the three sides measuring approximately 1.5 meters. Apart from this bench, the *voronok* has two tiny booths in which "especially dangerous" prisoners, including political prisoners in some instances, are placed for the journey.

One of the most common criticisms of transportation in the *voronok* is overcrowding. The vehicle is built to hold 11 prisoners at most, often it carries more than twice that number. One witness told Amnesty International that she had seen 25 women prisoners, one with a child, unloaded from one of these vehicles in the corrective labour colony complex in the Mordovia ASSR. The discomfort of overcrowding is usually aggravated by lack of ventilation. In mid-1979 prisoners reported that in April 1979 in Kazan 17 prisoners had died of suffocation in a *voronok* which had been left standing in the sun without anyone attending to the prisoners' requests to be let out.

Another criticism of the *voronok* is that since the interior fittings are all of metal and trips are often made over very rough rural roads, prisoners are liable to suffer physical injuries as a result of fast or violent driving. Cases have been reported to Amnesty International of prisoners' suffering broken limbs or heart attacks as a result of these conditions.

Prisoners are often transported over long distances to and from their place of imprisonment or exile. Over long distances prisoners are usually transported in trains, although aircraft may be used in some circumstances, for example if the place of imprisonment is not accessible by any other means of travel. The railway cars in which prisoners are transported are known as "Stolypin wagons". Normally there are other cars in the same train, usually goods wagons or passenger cars.

According to detailed first-hand accounts, a "Stolypin wagon" contains 10 compartments, some meant to hold eight (10 according to some accounts) people and others meant to hold three. Usually there is overcrowding—15 or more and sometimes as many as 30 people travel in a compartment meant for eight or 10 prisoners and remain in these conditions for stretches of three or four days at a time.

The toilet is not in the prisoners' compartment but at the end of the corridor. Normally the guards take the prisoners one by one to the toilet once or twice a day. Other than that the prisoner must ask special permission to be taken there. In this, as in much else throughout their imprisonment, the prisoners are at the mercy of arbitrary treatment by the guards.

According to unpublished regulations, the guards are supposed to give the prisoners water either on request or every four hours (accounts vary on this point) but prisoners regularly report that in practice they are given water only irregularly, after a long wait. Deprivation of water is one of the most common complaints regarding transport over long distances, partly because the prisoners' diet normally contains salted fish.

Prisoners in transit receive inadequate nourishment. According to the regulations governing their feeding, they are to receive a warm meal only every fourth day. Otherwise they are issued cold rations to last them for three days, the normal ration consisting only of a small portion of salted fish and some bread. Often prisoners do not receive even these inadequate rations. For example, one unnamed Baptist prisoner in transit from Voroshilovgrad (in the Ukraine) to Khabarovsk territory (on the Pacific coast) in 1977 received "three small loaves of bread and 100 grams of fat" for one three-day stage of his journey. The worker Yevgeny Buzinnikov, on his journey from Byelorussia to serve his sentence in a camp in Sverdlovsk in 1978, received at one stage only half a loaf of bread and a jar of jam—one day's rations to last three days. Prisoners also regularly report that the food they receive is badly prepared and often spoiled.

Lack of water becomes a serious problem in the summer months. The "Stolypin wagons" are made of metal and become very hot on warm days. The trains often move slowly and make long stops at numerous stations along the way. During such stops the windows (which are across the corridor from the prisoners' compartments, separated from them by locked grill-doors) may not be opened.

It is quite normal for prisoners in transit to remain in these conditions for a month or more.

One of the best known instances of infliction of suffering on prisoners during transportation occurred in July 1972, when several hundred prisoners—including a number of known prisoners of conscience—were transferred from the corrective labour complex in Mordovia northwards to the complex of camps in the Perm region. According to accounts by prisoners who were there, the transfer took place during a heat wave. The train travelled mainly at night and was left standing during the daytime.

One *samizdat* account described the conditions on this transfer as follows:

Fifteen people in a sleeping compartment. Everybody bathed in sweat.

Food spoiled. For two days they did not take prisoners to the lavatory.
People had to use the corridors . . . The windows were sealed shut.
Only at the end of the deportation did they open the windows a little,
but it did not help. People were lying naked on the floor. Dirt. Stink.
Suffocation. One man died during the deportation. It was a terrible
torture.

According to another account:

Even the smallest concession—a drop of water, a gulp of fresh air—could
be gained only be collective screaming whenever the train was passing
through a populated area. Some prisoners lost consciousness . . .
Nikolai Nikolayenko was taken from the train to a hospital. No medical
service was provided on the journey. Illiterate guards were indiscriminately
handing out the same pills to everybody . . .

This particular mass transfer has become notorious among Soviet dissenters
because it involved many prisoners of conscience, but the severity of ill-treatment
it involved was by no means exceptional.

Prisoners transported over long distances normally spend some time,
occasionally just overnight, but usually longer, in various prisons along the way.
Commonly referred to as "transit prisons" these stop-over places are actually
local MVD prisons, both investigation prisons and prisons for serving sentence in.
Prisoners' accounts of such places are an important source of information on
aspects of the Soviet prison system that is not otherwise available. For example,
some prisoners of conscience in transit have been housed temporarily in cells
designated for people under sentence of death, and thus saw at first-hand an
aspect of one of the more secretive of Soviet penal practices. From available
accounts, it would appear that prisoners under sentence of death are held in even
worse physical conditions than other convicted prisoners. For example Georgy
Davydov, a Leningrad geological engineer sentenced in 1973 to 7 years' imprisonment and exile for "anti-Soviet agitation and propaganda", was kept in a death
cell in a prison in Kirov while he was in transit from his Perm camp to Vladimir
prison in 1974. According to Davydov's account, another prisoner was awaiting
execution in a nearby cell. The death cell where Davydov was kept was a
basement cell. It had an arched ceiling, so that a person could stand upright only
in the middle of the cell. The furniture consisted of a low plank bed and a tiny
rudimentary table. There was no toilet, only a bucket (*parasha*) without a handle
or lid. The cell was damp, and there were woodlice on the walls. The cell had
only a tiny window and was lit by a 40-watt bulb.

Prisoners usually find transit prisons overcrowded, dirty and infested with
insects. The Ukrainian Mykola Gandzyuk, sent into exile in early 1976 after
serving 12 years' imprisonment for nationalist activities, wrote to a friend that
in a transit prison in Sverdlovsk he was kept with about 80 other prisoners in a
cell meant for 20 people. Prisoners had to find space even under the plank beds
and immediately next to the toilet, and it was difficult for them even to get to
the door when their food was delivered through the food trough. Gandzyuk also
spent part of his journey in a *voronok* into which 30 prisoners were packed.

When Niole Sadunaite was in transit from Lithuania to Mordovia in 1975 to serve 6 years' imprisonment and exile for "anti-Soviet agitation and propaganda" she spent seven days in a transit prison in Pskov. According to a subsequent letter from her, she was kept in a "damp, cold, dark, filthy and stuffy basement cell". She was issued a dirty mattress and, typically, no sheet or blankets. She received no medical attention there when she caught a cold. In another prison on the same journey she had to sleep on the floor, since the mattress she was issued had bedbugs.

Another woman prisoner of conscience, the Ukrainian poet Irina Stasiv-Kalynets, said after her transportation in 1978 to serve 3 years' exile after serving 6 years' imprisonment that conditions in the transit prisons were "filthy" and that the cells were often underground and infested with insects. Ilya Glezer, a biologist sentenced in 1972 to 6 years' imprisonment and exile has confirmed all this and reported that in one prison he had been kept with 25 people in a cell meant for four.

Sometimes prisoners of conscience, especially if they are convicted of "especially dangerous" crimes such as "anti-Soviet agitation and propaganda" are put in cells by themselves or with only one or two other prisoners also convicted of serious crimes, and thus are able to avoid the worst excesses of overcrowding. Kronid Lyubarsky, a Moscow astronomer sentenced in 1972 to 5 years' imprisonment for "anti-Soviet agitation and propaganda", was kept alone in a cell in Moscow's Krasnaya Presnya prison. His cell had a toilet, but the cell light was left burning all night and the mattress he was issued was "filthy and evil-smelling".

Another subject of constant complaint regarding conditions in transit (both in transit prisons and in transportation vehicles) is the behaviour of the guards and the criminal prisoners. While in transit prisoners are subjected to rigid security measures, which include repeated personal searches, the use of guard dogs and the requirement that whenever outside their compartment or cell they must keep their hands clasped behind their backs. Prisoners also refer to the rude, unpleasant, often threatening and sometimes violent behaviour of the guards.

In 1977 nine political prisoners in the Mordovia special regime camp said in a statement that in future they would collectively resist the transportation of prisoners away from their camp. They gave as their grounds that two of the prisoners in their camp (Mikhail Osadchy and Bohdan Rebrik) had recently been beaten up by guards while in transit, while another prisoner had been thrown into a *voronok* completely naked. They expressed fear that prisoners were more likely to be beaten when taken away and separated from their fellow political prisoners, who could offer protection by collective hunger strikes and similar actions.

The Leningrad poet Yuliya Okulova (Voznessenskaya), who had been sentenced to serve 2 years' imprisonment, reported that while in a transit prison in Novosibirsk in 1977 she had witnessed very serious mistreatment of a group of young female prisoners. According to a lengthy statement by her partially reproduced in issue 47 of *A Chronicle of Current Events*, the guards had tormented the prisoners by making their shower water alternately boiling hot and cold, and had then driven them naked down a corridor in front of male guards and prisoners. The girls were subsequently made to run a gauntlet of guards who beat them with fists, keys and a hosepipe. They were then crowded into tiny "box" cells and ill-treated in other ways.

Numerous similar incidents have been reported in which guards have deliberately ill-treated prisoners. Attacks by criminal prisoners are also common. By all accounts it is virtually routine for criminal prisoners to forcibly steal all valuables from weaker prisoners and prisoners who are on their own, sometimes including the clothes off their backs. Some former prisoners of conscience have reported seeing prisoners rape or attempt to rape their victims.

## Prisoners' Accommodation and Other Facilities

### Prisons

The prison in the corrective labour system on which Amnesty International has the most detailed information is Vladimir prison, where prisoners of conscience were held until 1978.

Prisoners in Vladimir prison (as in any other institution of this type) are confined to cells, most holding from two to six prisoners but some holding 10 or more. Except when undergoing punishment in a punishment cell, prisoners may not be held in solitary confinement unless "exceptional circumstances" require a prisoner's isolation from other prisoners. (Article 68, RSFSR Corrective Labour Code.)

According to the law, there must be 2.5 square meters' living space for each occupant of a cell. Prisoners assert that this norm is often violated and that many cells are overcrowded. The door to each cell has an aperture through which guards may observe the inmates. The window of each cell is covered by iron blinds so that daylight is cut off and the prisoners cannot see out. A light burns all day and night in every cell. Some cells have a sink with running water and a toilet. Others have neither, and prisoners must resort to a toilet bucket (*parasha*) in the cell. Prisoners are fed through a food trough (*kormushka*) in the cell door. The floors of most cells are of cement, and prisoners have fruitlessly asked that they be covered with some sort of tile to make them less uncomfortable. A light (either 40 or 100 watts, depending on the size of the cell) burns all night.

The cells are fitted with loudspeakers, and prisoners complain that these are a source of constant disturbance. They provide important information not otherwise available. For example, prisoners of conscience who were held in Vladimir prison between 1974 and 1977 have told Amnesty International that reports of death sentences were broadcast over the loudspeaker system there "almost every week". According to this source, most of the death sentences were announced as having been executed, all were for violent crimes such as murder and none were for war crimes. This information suggests that the annual number of death sentences in the USSR is much higher than the approximately 30 announced each year in Soviet media.

Prisoners have complained that a number of cells in Vladimir prison lack proper ventilation or any ventilation at all and that this, combined with bad or non-existent plumbing facilities, makes the cells reek. There have also been complaints about the dampness of the cells and the inefficient heating, which often causes the cells to be either uncomfortably hot or too cold, depending on the season. Prisoners have complained that the cells are inadequately lit and that inmates suffer eye-strain because of this since no daylight enters the cells on account of the iron blinds on the window.

Prisoners in Vladimir prison are allowed 60 or 30 minutes of exercise each day, depending on their regime. The following description of the exercise area (in a 1976 report by the Moscow Helsinki monitoring group) sums up descriptions of the exercise facilities by inmates themselves:

> The exercise yards are small stone pits. Each exercise yard is 5 or 6 by
> 3 or 4 meters, little larger than the cells, and is surrounded by high brick
> walls. Above there is an iron grill. (When he is in his cell the prisoner
> never sees the sky, and when he takes his exercise, he sees the sky in a
> cage. Grass and vegetation he never sees.) Sunlight does not normally
> fall in the area of the exercise yard.

The first available accounts of Chistopol prison suggest that conditions there are similar to those in Vladimir prison.

## Corrective labour colonies

Most prisoners of conscience are kept in corrective labour colonies (camps). Like prisons, they are surrounded by barbed wire and walls with watch towers and are guarded by armed MVD personnel and dogs.

Prisoners in special regime camps, like those in prisons, are confined in cells, although in theory they may be transferred to barrack-type accommodation for "good behaviour". Political prisoners in the Mordovia special regime camp are confined to cells holding between three and five prisoners each. The cells do not have toilets, so prisoners must use a bucket in their cell. Reportedly the roof of the cell-block where prisoners of conscience are held leaks badly, and has not been repaired despite years of complaints by the prisoners. Irina Zholkovskaya, the wife of the prisoner of conscience Alexander Ginzburg, reported after visiting him at the camp in 1978:

> The cell in which my husband and other prisoners is kept is so damp
> that water drips down the walls and the plaster is crumbling off. Mice
> run about in the cell.

Prisoners in this camp are permitted one hour's exercise each day in covered exercise yards measuring 6 by 9 meters. According to reports from prisoners, the exercise areas are completely unhygienic: some have filthy toilets and rubbish areas in them. There are also detailed reports that the prisoners' bathing and washing areas are likewise unhygienic and primitive.

Prisoners in ordinary, reinforced and strict regime camps have barrack-type accommodation. A single barrack may hold as many as 200 prisoners, often in overcrowded conditions. They sleep on double bunk beds and keep their meagre belongings (toilet articles, food they may have purchased at the camp shop, books) in a small night-table, which must be shared by prisoners in the same bunk.

Prisoners have complained about numerous features of these barracks: the overcrowding and total lack of privacy; the difficulty in studying or even reading because of noise made by the large number of fellow inmates; lack of ventilation; insufficient heating during the cold months (indoor temperatures of around $8^{\circ}C$ have been reported from a number of camps, although the official norm is that barracks must be heated to $18\text{-}20^{\circ}C$); constant disturbance by the public address system; toilet facilities which are inadequate or situated so far from the barracks that elderly or invalid prisoners have difficulty in reaching them.

Many of the camps known to Amnesty International are located in areas affected by severe cold during the winter months. Nonetheless the authorities forbid the prisoners to use more than the standard issue of one blanket, even in winter. The same applies to prisoners' clothing. All prisoners must wear uniform clothing, which is black when issued but becomes grey with washing. Prisoners' underwear is black too. Prisoners who are categorized as "especially dangerous recidivists" (such as the political prisoners in the Mordovia special regime camp) wear special striped uniforms. All are expected to wear this standard clothing during the working day, and a number of cases have been reported in which prisoners of conscience were punished for wearing additional clothing during the winter or for removing part of their regulation clothing during the summer.

Prisoners are woken daily at 6.00 am. They may be punished for not getting out of bed immediately or for lying down on their bed again after they have risen. After they have left the barracks for their morning meal they may not return there again until after work. Lights out is at 10.00 pm and prisoners may be punished for not being in their sleeping quarters at that time.

Prisoners are generally permitted to launder their clothes once a week, often in primitive conditions. They are permitted to have a bath once every week or 10 days. There have been complaints about the infrequency of baths, shortage of soap and unhygienic conditions in the bathing areas. There have been other complaints about lack of hygiene. For example, it has been reported that there were lice in the barracks of ordinary regime camp OR-318/76 in Rovno region in the Ukraine, where the prisoners of conscience Vasyl Barladyanu and Pyotr Vins were both held at the same time in 1978.

## Food

Hunger as a permanent feature of camp and prison life is provided for in the corrective labour legislation. Not only is hunger an essential part of most of the punishments which are regularly imposed on prisoners, but prisoners' regular diet is also such as to cause hunger and malnutrition.

Article 56 of the RSFSR Corrective Labour Code states in part:

Convicted people shall receive food ensuring the normal vital activity of the human organism. Food rations shall be differentiated according to the climatic conditions at the location of the corrective labour colony, the nature of the work done by the convicted person and his attitude to work. People who are put in a punishment- or discipline-isolation cell, in a punishment cell, in the cell-type premises of colonies with ordinary, reinforced and strict regime and in a solitary cell in a colony with special regime shall receive reduced food rations.

The Commentary to Article 56 goes further:

> Convicted persons who systematically and maliciously do not fulfil
> their output norms at work may be put on reduced food rations.[1]

The law permits prisoners to obtain supplementary food from two sources: periodic food purchases with the camp or prison and parcels from people outside the camp or prison. However the amount and nature of food which may be obtained in these ways is closely regulated so that it does not enable the prisoner to evade the regime of hunger. Furthermore, prisoners are frequently deprived of these supplementary sources of food as a punishment.

The authorities take other measures to ensure that prisoners are entirely dependent on the administration for their food. They are never, to Amnesty International's knowledge, employed in agricultural work, in spite of the chronic annual shortage of farm labour in many parts of the country during the sowing and harvest seasons. This was partly explained in 1968 in an officially-published monograph on penal theory. The authors strongly recommended against putting prisoners to work on farms, partly because:

> . . . it is impossible to limit prisoners' consumption of many food items
> which are produced in such colonies (milk, eggs, vegetables, fruit, etc.).
> Thus the food rationing levels which exist for prisoners and also the
> regulations on parcels and hand-delivered packets lose their educational
> significance.[2]

The camp and prison authorities are obliged to confiscate from prisoners "food products obtained by them in violation of the established procedures for purchasing or receiving them."[3] To the same end the Presidium of the RSFSR Supreme Soviet issued a decree in 1972 making it a punishable administrative offence to transmit food illegally to convicted people serving terms of imprisonment.[4] When this decree was announced in 1972 Academicians Sakharov and Leontiyev said in an appeal to the RSFSR Supreme Soviet:

> The culpability for illegal transmission of food products to prisoners which
> is established by the decree is an official indication of the existence of a
> regime of chronic starvation in our camps and prisons. No one would resort
> to illegal transmission if there were no necessity for it. The decree opens
> up possibilities of making the tragic situation of prisoners . . . even worse, by
> instituting searches of prisoners and their visitors. We call upon deputies of
> the Supreme Soviet to speak out for a reform of corrective labour
> legislation, with the aim of putting an end to the intolerable torturing of
> prisoners through starvation.[5]

The determination of food rations for convicted prisoners is the responsibility of the USSR Council of Ministers. The current diets for prisoners are laid down in an unpublished decree (MVD Directive 0225), issued in 1972. According to reports from prisoners, the decree establishes 13 different diets, each intended for a particular category of prisoners according to the regime to which they have been sentenced, the nature and location of their work, any punishment they may be undergoing and any authorization they may have for supplementary diet on medical grounds.[6]

"Norm 1" has been described in *samizdat* sources as "the standard, 'guaranteed' norm" in corrective labour colonies of all regimes. The daily menu under Norm 1 is as follows:

| | |
|---|---|
| Rye bread — 650g. | Fat — 10g. |
| Wheatmeal flour — 10g. | Vegetable oil — 15g. |
| Groats — 110g. | Sugar — 20g. |
| Macaroni — 20g. | Potato — 450g. |
| Meat — 50g. | Cabbage and other vegetables — 200g. |
| Fish — 85g. | Tomato Paste — 5g. |

This diet contains 2500 calories and 65 grams of protein, although prisoners doing particularly strenuous labour may be given an additional several hundred calories in the form of an extra helping of porridge, some oil and some sugar.

Mikhail Shtern, an endocrinologist who was imprisoned in a reinforced regime camp near Kharkov from 1975 to 1977, has described this "standard" diet thus: "The food was like animal fodder. No vegetables or fruit for years on end, and microscopic portions of meat."[7]

This diet is not adequate for prisoners doing most of the types of compulsory labour demanded in camps and prisons, and in practice is made up of low quality food lacking in vitamins and fats. Prisoners of conscience are frequently fed for long periods at norms even lower than "Norm 1".

It is common for prisoners of conscience in camps to be confined for periods of 15 days, in many cases repeatedly, to punishment-isolation cells, and for inmates of prisons to be confined to punishment cells. Chapter 6 describes in more detail these and other forms of punishment in camps and prisons. Prisoners subjected to these punishments are fed as follows.

Every second day they are fed according to "Norm 9b". This diet contains between 1300 and 1400 calories and about 38 grams of protein and consists of the following:

| | |
|---|---|
| Rye bread — 450g. | Fat or Vegetable oil — 6g. |
| Wheatmeal flour — 10g. | Potato — 250g. |
| Groats — 50g. | Cabbage — 200g. |
| Fish — 60g. | Tomato paste — 5g. |

There is no meat in this diet.

On alternate days (known to prisoners as "skip days" or "hungry days") prisoners in punishment-isolation cells or punishment cells receive no warm food, but only 450 grams of rye bread, hot water and salt. Prisoners in punishment isolation cells who work receive the 1300-1400 calorie diet each day.

Prisoners in camps may also be punished by being kept for up to six months (sometimes for repeated terms) in "cell-type premises" within their camp. If they work, as is expected of them, they are fed at "Norm 9a":

| | |
|---|---|
| Rye bread — 600g. | Vegetable oil — 15g. |
| Wheat flour — 10g. | Sugar — 10g. |
| Groats — 80g. | Potato — 350g. |
| Macaroni — 10g. | Cabbage and other vegetables — 200g. |
| Meat — 30g. | Tomato paste — 5g. |
| Fish — 75g. | |

According to some accounts this diet contains about 2100 calories and 55 grams of protein,[8] but according to other accounts it contains only about 1700 calories.[9] The same diet is given to inmates of special regime camps who are punished by a term in a solitary cell. This punishment may last one year.

According to an unpublished MVD directive, prisoners in camps who while serving punishment in "cell-type premises" "maliciously" refuse to work or "deliberately" do not fulfil their output norms are to be fed at the "Norm 9b" ration described above: about 1300 calories per day. As further punishment they may be put on rations like those in the punishment-isolation cell and punishment cell: the "9b" diet one day, bread and water the next.

Inmates of prisons (except when they are in punishment cells—see above) are fed differently according to whether they are on ordinary or strict regime. Those on ordinary regime in prisons are on a diet which contains around 2000 calories and 51 grams of protein. However most inmates of prisons spend part of their sentence on strict regime, especially if they are prisoners of conscience who engage in any form of protest against their conditions of confinement. All "recidivists" who are sentenced to a term in a prison, and similarly all prisoners who are transferred to a prison from a camp as a form of punishment, spend their first two to six months in the prison on strict regime. In addition, a term of up to six months' strict regime is frequently imposed on prison inmates as a form of punishment. As with other punishments, the legal limit of six months is frequently violated in the cases of prisoners of conscience. The strict regime diet contains about 1750 calories per day and 49 grams of protein, according to the most detailed available accounts. Furthermore, all prisoners who are put on strict regime serve their first month of this punishment on "reduced rations". This diet, which is nowhere mentioned in any published legal texts, reportedly contains around 1300 calories.

The Moscow Helsinki monitoring group has described this "reduced rations" diet as follows:

450 grams of underbaked, damp, sour and heavy bread and besides this:
Breakfast—60 grams of sprats or sardelle, not rarely completely spoiled and inedible.
Lunch—About half a litre of meatless, watery cabbage soup or meatless watery broth (in the soup, apart from the spoiled smelly cabbage there swim a few bits of potato, often black; in the broth there are likewise a few bits of potato and a few groats, either pearl barley or oats).
Dinner—About a glassful of cooked groats (oats, pearl barley or wheat, boiled in water).
Figures on the general quantity of fat (or vegetable oil) [sic] vary; according to some figures it is 3-4 grams per day, according to others 5-6 grams per day. (The fat is added to the food.)

It should be borne in mind that prisoners are expected to do compulsory work, normally of a heavy nature, even when they are on the various punishment diets, except for prisoners in punishment cells and punishment-isolation cells who are receiving warm food only on alternate days and those in "cell-type premises" who are on "9b" rations. (See Chapter 5.) Even the best of the above diets contains no more than about 2500 calories (or 2900 for some prisoners). Yet according to standards issued by the World Health Organization in 1973, a man working "very actively" requires a daily calorie intake of between 3100 and 3900 calories.[10] Also according to international standards, the human organism requires daily protein intake of one gram for every kilo of body weight (provided the daily calorie intake is adequate). The camp and prison diets fall far short of these standards, with severe consequences for the health of the prisoners. The law permits granting a diet supplement to prisoners doing heavy work, but it is rarely granted to prisoners of conscience. When political prisoners in Vladimir prison were first required to work, in 1975, their diet was increased only by 100 grams of bread per day. The diets for prison strict regime, prison reduced rations, punishment cell, punishment-isolation cell and "cell-type premises" are simply starvation diets.

Prisoners' food is normally both monotonous and of very poor quality, so that the calorie content estimates cited above are actually higher than the real calorie content of prisoners' diets. The Moscow Helsinki monitoring group reported in 1976:

Thus the black (rye) bread is usually underbaked, damp and heavy; it is quite different from the bread sold outside. The fish (in the prisons: sprats, sardelle, very salty; in the camps: salted cod or some other kind of salted fish) is not rarely completely spoiled and rotten. The meat is of the lowest quality, scrap meats. The sauerkraut, which is used in making the cabbage soup or borshch with which the prisoners are fed several times a week, is foul-smelling or completely rotten. The potatoes are during much of the year dried out and long past the time of keeping. And so on.

An anonymous account from the Mordovia special regime camp in 1978 described the daily diet there:

Day after day we eat the same fodder: in the morning five days a week we get 55 grams of fish—rotten fish—and a bowl of watery gruel; at midday 21 grams of rotten *sboi* [the entrails, head and legs of a slaughtered animal— *AI note*] or lard, some watery, smelly soup of some borshch made of spoiled cabbage; in the evening smelly soup. We get damp bread with [illegible in the original—*AI note*] the thickness of a finger. We do not in practice get any of the vegetables authorized for our rations.

Ona Pranskunaite, a Lithuanian prisoner of conscience, wrote in late 1977 or early 1978 that in her women's ordinary regime camp in the Gorky region, the bread served to prisoners contained sawdust and was used for feeding livestock as well.

An entry for 1977 in a regular "diary"-type account by prisoners in a Perm camp says:

May 2, 6, 13, 16, 23, 26, 27, 30: rotten fish for supper.

According to another detailed account by prisoners in Perm in late 1978:

The food in camp 35 has improved. The older prisoners say that this is the first time in 25 years that they've eaten tomatoes or eggs.

Yury Orlov

Danylo Shumuk, who at the time of writing had served 35 years in prison

Valery Marchenko

118

Ukrainian Helsinki monitor Oksana Meshko (left) with her son Alexander
Sergiyenko in 1979

A camp in the city of Baku, in the Azerbaidzhan SSR

The same report went on to say that the improvement was only temporary, and speculated that it might have been somehow connected with the fact that Yury Orlov, Chairman of the Moscow Helsinki monitoring group, had recently arrived in the camp to serve his 12-year sentence for "anti-Soviet agitation and propaganda". Orlov, whose case had become very well-known internationally, had announced that while in the camp he would closely monitor conditions there on behalf of the unofficial Helsinki group.

Obviously feeding practices of this sort eventually cause considerable suffering and risk to the health of the prisoners. Vladimir Bukovsky described the effects as follows in the memoirs he wrote after spending from 1972 to 1976 in Vladimir prison and the Perm camps:

I can't say that prison hunger was particularly agonizing—it wasn't a
biting hunger but, rather, a prolonged process of chronic under-nourishment.
You very quickly stopped feeling it badly and were left with a kind of
gnawing pain, rather like a quietly throbbing toothache. You even lost
awareness that it was hunger, and only after several months did you notice
that it hurt to sit on a wooden bench, and at night, no matter which way
you turned, something hard seemed to be pressing into you or against you—
you would get up several times in the night and shake the mattress, toss
and turn from side to side, and still it hurt. Only then did you realize that
your bones were sticking out. But by then you didn't care any longer.
Nevertheless, you didn't get out of your bunk too quickly in the
mornings, otherwise your head would spin.[11]

Issue number 42 of *A Chronicle of Current Events* (8 October 1976) reported as regards Vladimir prison:

Because of underfeeding prisoners on strict regime suffer from swelling
of their finger joints and swellings and red patches show up on their
bodies.

The same issue of the *Chronicle* reported as follows on the condition of the prisoner of conscience Gabriel Superfin at the end of a period on strict regime in Vladimir prison:

On 26 August Superfin finished three months on strict regime. In the
evenings his legs swell up, and he is having difficulty with his stomach
and liver; he has persistent pains.

Prisoners normally suffer severe weight loss while serving their sentences and as well as the stomach ulcers from which many prisoners suffer after a few years of imprisonment vitamin starvation and related ailments are common. Prisoners in Perm camp 36 reported in 1976 that some prisoners there were suffering from scurvy.

It is not uncommon for prisoners to resort to eating grass, wild flowers, nettles and the like in order to compensate for the deficiencies of their diet. The Ukrainian journalist Valery Marchenko reported in 1976 from his camp in Perm that he had gathered and dried some birch tree buds to eat as a complement to his diet, but the guards took them away from him as "not authorized". Similarly, the prisoner of conscience Nikolai Budulak-Sharygin reported after his release in 1978 that he had resorted to collecting nettles to improve his diet and that of other prisoners in Mordovia.

However, the authorities are careful to prevent prisoners from supplementing their diets in these and other ways. According to information given to Amnesty International by Nadezhda Svetlichnaya after she emigrated in 1978 at the end of a four-year sentence, the women prisoners in Mordovia camp 3 were permitted to cultivate a small flower garden, but were expressly forbidden to grow any vegetables in it. Prisoners from other camps in Mordovia and in Perm have reported that the authorities there took considerable trouble to stop the growth of grass and other vegetation in the areas used by the prisoners.

Prisoners are permitted to spend a small amount of money each month on "food products and basic necessities". The amount they may spend in this way varies from regime to regime. In ordinary regime camps prisoners may spend up to 7 rubles per month, in reinforced regime camps up to 6 rubles, in strict regime camps up to 5 rubles and in special regime camps up to 4 rubles. Prison inmates may spend up to 3 rubles a month when on ordinary regime and up to 2 rubles a month when on strict regime. (Articles 62 to 70, RSFSR Corrective Labour Code.)

Prisoners' meagre shopping allowance must cover not only any food they may purchase but also "basic necessities", such as toilet items, stationery, tobacco, etc. For purchases of food and basic necessities prisoners may spend only money they receive for their work while serving their sentence.

After serving a specified part of their sentence "model" prisoners and prisoners who over-fulfil their output norms may benefit, according to the law, from a small increase in their shopping allowance. Few prisoners of conscience are known ever to have benefited from this provision of the law.

On the other hand prisoners of conscience have regularly been punished by being deprived of their monthly shopping allowance. Often this happens repeatedly to the same prisoner. The Armenian prisoner of conscience Razmik Markosian, for example, reported in 1977 that he had been deprived of his shopping allowance for nine out of the previous 12 months. Prisoners in punishment cells and punishment-isolation cells are not permitted to buy food, "since part of their punishment is that they receive food at reduced rations".[12] Other prisoners of conscience have been unable to make shop purchases because there was no money left over after deductions from their work earnings. Thus the Ukrainian prisoner of conscience Irina Stasiv-Kalynets could make no shop purchases for more than a year in 1976-1977.

Even when prisoners are permitted to use the shop, this enables them to acquire only a very limited diet supplement. The range of products available in camp and prison shops is laid down in the unpublished Rules of Internal Order.

Among the products whose sale was forbidden under the Rules of Internal Order prior to 1978 were meat and milk products, sugar, honey and chocolate. According to some reports the Rules of Internal Order which came into effect in 1978 added oil, fat and margarine to the forbidden list and reduced the monthly limit on purchase of tea from 100 grams to 50 grams. According to other reports the new Rules of Internal Order make it permissible at least in principle for milk products to be sold to prisoners. According to reports by prisoners the food products sold are usually of low quality and often stale or beginning to spoil.

In 1977 Bukovsky listed 36 products which were available in the shop in Vladimir prison. Of these 19 were food products. The prices of some of the foods on the list were.

*Apple jam* — .60 rubles for a jar of ½ kilogram
*Margarine* — .36 rubles for 200 grams
*Mushroom solyanka* (a soup) — .34 rubles for a jar of ½ kilogram
*Vegetable solyanka* — .32 rubles for ½ kilogram
*Cheese* (depending on the sort) — from 1.60 to 3.60 rubles per kilogram

At these prices, a prison inmate on ordinary regime, with a monthly spending allowance of 3 rubles, would be able to supplement his or her diet each month with at most 2½ kilograms of apple jam or less than 2 kilograms of the cheapest cheese if he or she were to spend all his or her allowance on food products alone.

Bread is also available from the shop, at the following prices according to Bukovsky's detailed 1977 report:

Rye bread — .15 rubles per kilogram
White bread — .15 rubles per ½ kilogram
White bread — .22 rubles per 800 grams

However the prisoners are allowed to purchase bread only twice a month, buying a maximum of two kilograms each time.

The only other means by which prisoners may supplement their diet is through parcels sent or brought to them by friends and relatives. This source of food is even more limited. No prisoner may receive a parcel until he or she has served half his or her sentence. Thereafter prisoners in ordinary regime camps may receive three parcels per year, prisoners on reinforced regime two and those on strict and special regime one. Inmates of prisons may not receive any parcels.

The maximum weight of a parcel is five kilograms. The permitted contents are tightly regulated by the MVD's Rules of Internal Order. Reportedly bread, salted fish, fish preserves, fruit and vegetables, vegetable and fruit oils, fat, cheese, confections, jam, onions and garlic are permitted. Sugar, honey, chocolate, meat products, food concentrates and vitamins are among the products which may not be included in parcels.

All prisoners may also receive two one-kilogram packets per year. These are meant to contain mostly printed matter, but may also contain dry confections (but nothing made of chocolate).

Cancellation of the prisoner's right to receive his or her next parcel is a punishment commonly inflicted on prisoners of conscience.


In spite of their constant undernourishment, prisoners of conscience frequently resort to hunger strikes as a means of protest.

The authorities use various techniques to try to discourage and break hunger strikes. There are numerous reports of hunger striking prisoners of conscience being beaten, put in punishment cells, forced to go to work while on hunger strike, sent into transit while on hunger strike or put into cells with criminal prisoners who tried to induce them to take food either by force or by persuasion.

The authorities invariably force-feed hunger striking prisoners after they have gone a certain time without food. Whereas until the mid-1970s the official policy reportedly was to feed hunger-strikers after 17 days, the current practice (laid down in an unpublished MVD directive) is to begin feeding "when the body begins to smell of acetone".

Hunger strikers are supposed to be fed daily with an enriched gruel consisting of 800 grams of milk, 30 grams of butter, 100 grams of sugar, two eggs, 50 grams of meat and 15 grams of groats. However, according to various accounts, prisoners are often force-fed only once or twice a week and are unlikely to get the full diet since the staff normally steal the better products. The process of force-feeding is unpleasant under any circumstances, but there are also reports that in many cases it is carried out clumsily and with unnecessary use of violence.

## Medical Conditions

Obviously lengthy subjection to undernourishment can, and in many cases does, have serious consequences for prisoners' health. The combination of low-grade, badly cooked and hastily eaten food with heavy labour in unhealthy conditions and a harsh climate causes some prisoners to emerge as chronic invalids. Most inmates suffer from stomach ulcers and other gastric complaints after two or three years. Colony and prison medical facilities are inadequate to cope with the health problems of prisoners subjected for long periods to these harmful conditions.

Article 37 of the Fundamentals of Corrective Labour Legislation of the USSR and Union Republics states:

The procedure for rendering medical aid to people deprived of liberty, the use of public health medical institutions and agencies and the enlistment for this purpose of medical personnel shall be determined by the Ministry of the Interior of the USSR and the Ministry of Public Health of the USSR.

In practice, however, the medical system for prisoners is entirely contained within the MVD. All doctors in camps and prisons are officers of the MVD which has its own Medical Administration in Moscow and locally. The MVD operates the medical units in camps and prisons and has its own hospital facilities for prisoners. The medical commissions which rule on whether individual prisoners are fit to work or to continue serving their sentences are also administered by the MVD. As far as is known to Amnesty International, prisoners never see doctors from outside the MVD except in the rare case when, for want of facilities within the corrective labour system, they are treated in public hospitals.

Every camp and prison has its own medical unit. As well, there are larger hospital units to serve complexes of colonies such as those in Mordovia and Perm. The MVD also maintains at least one central hospital (the Leningrad Gaaz

Central Hospital) for prisoners with serious illnesses from camps and prisons throughout the corrective labour system. When the prisoner of conscience Sergei Kovalyov asked to be sent there in 1977 for treatment, he was reportedly told by officials in his Perm camp that no political prisoner had ever been sent there. Kovalyov was eventually sent there for treatment, as were the Ukrainian prisoner of conscience Vasyl Stus in 1976 and the Latvian prisoner of conscience Maigonis Ravinish in 1979.

By all accounts the medical facilities in camps and prisons are inadequately staffed. There are numerous reports that many staff doctors are either newly qualified or under-qualified, and that medical staff posts are often unfilled. For example, former prisoners have told Amnesty International that in the mid-1970s Mordovia camp 19, a strict regime camp many of whose inmates are serving lengthy terms of imprisonment, had the services of a doctor for a time only because the wife of the camp director was a doctor. When her husband was replaced and she left the camp, the prisoners' medical care was left in the hands of a man named Seksyasov, who had trained as a *feldsher* (a semi-skilled practitioner without graduate qualifications) while working in the camp's administration. According to frequent reports Seksyasov was neither medically competent nor of good will, but he was left in charge of deciding whether prisoners needed treatment, whether they were fit to go out to work and whether they were fit for punishment.

For 18 months in 1977 and 1978, Perm camp 36 did not have any medical staff competent to do dental and stomatological work. Occasionally a stomatologist from outside the camp would visit, but she refused to treat some patients because of lack of time. The effect of this on prisoners is reflected in the following report by the Ukrainian literary critic Ivan Svetlichny:

Two days ago the prisoner Ya. I. Korizor, who for months had been asking in vain for dental treatment, pulled out two of his teeth with a pair of pliers. This is typical of the nature of the medical service available to us. Other prisoners are in the same situation as Korizor, and if they do not do what he did it is only because they do not have his will power or because this would not help them.

In 1976 inmates of the same camp said of the camp doctor Sheliya: " . . . his loutishness and low competence are such that the residents of the camp settlement regard him with the same contempt as the prisoners". Some prisoners in the camp refused to go to him for treatment, and in 1977 it was reported that the prisoners were preparing some sort of strike action to try to have him removed from his post. In 1978 this same Dr Sheliya testified at the trial of Yury Orlov that the treatment of prisoners in the camp was adequate from a medical point of view. The former Ukrainian prisoner of conscience Nadezhda Svetlichnaya told Amnesty International in 1978, after serving 4 years' imprisonment, that in the women's strict regime camp in Mordovia a doctor came around the camp approximately every week, and the nurse came every day, but the prisoners avoided going to the medical personnel because of the low quality of the medical assistance they provided.

One prisoner whose health and lack of medical treatment caused special concern in 1978 and 1979 is Igor Ogurtsov, a Leningrad orientalist who was sentenced in 1968 to 20 years' imprisonment and exile for leadership of an underground group. According to numerous accounts Ogurtsov was an exceptionally tough and fit man at the time of his arrest. By 1978 it was known that he was suffering from a complex of serious ailments. Both he and other prisoners have attributed his decline in health directly to his conditions of imprisonment. His mother said in early 1979 in an appeal to the World Medical Association that she had despaired of his receiving a proper diagnosis in his camp and had consulted several Leningrad physicians. On the basis of the symptoms described by Ogurtsov in his letters, these doctors formed the opinion that he was suffering from calcium deficiency leading to porosity of the bones, prolapse of the stomach and the pancreas and infectious mononucleosis that had been neglected for years.

In one of his letters in early 1979 Ogurtsov said:

I feel quite poorly. It's very difficult to work. I have constant pain
around the waist and below the belly, and my pelvic bones are breaking.
Since I can't be certain what's wrong with me I can't take any measures
to help myself. I can't put any faith in the camp medical unit since I
got absolutely no help from there and not even a diagnosis when I went
there with the same symptoms a year ago.

MVD officials in April 1979 turned down requests by Ogurtsov and his family that he be sent to Leningrad for diagnosis and treatment in the general hospital for prisoners, justifying their refusal by reference to his "satisfactory state of health". As of early 1979 Ogurtsov was still being required to do heavy physical work. In the first half of 1979 he reportedly spent 42 days in punishment-isolation cells. In the summer of 1979 he was transferred to Chistopol prison as a punishment.

Camp and prison medical facilities normally lack not only adequate trained staff but also basic medical equipment and supplies. Prisoners frequently report that medical units in camps have only few medicines in stock and that what few there are are usually past their date of recommended use by the time they arrive in the camp. Families and friends of prisoners have frequently tried to send medicines necessary for their treatment in the camp. These are almost invariably refused by the camp authorities. There have been rare exceptions where the administration has let through medicine sent by private sources (for example, to the prisoners Vasyl Barladyanu and Valery Marchenko) but these exceptions, welcome though they are, serve to underscore the deficiency of the authorized medical provisions.

An anonymous report from the Mordovia special regime colony in 1978 described the local medical unit for prisoners there, most of them serving sentences of more than 10 years' hard labour:

It is a small . . . cell. And in this medical unit there is no *feldsher*, no
medication, but only an orderly, a former policeman [for the German
occupation forces during World War II—*AI note*] . This policeman can't
distinguish a headache from a carbuncle or aspirin from vaseline,
but he's all we have for medical assistance.

Prisoners commonly complain that it is difficult for them to obtain even what limited medical treatment is available.

Prisoners in the Mordovia special regime camp have said that, while in theory a camp doctor is supposed to tour the hospital regularly, in practice they have to wait a month to see a doctor, even after they have reported that they are ill. Vladimir Bukovsky wrote about Vladimir prison after he was released from there in 1976:

> Beginning in the morning (only beginning in the morning) it is possible
> to register to see the doctor. But this doesn't mean that they will call you
> on the same day; they can call you after a considerable delay, sometimes
> a week or two later. In a case of urgent necessity for medical help guards
> may call a medical assistant, but even for this it is necessary to bang on
> the door and wait a long time before they call him.

Prisoners frequently have to submit complaints or make some sort of demonstration in order to get medical attention. For example, in Perm camp 36, Mykola Slobodian, a Ukrainian imprisoned for "anti-Soviet agitation and propaganda", was put in a punishment-isolation cell in the spring of 1978 for not meeting his output norms. At the time he was suffering from a bleeding stomach ulcer. Twelve other prisoners of conscience went on hunger strike until a medical commission came to examine him.

Another illustration of the difficulty prisoners commonly have in being seen by a doctor is the following report of an incident in Vladimir prison in 1975:

> During the night of 17-18 October Gunnar Rode, a prisoner in cell 31 in
> block 4, became ill. Apparently he had developed twisted bowels, as
> had already happened to him in 1971 (*Chronicle* 20). Mikhailov, the same
> guard who on 18 May beat the hunger-striking Abankin in the punishment
> cell (*Chronicle* 37), refused to call a doctor. Then the prisoners of cell 31—
> Vitold Abankin, Vladimir Bukovsky, Yury Grodetsky, Alexei Safronov,
> Babur Shakirov—made a lot of noise, beat on the peep-hole and food-
> trough in the door. The assistant duty officer for the prison and a medical
> assistant ran in and took Rode off to the medical unit. They gave him
> treatment and returned him to his cell within a day.

According to Bukovsky's subsequent account of the incident, in order finally to attract medical attention "Rode's cell-mates had to tear a bench from the cement floor, kick through the food-trough and split the door". Four of them were punished for the incident.

Even when prisoners do see a doctor, treatment is likely to be perfunctory. Prisoners have frequently said that the medical staff give more satisfactory treatment only if there is a conspicuous danger that the prisoner might die. Bukovsky explained this as follows:

> Under the conditions of prison medical practice . . . the prison doctors
> cannot undertake to cure patients. The role of prison medicine amounts
> only to relieving the acuteness of an illness and preventing the impermissible
> outcome of death. Consequently illnesses take on a chronic form, are
> difficult to treat and lead to disablement.

Zamovskaya (a doctor in Vladimir prison) said plainly: "It's a prison you are in, I don't intend to give you serious treatment, and anyway you are our enemies. I am not about to spend my time on turncoats and traitors." She told me personally (when I requested treatment for a liver ailment): "I didn't put you in prison, you are undergoing punishment; you didn't have to get yourself into prison."[13]

Some prisoners of conscience have been told by medical or administration staff that they would receive treatment only if they "behaved well" (Sergei Kovalyov in 1976) or if they acted as informers (the Lithuanian prisoner Sarunas Zukauskas, himself a doctor, in 1976).

Prisoners have repeatedly charged that the medical personnel in the camps and prisons frequently put their loyalty to the MVD and the corrective labour system ahead of medical ethics. In at least one case it has been reported that a camp doctor acted as an intermediary between a KGB officer in a Perm camp and a prisoner who was acting as an informer. According to the prisoner, the doctor paid him off with chocolate and a recommendation that he receive a medical diet and be sent to the camp hospital.[14]

Until 1977, reportedly, camp and prison doctors were required to counter-sign the orders for prisoners to be confined to punishment cells and punishment-isolation cells. In this as in other matters such as checking prisoners' fitness for compulsory labour, camp and prison doctors are known to have routinely failed to protect prisoners from harmful decisions of the administration, even where reportedly there were conspicuous reasons for intervening on the prisoners' behalf on medical grounds.

Thus Alexander Sergiyenko, a specialist in Ukrainian culture imprisoned for "anti-Soviet agitation and propaganda", suffers from active tuberculosis of both lungs, which his mother has stated was officially diagnosed years ago and served as grounds for deferment of his military call-up. After serving almost two years of his seven-year sentence he was transferred as a disciplinary measure to Vladimir prison in 1973. Among other punishments to which he was subjected in Vladimir prison was strict regime for six months from June 1975, the first month on reduced rations; he was placed in a punishment cell for eight days in May 1975, for 15 days in October 1975 and for 15 days in March 1976. In an appeal to Amnesty International in June 1975 his mother described his condition when she visited him that month:

In a visit on 20 June this year I saw my son. He was grown very thin, as wasted and emaciated as could be. With a height of 179 centimeters he weighs 67 kilograms. It was difficult for him to speak—his voice had grown so weak and faint.

Reportedly, when Sergiyenko's mother asked that her son be permitted more than the one hour's authorized daily exercise, on the grounds that cell accommodation in the conditions of Vladimir prison was dangerous for him in his tubercular condition, officials of the MVD's Medical Administration replied that they were "not competent to change the regime of someone sick with tuberculosis" by changing his permitted exercise period or preventing his being put in a punishment cell. In a number of other known cases too, doctors and medical authorities have told prisoners or their relatives that they were "not competent" to get involved in "regime matters", these being within the competence only of the camp and prison administrations.

In a number of cases, prisoners of conscience who have reported ill and asked to be given treatment and relieved from work have been treated as malingerers and punished. The treatment of Yury Litvin while he was serving 3 years' imprisonment for "anti-Soviet slander" in an ordinary regime camp in the Komi ASSR is representative. In 1975, while serving his sentence, Litvin had surgery for a perforated ulcer. In 1977, reportedly, he asked to be released "with obligatory induction to labour" (see Chapter 2) because of his ill health, but the camp doctor recommended against this. The doctor also refused Litvin a special medical diet on the grounds that he was "absolutely healthy". Litvin was put in the punishment-isolation cell for 10 days for "simulating" illness. While he was there his ulcer perforated. He was made to finish his term in the punishment cell, and from there he was taken directly to a hospital. According to *A Chronicle of Current Events* (issue 47), Litvin was sent to the punishment-isolation cell again the following month for submitting a complaint to the local Communist Party authorities alleging that a 20-year-old fellow inmate had died of a heart attack without receiving any medical assistance.

Mikhail Shtern, himself a doctor, reported the following incident in a reinforced regime camp near Kharkov, where he had been imprisoned until 1977:

There was a tragic case of a young man called Sotnikov, who had served nine years and had less than a year to go. His family—wife, two children and old mother—were waiting for him at home. In September 1975 he asked the head of the medical centre of the camp, Dr Gregory Stepanovich Naidovsky, for treatment.

I remember this so-called medical colleague with horror. For three days running Sotnikov was shouting to Naidovsky: "I'm dying from a terrible stomach disease. Save me! Send me to a hospital!" But Naidovsky answered: "You're malingering. Get out, or I'll put you in a punishment cell." On the fourth day another doctor, a decent man, diagnosed an intestinal obstruction. It was too late. Sotnikov died the same day." [15]

It has often happened that in cases where camp or prison doctors have recommended that a prisoner be relieved from work, given light work, or sent to a hospital, the camp or prison administration has overruled the recommendation.

There are also numerous reports that inadequate measures are taken in camps and prisons to isolate inmates with tuberculosis or other infectious diseases. From the available information it is evident that a disturbingly high proportion of prisoners suffer from tuberculosis—as many as 25 per cent, according to Bukovsky. *A Chronicle of Current Events* reported in 1975 about Vladimir prison:

For one and a half years Mikhail Makarenko has been in the same cell with a man suffering from tuberculosis. Now he himself has an active [*otkrytaya*] form of tuberculosis.

Similar reports have been received from camps in Perm and Mordovia.

Prisoners who find it difficult to get treatment, a medical diet or relief from work in their camp find it even more difficult to obtain a recommendation that they be transferred to the hospital within their complex of camps or a civilian hospital in the area. Again, such a recommendation is given only if the patient is recognized as seriously ill.

The central camp hospital for the Mordovia camp complex is in camp ZhKh 385/3 at Barashevo. The central camp hospital for the Perm camp complex is in camp VS 389/35 at Vsesvyatskoye. By all accounts prisoners are transferred from their camp to the hospital in the same harsh conditions of transport as those described in this chapter. There have been reports of prisoners being transferred to hospital in handcuffs, even when seriously ill, and of prisoners with tuberculosis being transferred in the same vehicle with others.

According to a report from a group of inmates of the Perm camps in early 1979, the central hospital for the Perm camps is a small, two-storey building. It is clean inside, the cleaning being done by prisoners. There are medical staff on duty until 8.00 pm, but not after hours. The staff consists of a surgeon (the chief doctor), a therapist and from three to six nurses. There is an operating theatre, a laboratory and an X-ray unit, which enable basic surgical operations and examinations to be carried out. Eye-witness testimony about the camp hospital at Barashevo in the Mordovia camp complex indicates that it is more or less similar to the Perm hospital in staffing and equipment.

According to first-hand accounts, prisoners who are admitted to the hospital are kept under lock and key. The rooms where they are held do not normally have toilets, and prisoners are let out at intervals to go to the lavatory, having otherwise to use a bucket in their room.

Prisoners in Mordovia have complained that the doctors in the hospital there do not make regular rounds of the patients, that prisoners are likely to see the doctor only once or twice while they are there and that prisoners often receive little or no treatment.

The following is one former prisoner's account of conditions in the hospital unit in Vladimir prison in 1975:

The hospital is on two floors in the second block. This is the oldest block of the prison. Transfer to the hospital is regarded not as a medical measure but as a reward, inasmuch as hospital food is given there. The decision on transfer to the hospital depends not so much on the doctors as on the Operations Department. There are 40 wards in the hospital, including the psychiatric wards. The wards hold no more than three people. And there are altogether 1300 prisoners in the prison, of whom, at a minimum estimate, around one-third suffer from ulcer ailments and no less than 25 per cent from tuberculosis. The hospital ward has an area of 7.5 square meters and is not fitted with a lavatory pan or sink. They take the prisoners out to the toilets twice a day. The ward is locked all day. In the hospital wards just as in all the cells there are solid blinds on the windows and cement floors.

In the hospital the exercise period (for those who wish it) is two hours, not one hour as for the other prisoners. There is one guard for the whole corridor, and no matter what the nature of the illness it is impossible to get to the toilet area outside the prescribed time. At the very top of the hospital block there is a polyclinic section with the doctors' offices. Therefore it is easier to knock and summon a doctor than it is in the ordinary cells, but it is still difficult.

The dispensation of medications and injections takes place in the corridor, since there is no room for this in the wards. They call the patient into the corridor and administer the intramuscular or intravenous infusion right there. (In the ordinary cells injections, when they are prescribed, are generally made through the food-trough.) . . . Treatment, the prescription of diet rations and generally all medical measures, including transfer to the hospital, are used as a means of pressure on the prisoners, since they are put in direct relation with their behaviour.[16]

One benefit of a stay in the hospital is the improved diet. The medical diet ("Norm 5b" under the 1972 MVD directive) reportedly contains between 3100 and 3300 calories and is intended to contain some products not normally given to prisoners, including milk. Prisoners have said that the main difference between this diet and the normal diets is that it has larger portions. There have also been reports that the staff in the camp hospital kitchens regularly steal the better products from the hospital diet. Nonetheless, the increase in calorie intake, together with a spell away from compulsory labour, may make a stay in the camp hospital important for the physical well-being of a prisoner.

However, under an unpublished MVD directive (Number 125, 1 October 1975), prisoners in camp and prison hospitals and medical units may, for violating discipline, be punished by all the normal means, including punishment cell, punishment-isolation cell and "cell-type premises". Furthermore, inmates have reported that prisoners in the hospital may in practice be sent back to their camp on the slightest pretext, whether or not they have recovered from the ailment for which they were sent there.

### Early release on grounds of illness

Soviet law provides a device for early release of prisoners who are seriously ill. Article 100 of the RSFSR Corrective Labour Code states:

> Convicted people who are suffering from chronic mental illness or other serious illness preventing the further serving of their sentence can be freed by a court from further serving their sentence. The procedure for freeing such people from further serving their sentence is defined by legislation of the USSR and RSFSR.

> An application for release from further serving of sentence shall be brought to the court by the head of the organ charged with execution of the punishment. Together with this application there shall be sent to the court the conclusion of a medical commission and the personal file of the convicted person.

The official Commentary to the RSFSR Corrective Labour Code indicates that this article is meant to have only a restricted application. According to this source, the USSR Ministry of Health has established a list of ailments categorized as "preventing further serving of sentence". The Commentary mentions a few of these illnesses: schizophrenia, epileptic dementia, inoperable tumour of the brain and spinal column accompanied by a tendency to paralysis and severe psychiatric disturbance, persistent quadraplegia, and similar conditions.[17]

In 1976 MVD medical officials told the mother of the prisoner of conscience Alexander Sergiyenko, who had appealed for her son to be released under Article 100, that prisoners are released in this way only if they are chronically incapable of moving about by themselves.

Furthermore, by requiring that the court deciding cases of possible release under Article 100 study the prisoner's personal file, the law invites consideration of the applicant's "behaviour" or "attitude to work" as well as his or her state of health.

In some cases where the families of prisoners of conscience have applied for release on grounds of illness the authorities have refused to grant this, referring to just such considerations. For example, the relatives of Yevgen Pronyuk, a Ukrainian philosopher, applied in the mid-1970s for his release, referring to the fact that before being imprisoned he had had one lung removed because of tuberculosis and during imprisonment his condition had worsened and a cavity had developed in his other lung. They received the reply that he could not be released because of the "negative character reference from his corrective labour institution".

Mikhail Dyak, a Ukrainian who was sentenced in 1967 to 17 years' imprisonment and exile, developed Hodgkin's disease (lymphogranulomatosis) while serving his sentence. For three years during the mid-1970s the authorities refused to recommend him for early release, although his ailment was most grave. According to numerous accounts from former prisoners, the authorities insisted that he first ask for a pardon. In January 1975 the Chusovoi district court (near the Perm camps) justified their refusal to order his release by saying he had not "gone on the path of correction". He was finally released in May 1975 after he reportedly agreed to say that the acts for which he was imprisoned were criminal. He died within the year of being released.

In spite of numerous appeals that have been lodged with the Soviet authorities to recommend the release of ill prisoners of conscience under Article 100, it is almost unheard of for prisoners of conscience to be released this way. In almost none of the cases known to Amnesty International has the matter even come before a court.

On the other hand, Article 100 may have been invoked in some of the numerous transfers of troublesome political prisoners to psychiatric hospitals on the grounds of their alleged "mental illness".

For example, Yury Belov, who was sentenced in 1967 to 5 years' imprisonment for having written a *samizdat* essay "Report from the Darkness", was transferred in 1970 from a colony to Vladimir prison, apparently as a disciplinary measure. In the autumn of 1971, new criminal proceedings were initiated against him for "anti-Soviet agitation" allegedly carried out within the prison. However, in December 1971 he was sent to the Serbsky Institute of Forensic Psychiatry in Moscow for a psychiatric examination. He was diagnosed as "mentally ill" and in May 1972 transported from Vladimir to the special psychiatric hospital in Sychyovka, in the Smolensk region. According to *A Chronicle of Current Events* the head doctor of this institution told Belov "that they would treat him until he changed his opinions". Belov was eventually released from a psychiatric hospital in 1977.

Another prisoner to whose disadvantage Article 100 has been applied is Algirdas Zypre. Zypre, a Lithuanian, joined a group of Lithuanian partisans in 1944 while German and Soviet troops fought for possession of the Baltic republic. At the time he was 14 years of age, and he was reportedly moved to join the partisans both by nationalist sentiment and by the fact that his mother had been sent to a Siberian prison colony in 1944 because she owned a farm.

In 1958 Zypre's former partisan activities were discovered and he was sentenced to 25 years' imprisonment. Shortly thereafter new criminal legislation came into force setting the maximum term of imprisonment at 15 years. In 1973, having served 15 years' imprisonment, Zypre began petitioning legal authorities for his release. His petitions were rejected in the summer of 1973. When he persisted in his efforts to obtain release, he was taken in September 1973 from Perm colony VS 389/36 to Moscow's Serbsky Institute for psychiatric diagnosis. According to an anonymous *samizdat* document, Zypre was first diagnosed by local psychiatrists employed in the corrective labour system. In 1974 he was transferred from Moscow to a hospital psychiatric ward in Mordovian corrective labour colony ZhKh 385/3. He was subsequently sent to the Kazan Special Psychiatric Hospital. Former prisoners who knew him in the Mordovian camps have said that he was in no need of psychiatric treatment.

Other prisoners of conscience who have been sent from camps or prisons to psychiatric institutions in recent years are Vladimir Balakhonov, Levko Lukyanenko and Valentin Moroz.

Accounts by prisoners have referred to a high mortality rate in the camps in Perm and Mordovia. One such account written anonymously in 1976 said that 135 prisoners had died in the Mordovian camps in 1975, 34 of them (including 17 women) by suicide, 12 of the 135 in punishment-isolation cells. In 1977 *A Chronicle of Current Events* reported that 11 of the approximately 100 inmates of the Mordovia special regime camp had died in the past year and supplied details suggesting that many of these deaths were attributable to conditions in the camp. A report from a prisoner there in 1978 said that older prisoners in the Mordovian special regime camp "die like flies". In 1978 the prisoner Vladimir Gandzyuk reported that during two months that he spent in the central hospital for the Mordovian complex of camps "no less than 50 prisoners" were brought from Mordovian camps 17 and 19 and died there. In early 1979 a group of prisoners in the Perm camps reported that in the preceding seven years 13 inmates of the Perm camps had died "ahead of their time" because of lack of medical assistance.

Over the years there have been persistent individual reports of prisoners in these and other places of imprisonment dying in conditions of medical neglect or as a consequence of other aspects of their conditions.

According to numerous accounts by prisoners the authorities do not give the body of a deceased prisoner to his or her family, but instead bury it in or near the camp or prison, marking the grave not with the prisoner's name but with the official number of his or her case.

The medical facilities provided for Soviet prisoners deviate sharply from legal stipulations that prisoners are to receive all necessary medical treatment. Even more do they conflict with claims that Soviet penal policy reduces to a minimum the infliction of suffering on prisoners. This is incurred in part by omission—the shortage of trained personnel and facilities—and in part by commission—the reluctance to give serious consideration to the real medical needs of many prisoners. Medical neglect dovetails with chronic hunger and with overwork to give to Soviet penal institutions a more punitive character than is justified by any standards, let alone by the high standards proclaimed by Soviet authorities.

# Notes

1. *Commentary to RSFSR Corrective Labour Code*, Moscow, 1973, page 146.
2. I.V. Shmarov, F.T. Kuznetsov and P.E. Podymov, *The Effectiveness of the Work of Corrective Labour Institutions*, Moscow, 1968, page 158.
3. *Commentary to the RSFSR Corrective Labour Code*, Moscow, 1973, page 65.
4. The text of this decree appears in *Vedemosti Verkhovnogo Soveta RSFSR*, Moscow, 15 June 1972. See also *Commentary to RSFSR Corrective Labour Code*, Moscow, 1973, page 83.
5. *A Chronicle of Current Events*, Number 26, pages 263-264.
6. The following detailed descriptions of the various diets refer most often to reports issued by the Moscow Helsinki Monitoring Group in the period 1975-1979. Numerous reports by prisoners in various regimes of corrective labour institutions corroborate in detail the Helsinki group's accounts. Where there are any discrepancies in the available information, these are indicated in the present Amnesty International report.
7. *The Observer*, London, 24 April 1977.
8. Document Number 3 of the Moscow Helsinki Monitoring Group; Number 33 of *A Chronicle of Current Events*.
9. Malva Landa, Tatyana Khodorovich and Tatyana Velikanova, "The Torture of Prisoners of Conscience in the USSR With Hunger and Cold Continues", in Vladimir Bukovsky (editor), *Vladimir Prison: A Collection of Articles and Materials*, Khronika Press, New York, 1977.
10. On internationally accepted standards in this regard see *Energy and Protein Requirements*, World Health Organization Technical Report, Series Number 522, Geneva, 1973; and *Nutrition and Working Energy*, FAO Freedom from Hunger Campaign, Basic Studies Number 5, Rome, 1972.
11. Vladimir Bukovsky, *To Build a Castle*, Andre Deutsch, London, 1978, pages 17-18.
12. *Commentary to RSFSR Corrective Labour Code*, Moscow, 1973, page 64.
13. *Vladimir Prison: A Collection of Articles and Materials, op cit*, pages 74-75.
14. Number 52, *A Chronicle of Current Events*.
15. *The Observer*, London, 24 April 1977.
16. *Vladimir Prison: A Collection of Articles and Materials, op cit.*
17. *Commentary to RSFSR Corrective Labour Code*, Moscow, 1973, pages 243-244.

# CHAPTER 5

# Reform of Prisoners

Soviet corrective labour law and all official statements on the subject insist that imprisonment in the USSR has as a goal the correction and re-education of the prisoner.

Contemporary corrective labour law and theory call not merely for reform of prisoners in the sense that they should not repeat their crimes in the future, but also in the sense that their moral outlook, their relations with society and their attitude to work should be radically altered by their experiences while serving sentence.

In pursuit of such thorough reform of the prisoners, the law requires the personnel of corrective labour institutions to study exhaustively each prisoner so that an "individual program" of rehabilitation can be worked out for each one.

According to Article 7 of the Fundamentals of Corrective Labour Legislation, there are four basic means of "correction and re-education" of prisoners: "the regime of serving sentence"; "socially useful work"; "political education work"; "vocational instruction".

The "regime of serving sentence" is starkly punitive in its most essential characteristic – the systematic deprivation of food – as well as in the rigorous discipline and security restraints to which prisoners are routinely subjected. Official literature on the subject treats the punitive aspect of the regime as part of the process of reforming of prisoners.

The other three methods of reforming prisoners are in theory supposed not to inflict suffering on prisoners.[1] In practice, "socially useful labour" is compulsory and normally of such a nature as to be punitive in character. "Political education" is compulsory and, at least for prisoners of conscience, a degrading exercise in attempting to force people to change their beliefs. Both of these methods provide the authorities with countless opportunities to impose additional punishments on prisoners who have not "gone on the path of correction". As for "vocational instruction", few prisoners of conscience seem ever to have left imprisonment more qualified for employment than when they started their sentence. On the contrary: many lose touch with their original profession or trade while imprisoned and most suffer systematic job discrimination after completing their sentence.

A study of material available on conditions of imprisonment leaves the net impression that the goal of rehabilitating prisoners is not taken seriously either by administrators or prisoners. This goal is totally outweighed in the administration of colonies and prisons by considerations of security and by the "punitive" element. Prisoners have been given to understand clearly that this is the case.

For example, in Mordovian special regime colony ZhKh 385/1, KGB Captain Kochetkov told Edward Kuznetsov in 1971:

You're on "special" here. This is not a corrective but a punitive institution. Our job is to bend you, until you're like putty in our hands. Do you understand?[2]

## Work

According to the law, "every convicted person shall have the duty to work". The place assigned to prisoners' labour in Soviet corrective labour law and theory is explained in part by the high esteem given to labour in general by Marxist-Leninist doctrine: according to the official Commentary to the Fundamentals of Corrective Labour Legislation:

Labour is a universal means of education for people. On the basis of participation in socially useful labour is formulated the psychology of a toiler, the feeling of comradeship and collectivism. In labour the socially useful qualities of man are moulded. Also by means of socially useful labour reform of convicted people is gained.[3]

To this end Article 37 of the RSFSR Corrective Labour Code stipulates:

The production and economic activity of corrective labour institutions must be subordinated to their basic task — the correction and re-education of convicted people.

The Commentary to the RSFSR Criminal Code explains:

In a socialist society, where the principle operates that "he who doesn't work doesn't eat", labour is not only the right but also the obligation of every citizen. . . . The induction of convicted persons to labour is necessary for rooting out their habit of a parasitic existence or their unconscientious attitude to work.[4]

Prisoners are required to pay from their work as much as possible towards the financial cost of their imprisonment.

Articles 37-42 of the RSFSR Corrective Labour Code lay down in broad terms the conditions under which prisoners are to work. However, the Commentary to the Fundamentals of Corrective Labour Legislation of the USSR and Union Republics acknowledges that these regulations are only general in character. Specific details of prisoners' labour are determined by the administration of each corrective labour institution.

In practice, the prisoners' work in no way leads to the enhancement of their consciousness or to their "reform", as called for by corrective labour theory. Prisoners' work is a form of punishment, a fact acknowledged by the Soviet newspaper *Kazakhstanskaya Pravda* (14 March 1973) in a rare public reference to such labour:

The work carried out by prisoners is basically hard labour, and output norms are maximal. But there is nothing to be done about this. A labour colony is not a rest home. It is a place for serving out punishment. Here it is necessary to work. By the sweat of one's brow.

A different sort of reaction to prisoners' conditions of labour was reported in issue 42 of *A Chronicle of Current Events*. According to this report, in 1976 about 400 workers in the Kirov factory in Leningrad undertook a "go-slow" strike in protest against bad treatment of prisoners working in the factory.

Corrective labour colonies and prisons serve as economic enterprises. The law (Article 37 of the RSFSR Corrective Labour Code) states that the economic activity of camps and prisons must be subordinated to their "basic tasks", the "correction and re-education" of prisoners. However the official Commentary says the following about this principle:

> The law's general position of principle that the economic production activity of corrective labour institutions must be subordinated to the task of correcting and re-educating prisoners cannot, of course, be interpreted as any belittlement of the economic activity of the corrective labour institutions. Fulfilling the production plans in all their quantitative and qualitative indices, including productivity of labour and profit making, has important significance not only economically but also in an educative sense. The indicators of the production activity of the corrective labour institutions are established in the economic plans of the Union Republics. Therefore prisoners' work has a certain economic significance.[5]

In practice, the administrations of camps and prisons are obliged to make prisoners' work as profitable as possible. The characteristic ways of achieving this are the keeping down of expenditure on prisoners' accommodation, food and medical care, the fixing of high output norms, the investing of little in machinery and work facilities and the punishing of prisoners for not achieving the output norms.

Many camps and prisons specialize in one particular type of production: timber cutting, woodwork, sewing and supplying parts for factories are particularly common, but the range of types of production is quite broad. Camps and prisons which operate as production enterprises normally have a work area separate from the prisoners' barracks. In prisons normal cells may be converted into work areas (as happened in Vladimir prison in 1975), and prisoners may also be put to work in their own cells (as is the practice for political prisoners in Chistopol prison).

Some colonies (but never prisons) supply labour to enterprises outside the corrective labour system. The use of convict labour is reportedly still quite common in the construction industry in particular. A report from Latvia in 1975 or 1976 said that prisoners were being brought daily to Riga from as far as 50 or 60 kilometers away for work on construction sites there.

Political prisoners in Vladimir prison were not required to work prior to 1975 because, reportedly, there were not enough of them to make their work economically profitable. After 1975 they were put to work at assembling radio parts. In Chistopol prison, which has replaced Vladimir prison as the main prison-type institution for convicted political prisoners, some inmates were working at sewing potato sacks by hand in 1978 and 1979, while others were assembling parts for wrist-watches.

Inmates of the special regime camp in Mordovia work at polishing crystal for chandeliers. Inmates of the strict regime camp 19 in the Mordovian complex of colonies produce wooden clock frames, and do all the work from sawing the logs to polishing the finished product with fine abrasives. Women in camp 3 in Mordovia – also strict regime – sew gloves and other products.

In the Perm region complex of colonies, inmates in the three different camps for political prisoners have worked variously at assembling metal panels, preparing parts for flat-irons, doing other metal work and sewing.

The law (Article 37 of the RSFSR Corrective Labour Code) states that prisoners on "special regime" must work at "heavy labour", but does not give any indication of the relative intensity of compulsory work on the other regimes. The copious available information does not suggest a clear distinction in this respect between camps of different regimes. Some camps with ordinary regime – the mildest – are known to employ their inmates in very strenuous work in stone quarrying, timber cutting, mining or similar production.

In most camps, there is some flexibility as to the type of work to which a prisoner may be assigned insofar as there is need for "support work". Such work may range from heavy labour such as loading and unloading supplies and products and stoking furnaces to lighter tasks such as cleaning and maintenance. In many cases—particularly when political prisoners are involved—administrators have required ill or aged prisoners to work at heavier rather than lighter tasks, assigning the easier work to prisoners who have "gone on the path of correction" by acting as informers or otherwise cooperating with the authorities.

Article 37 of the RSFSR Corrective Labour Code states that "where possible" prisoners are to be assigned work taking into account their professional or other speciality. The law allows corrective labour administrations considerable discretion to neglect this principle. Most of the available jobs involve manual labour. Many prisoners of conscience are trained for and accustomed to non-physical labour, and suffer from compulsory physical labour not only because of its difficulty for them but also because they are cut off from their professional and intellectual activities. However, there are very few jobs available to accommodate such needs, and most prisoners are required to do heavy work or piece-work whether it is suited to them or not.

According to Article 37 of the RSFSR Corrective Labour Code, prisoners are to be assigned work "with consideration of their work-capacity". The official Commentary to the Fundamentals of Corrective Labour Legislation elaborates this:

> Consideration of the convict's work capacity is obligatory for the administration . . . An insufficient workload, and even more so overtaxing work correspond neither to the educative nor the economic goals of labour nor to considerations of health. Putting convicts to overtaxing labour would contradict the law's position that the execution of punishment does not have as a goal the infliction of physical suffering.[6]

Medical commissions administered by the MVD annually examine prisoners to decide their fitness for work. These medical commissions have guidelines which do not encourage generosity even to ill or aged prisoners. The Commentary to Article 37 of the RSFSR Corrective Labour Code rejects the "mistaken opinion" of some officials that invalids may be put to work only with their own consent, and requires that even severely disabled prisoners be assigned work which is suited to their "residual fitness for work". The same Commentary reaffirms that prisoners above the legal retirement age (60 years for men, 55 years for women) must work.[7]

It is evident from prisoners' accounts that the annual medical examinations have freed very few prisoners from compulsory work on grounds of disablement or illness. As a rule, these commissions simply label prisoners "fit for work", and leave it to the discretion of the camp or prison authorities to decide the type of work each prisoner should have. Apart from these annual fitness checks, prisoners may in theory be relieved from work for medical reasons at any time on the recommendation of the medical staff in their camp or prison. However, as indicated in Chapter 4, the medical staff as a rule do not recommend even ill prisoners for release from compulsory work, and are liable to be overruled by the administration if they do so. Prisoners who report ill and are ruled fit to work are liable to be punished for "simulating".

It is a constant theme of reports from camps and prisons that inmates who are ill, seriously disabled or aged are required to work and assigned labour for which they are manifestly unfit. Examples of this are recorded in virtually every issue of *A Chronicle of Current Events*. Representative of this practice was the treatment of the Lithuanian Vladas Lapienis, born in 1906, who was sentenced in 1977 to 5 years' imprisonment and exile for "anti-Soviet agitation and propaganda" in the form of writing and circulating *samizdat*. Lapienis was sent to serve his sentence in Mordovian colony ZhKh 385/3-5. Twice within his first year there he was punished by a term in "cell-type premises" for not doing the work assigned to him. His wife described the circumstances as follows:

> My husband has been a pensioner since 1966 and is often ill. One-and-
> a-half years of imprisonment have completely undermined his health.
> The camp doctor talked to him for a few minutes and then wrote down
> that a "medical commission" had established that he was capable of
> doing heavy physical work. The camp administration forces him to carry
> coal, stoke the furnace and do similar work which only a healthy man
> can do. Moreover, they force my husband to do such work as sewing
> mittens, although they know that he can't do this on account of his
> weak eyesight. When my husband refused to do this work on account
> of his state of health, the camp administration began to impose various
> punishments on him.

By law (Article 38 of the RSFSR Corrective Labour Code) prisoners on all regimes must work an eight-hour day, six days a week. The prisoners' working day or week is often extended by several hours because of the need to meet time schedules and monthly output norms. Whenever this happens prisoners are legally supposed to be compensated with extra free time on other days, but this principle is sometimes violated. For example, Ona Pranskunaite, a Lithuanian woman sentenced in 1977 to 2 years' imprisonment for "anti-Soviet slander", reported from her ordinary regime camp in Gorky region in late 1977 or early 1978 that she sometimes had to work 14 or 15 hours a day and had only one free Sunday a month. By law prisoners are not allowed any annual holidays.

In addition to their regular day's work, prisoners are obliged to do unpaid work at maintaining and improving their camp or prison premises. According to Article 41 of the RSFSR Corrective Labour Code, this extra work should not be of more than two hours' duration per day. In some cases, prisoners' extra hours of labour have been used for basic construction of their camp or for heavy work such as surfacing roads or building fences.

The nature and long hours of work makes prisoners' labour gruelling. Through the interlocking systems of output norms, payment and punishments the camp and prison administrations ensure that prisoners work hard and do not relax on the job.

The camp or prison administration establishes an output target for each type of work done by the prisoners. In spite of the requirement of the law (Article 37 of the RSFSR Corrective Labour Code) that the economic activity of camps and prisons must be subordinate to their main task of correcting and re-educating their inmates, it is evident that the fixing of prisoners' output norms is strongly influenced by considerations of the profitability of their labour.

Prisoners of conscience have frequently complained that their output norms are excessively high, and that they were difficult to achieve both on account of their undernourished condition and because they were not trained in or accustomed to the work and had poor equipment.

The Lithuanian religious believer Niole Sadunaite, sentenced in 1975 to 6 years' imprisonment and exile for "anti-Soviet agitation and propaganda", reported from the strict regime women's camp in Mordovia in 1976 that the norm for sewing gloves was 70 pairs per day. (Other prisoners have reported that the norm was 60 per day.) She said that the norm was difficult to achieve because the machinery was constantly breaking down. She was ill at this time, and after returning to work from a period in the camp hospital she was permitted to rest for brief spells during the working day. However her norm was not adjusted to take these factors into account. The authorities "permitted" the prisoners in her shop to begin work ahead of their shift (at 6.30 am) and work late (until 10.30 pm), so she was able to fulfil her quota.

In the Mordovia special regime camp, the norm in 1979 was for prisoners to polish 35 pieces of crystal, 8 by 10 centimeters in size, each day, using machine-applied emery and metal abrasives. It was such a strain to meet this norm that prisoners sometimes discarded their heavy protective gloves and worked barehanded, at the price of continuously suffering abrasions. It was reported in 1979 that Anatoly Shcharansky, a mathematician, was having difficulty in fulfilling his daily norm of hand-sewing eight potato sacks per day in his cell in Chistopol prison.

Prisoners working to piecework norms of this sort are in a dilemma. Even if they can regularly meet their output norms, the administration may increase the norms as a consequence. The available information suggests that the administrations tend to push the norms up steadily (in some cases stating as their reason "economies in the wages fund" or some similar economic consideration) without making any compensation in the form of improving equipment and facilities or increasing prisoners' diet. Prisoners have met with little success in arguing that such increases in the output norm are as a rule inherently punitive because they can be met only by intensified labour.

On the other hand, if prisoners do not meet their output norms they are liable to be punished. In many known cases such prisoners have been punished for non-fulfillment of output norms even when they were ill or had not been given the parts or new material with which to work.

While the entire range of punishments may be used for this, those most commonly imposed involve deprivation of food. Article 56 of the RSFSR Corrective Labour Code says that prisoners' food rations shall vary according to, among other things, "their attitude to work". The official Commentary to this article goes considerably beyond the law itself by saying that prisoners who "systematically and maliciously do not fulfil their output norms at work" can be put on reduced rations.[8] Common punishments for this "offence" include confinement to punishment cells with reduction of rations to starvation level, deprivation of the monthly privilege of spending a few rubles on food products in the camp or prison shop and deprivation of the right to receive a parcel from outside the camp, with whatever food might be contained therein. Reduction in food by any of these means only makes it more difficult for prisoners to find the strength to meet their output norms.

The Commentary to Article 56 of the RSFSR Corrective Labour Code also states that prisoners performing "certain types of heavy labour" may be given extra rations. Former prisoners have described this diet supplement as consisting of an extra portion of gruel in the morning together with a spoonful of oil and two teaspoons of sugar. In addition, a cup of milk may be given to prisoners engaged in such work as stoking furnaces. However, as a rule these extra rations have been given only to prisoners trusted or favoured by the camp administration.

The law (Article 39 of the RSFSR Corrective Labour Code) states that prisoners are to be paid for their work at the rates for comparable work done outside the place of imprisonment. However most of the prisoners' wages disappear in automatic deductions for their upkeep. Prisoners are guaranteed receipt of only 10 per cent of their earnings. According to unofficial sources, the sum left to a prisoner usually comes to 14 or 15 rubles per month.

Prisoners are not allowed to be in possession of cash. The money left from their earnings after deductions goes into their personal account. They are allowed to spend a set amount of the money in their account on "food and basic necessities". The law says that these monthly purchases may be made only with money earned by the prisoner at his or her work in the camp or prison, the official explanation being that this is "with the aim of interesting convicted people in the results of their labour".[9]

Prisoners who over-fulfil their norms may be allowed to spend several rubles extra each month on "food and basic necessities". This extra food-purchasing privilege can mean a significant increase in the prisoner's nourishment. However, former inmates have remarked on the difficulty prisoners have in deciding

Niole Sadunaite

Vasyl Stus in exile

Vladas Lapienis                    Vasyl Lisovoi

Stepan Sapeliak at his abode in exile

whether the extra food purchased compensates for the additional expenditure of energy and physical strength necessary to fulfil high norms. The granting of this privilege is at the discretion of camp authorities, and it is normally granted only for exceptional labour output or as a reward for informers.

According to law, safety provisions for work in corrective labour institutions must meet the standards stipulated by labour legislation for all Soviet enterprises (Article 38 of the RSFSR Corrective Labour Code). In practice, prisoners' work conditions are usually unpleasant and often dangerous.

Mikhail Shtern, a Jewish doctor sentenced in 1974 to 8 years' imprisonment after his two sons had applied for permission to emigrate to Israel, described in 1977 the conditions of work in the reinforced regime camp near Kharkov where he served part of his sentence:

> The workshops at camp 12 are terribly contaminated by the gases given off
> by the production processes. In the workshop making air filters for tractors,
> vapour from epoxy resin causes skin diseases — dermatitis, skin ulcers. But
> prisoners are still left to work there.[10]

Numerous accounts of conditions in the special regime camp in Mordovia say that there too prisoners work in a thoroughly contaminated atmosphere. The prisoners polish glass with emery, sand and metal abrasives, and the air is consequently thick with harmful dust. The workshop lacks effective ventilation. The prisoners complained for years before finally getting a few respirators, but these are of such a design as to make breathing difficult, and prisoners do not always wear them at work.

Similar accounts of contamination and lack of ventilation have been made regarding work-places in a number of other places of imprisonment. The following account of working conditions in Vladimir prison is taken from an anonymous *samizdat* document written by an inmate there in the spring of 1975:

> In March 1975 they began to require the political prisoners to work . . .
> They set up machines in cell 1-28: there the prisoners both live and work.
> They temporarily transferred the criminal prisoners from cell 1-32 to other
> cells and set up machines, but they didn't take the bunk beds away. The
> working prisoners bump their heads on the top bunk. They provoke
> prisoners to refuse to do work so they can put them in the punishment
> cell. It is cold in the cell (10°C). There are iron blinds on the window, and
> no natural light. They refuse to install additional artificial lighting. The
> work consists of assembling resistors for radios from tiny parts. This
> demands maximum strain of the eyesight, which is already disturbed by
> the closeness of the walls and the round-the-clock burning of the electric
> light. It is difficult to predict what effect this will have on our eyes. They
> demand that we fulfil the output norms.

Pyotr Vins, a member of the Ukrainian Helsinki monitoring group, and Vasyl Barladyanu, a historian, both served sentences of imprisonment in a camp in Rovno region in the Ukraine during the late 1970s. There, prisoners were required to work at cutting and loading stone in a quarry. The floor of the quarry was covered with water, but the water wasn't pumped out; the prisoners were issued with only one pair of canvas shoes each year and they had no facilities for drying their clothing at the end of the working day.

The law provides for issuing prisoners with protective clothing necessary for their work, but very often this provision is not respected, even where prisoners are put to work on electric cutting machines. Such machinery often lacks basic safety guards. Kronid Lyubarsky, a Moscow astronomer imprisoned from 1972 to 1977 for "anti-Soviet agitation and propaganda", reported that it was common for prisoners to suffer hand cuts on the circular saw in camp 19 in the Mordovian complex. The two prisoners who had worked on this machine immediately before him had both cut their hands, as had the shop master. Kuzma Matvyuk, a Ukrainian imprisoned for "anti-Soviet agitation and propaganda", lost four fingers on this same machine, according to fellow prisoners. Similar reports have been received regarding workshops in Perm and elsewhere.

The risk of industrial accidents is certainly increased by the prisoners' physical condition. It is reasonable to expect that prisoners who are constantly under-nourished, often in need of medical attention which they are unlikely to receive and exhausted by punishments and the work itself will be particularly prone to injuries. When the prisoners are working at tasks for which they are not trained or accustomed, using equipment which is second-rate at best and operating under pressure to fulfil arbitrarily set output norms within monthly periods, the risk becomes particularly high.

The following extract from a letter by a group of prisoners in Mordovia camp 19 dates from 1972 but applies to prisoners' labour conditions in the late 1970s as well:

*In the machine tool shop the most dangerous part of the process is the removal of the finished piece and the installation of a new one. There is no provision for switching off the press during this technical operation, which is a serious infringement of technical safety completely inadmissable in an outside environment. The rotating reamer may easily injure the prisoner's hand: such injuries are fairly common. In addition, sharp, hot chips fly out from under the reamer. To work in gloves is forbidden in case the glove – and with it one's hand – becomes caught and pulled into the reamer. As well, there are splashes of emulsion which burn the skin, fumes, and horrible noise, not only from one's own press but also from the entire workshop. Shimon Levit has small cuts all over his hands. . . No one is able to fulfil the work quotas, which are tremendously high; failure to fulfil means punishment. . . The loading work is even worse. We all fear assignment to this particular job, which consists basically of loading and unloading railway wagons. The work is very difficult and dangerous, and one may be awakened (for work) at any time of the day or night without advance warning. Even on Sundays, one works.*

*. . .At first glance, sewing mittens in the camp workshop appears to be fairly light work. Such shops exist in almost all the camps. Women imprisoned for political reasons are engaged exclusively on this work, but even they find the job tiring. What can one say about those who have to do it? . . . Excessively high demands must be met in dimly lit buildings using machinery which is constantly breaking down. . . Sylva Zalmanson*

*suffers from constant backache and dizzy spells due to the continuous eye strain. Because of acute eye strain Yury Fyodorov (another political prisoner) has been transferred from sewing mittens to turning them inside out – work which is less conducive to strain and acute conjunctivitis. He is lucky, because the sewing norm can be fulfilled by few. Even healthy people are unable to achieve it, and all suffer the consequences.*

*. . .In outside construction work the situation is aggravated by the fact that it is almost impossible to endure the Mordovian frosts in the so-called "special work clothing". . . Changes and transfers are frequently made; at any time one may expect a transfer to even more difficult and strenuous work. This happened to Altman and Shepshelovich, who are now both working on a concrete mixer in penetrating winds. . .*

## Political Education

According to the law, "political education" work must be conducted with every prisoner.

The official aim of "political education" work with prisoners is to educate them "in the spirit of an honest attitude to labour, of exact fulfillment of the laws and respect for the rules of socialist communal life, of a protective attitude to socialist property. . ."[11]

A variety of "political education" measures are called for by law, including "agitation and propaganda work" and "explanation of Soviet legislation".

Guided by these general norms, the administration of each corrective labour institution "can apply any means and methods of pedagogical influence, provided these do not contradict the rules of regime established in the legal norms."[12] One method on which great emphasis is placed is the political education classes which are held at least once a week. These classes last up to two hours, and during them members of the colony administration discuss current affairs, political news and officially approved topics such as the history of the Communist Party. By all accounts these lectures and the discussions they provoke are conducted at a very low level and are universally resented. Political prisoners, many of whom are highly educated, find these political classes particularly degrading.

In an essay written in a Mordovian colony in 1966, the Ukrainian historian Valentyn Moroz wrote:

At the "political training" sessions conducted by semi-literate corporals
for artists and writers, the prisoners once began a discussion with Senior
Lieutenant Lyubayev (camp number 11) using the (United Nations)
Declaration of Human Rights as an argument. He retorted indulgently:
"Listen, but that is for Negroes."[13]

The writer Andrei Sinyavsky (who was sentenced in 1966 to 7 years' imprisonment for "anti-Soviet agitation and propaganda") has reported hearing from camp officials in Mordovia the same view that "human rights are for Negroes". Shimon Grilius (sentenced in 1970 to 5 years' imprisonment under the same article for his activities in a student group) has reported hearing the same thing from a procurator in a Perm camp in 1973.

Edward Kuznetsov, serving a 15 years' sentence in a special regime corrective labour colony, wrote in 1971 in his *Prison Diaries*:

> In the last class I went to, Lieutenant Bezzubov gave us the priceless
> information that "in China the Zionists and the Red Guards are on the
> rampage. But the Chinese people are not stupid — they'll show them!"
> The academic level of these lectures is truly breath-taking.[14]

Nonetheless, the attitudes which prisoners show in these classes can be used by the administration "in ascertaining the extent of their correction and reform". Prisoners of conscience commonly resist the pressure to conform to the official viewpoint in these classes. A minimum consequence of their continued "dissidence" is that they are easily disqualified from being considered for early release.

The corrective labour law does not make attendance at these classes compulsory, and the Commentary to the Fundamentals of Corrective Labour Legislation of the USSR and the Union Republics states that it is impermissible to treat attendance at them as obligatory.

However, the MVD's unpublished Rules of Internal Order permits punishment of prisoners for non-attendance at political education classes. To avoid formally contradicting the legal requirement that attendance at political classes must be voluntary, the directive categorizes political classes as part of the colony's "order of the day" and makes non-attendance punishable as violation of this routine.

In practice, colony and prison administrations do not generally strive for the "political re-education" of prisoners of conscience. Such prisoners usually have deep political or religious convictions which have been formed in the face of the highly-organized agitation and propaganda campaign aimed at all Soviet citizens and for which they were willing to risk imprisonment.

On the other hand, the authorities have very frequently punished political and religious prisoners for manifesting their "dissident" views. In the case of political prisoners, this punitive reaction is most directly aimed at prisoners' efforts to protest individually or collectively against their conditions of imprisonment or to send information out of the camps and prisons. Many prisoners of conscience have been punished for such actions by terms in punishment cells, by transfer from a camp to a prison or even by being brought to trial on new charges of "anti-Soviet agitation and propaganda" or "anti-Soviet slander". Prisoners of conscience have also been punished for "anti-Soviet" remarks in their letters of complaint to the Procuracy.

The attitude of colony officials to religious prisoners was described in 1973 by a group of former Soviet prisoners advocating better treatment for political prisoners in all countries of Europe:

> The hunt for religious literature is accompanied in prisons and camps by
> ferocious persecution of religious believers. The dispersal of prayer
> meetings in the camp areas, punishment by solitary confinement for
> failure to report for work on major religious holidays (such as Easter
> and Christmas), the forbidding of any kinds of rites, even preaching and

giving the sacrament to dying prisoners — these are the methods of "educational" influence with the help of which they try to eradicate religious dissent.

Many prisoners of conscience have had copies of the Bible and other religious literature confiscated and have been punished for the possession of such material. This applies to clergy as well as laity. The Orthodox priest Vasyl Romanyuk, a Ukrainian sentenced in 1972 to 15 years' imprisonment and exile for "anti-Soviet agitation and propaganda", said in a 1976 appeal to the World Council of Churches and other international organizations:

> For the past four years I have been asking that they allow me to use the Bible and the Journal of the Moscow Patriarchate, and this year I've gone on hunger strike to obtain this. But the camp administration told me: "You can hunger strike as much as you want but you'll die before you get a Bible, because the camp is a Soviet institution and religious literature is forbidden here."

Jewish prisoners are frequently singled out for special abuse. The following statement by a group of prisoners in Perm colony VS 389/35 in 1973 or 1974 is representative of many prisoners' criticisms on this subject:

> The camp authorities inculcate nationalistic conflicts and incite other inmates against Jews. KGB Captains Maruzan and Ivkin stress in their conversation with non-Jewish inmates that all nationalities of the USSR must take a stand against Jews, particularly in labour camps. The administration provokes anti-Jewish incidents, utilizes informers and spies, and uses false witnesses in order to be able to impose additional punishment upon the Jews. Inmates who have had contact with Jews are summoned for discussions during which anti-Semitic sentiments are expressed, and they are told that protests against arbitrariness in camp rules are only profitable to the Zionists . . . The Jews are forbidden to observe their religious traditions. . . and forbidden to congregate even for a few minutes; such gatherings are immediately regarded as a Jewish assembly, a synagogue. Conversation in Hebrew or Yiddish is subject to punishment because these languages are not understood by the guards and therefore their content cannot be checked. The study of Hebrew is prohibited. Internal letters in Hebrew or Yiddish are banned and confiscated.

Israel Zalmonson, a Jew sentenced in 1970 to 8 years' imprisonment for his part in a plan to steal an aircraft with which to leave the country, reported in 1978 from Perm camp 36:

> More than once prisoners have told me that representatives of the administration and the KGB had warned them to keep away from the Jews, usually referring to them as "yids". They do this so as to isolate the Jews from the other political prisoners and create a ghetto atmosphere. Specifically Lieutenant Salakhov, the former head of my detachment, told the prisoner Yury Dzyuba that "the Jews are our most bitter enemies" and for this reason he ought to keep away from

them. I was indignant about this behaviour and protested to the administration and the KGB. There was no reaction.

The open contempt with which the convictions of prisoners of conscience are treated is not conducive to their re-education in the spirit desired by the law. On the contrary, political prisoners' experiences in corrective labour institutions usually strengthen their convictions by providing what they regard as corroboration of their criticisms of institutionalized illegality and arbitrariness in the country.

The authorities also make considerable efforts to induce prisoners of conscience to condemn their own behaviour as dissenters. Frequently prisoners of conscience, especially those convicted under explicitly political articles of the criminal law, have been promised release from imprisonment on condition that they sign a statement asking for pardon, recognizing that they were justly convicted for criminal activity and thus effectively recanting their political views. Many of the prisoners of conscience in the Mordovia and Perm camps and in Vladimir prison have been taken briefly away to their home areas and given temporary luxury treatment in an attempt to persuade them to cooperate with the authorities in this way.

Representative of this means of forcing prisoners of conscience to compromise their beliefs is the following account of the treatment of Stepan Sapeliak, a young Ukrainian serving 8 years' imprisonment for "anti-Soviet agitation and propaganda", when he was taken away from Perm camp 35:

> In the spring and summer of 1975 they took Stepan Sapeliak to Kiev and Ternopol in the Ukraine. There they tried all means to get him to recant. They took him to the beach. They took him to his native village and said "Go home. We'll consider that you've repented and tomorrow you can sign the statement." When Stepan refused, they threatened to beat him and showed him their rubber truncheons. At this time a Canadian tourist, a Ukrainian by origin, was under arrest in Ternopol. They demanded of Sapeliak that he tell this Ukrainian lady that he was not a political prisoner but a simple hooligan, that he had never been imprisoned in the Urals but in Lvov, and that the story about his being beaten up was an invention. Stepan refused.

While some prisoners have accepted the terms offered them by the authorities and applied for pardon, most prisoners of conscience who are known to have been subjected to these "carrot and stick" methods have refused to recant their beliefs and have had to serve their sentences in full.

## Vocational Instruction

The fourth prescribed means of "correction and re-education" of prisoners is "general education and professional-technical study". By law, corrective labour institutions are required to provide general education up to the eighth grade for all prisoners who have not reached this level. The law further allows high school education for prisoners where facilities are available.

No information is available as to how these legal requirements covering general education are carried out. It is clear, however, that prisoners who have high professional qualifications do not receive further "professional-technical study" while in prison. Prisoners have complained that they are subject to "starvation of the intellect".

Prisoners are permitted to have only five books and journals in their possession at any one time, camp and prison libraries are invariably poorly stocked with literature and prisoners of conscience are regularly hindered from attempting to obtain scientific or academic literature from abroad or even from within the USSR. Prisoners have said that they find great difficulty in trying to study or write because of their complete lack of privacy or quiet in their barracks or cells and because they are exhausted by their work, the lack of proper nourishment and the constant strain of their relations with the administration.

The authorities conduct regular searches of the camps and prisons and the prisoners themselves. In numerous instances they have confiscated prisoners' writings, works of art, books and journals in excess of the permitted limit of five per prisoner — and even blank writing paper. The authorities are particularly keen to confiscate writings about conditions in the camp or other "prohibited subjects". However, even non-political works have been confiscated in numerous known cases. In 1977 the authorities in Perm camp 35 confiscated notes which the Ukrainian philosopher Vasyl Lisovoi was making for writing a philosophical dictionary in Ukrainian. In 1976, 300 poems by the Ukrainian poet Vasyl Stus and translations he had made from Goethe, Rilke, Kipling and other foreign poets were confiscated from him in Mordovia camp 17. In 1976 at least 150 drawings by the Ukrainian artist, Stefania Shabatura, were confiscated from her in the strict regime women's camp in Mordovia. Camp officials told her the drawings had been ordered to be burned. These are just a few examples of the steps taken by the authorities to prevent prisoners of conscience from studying or working on the subject of their professional training and interest.

A letter from political prisoners in Mordovia in the spring of 1974 stated: "Emerging from camp after many years of imprisonment, a man finds himself fully unqualified as a specialist."

The facts disprove official statements that the Soviet corrective labour system aims to make it possible for prisoners to take up a normal life in society. In the case of political prisoners with professional training, the prevailing conditions of imprisonment have the opposite effect. On emerging from a colony or prison, such individuals find themselves incapable of returning to their former profession, not only because of general discrimination against people with records of political dissidence, but as a rule also because they have been prevented from maintaining their technical or academic expertise.

150

## Notes

1. A.Ya. Natashev and N.A. Struchkov, *The Fundamental Principles of the Theory of Corrective Labour Law*, Moscow, 1967, pages 87-88.
2. Edward Kuznetsov, *Prison Diaries*, Vallentine, Mitchell, London, 1975, page 181.
3. *Commentary to the Fundamentals of Corrective Labour Legislation of the USSR and Union Republics*, Moscow, 1972, page 34.
4. *Commentary to the RSFSR Corrective Labour Code*, Moscow, 1973, page 18.
5. *Ibid*, page 96.
6. *Commentary to the Fundamentals of Corrective Labour Legislation of the USSR and Union Republics*, Moscow, 1972, page 102.
7. *Commentary to the RSFSR Corrective Labour Code*, Moscow, 1973.
8. *Ibid*, page 146.
9. *Commentary to the Fundamentals of Corrective Labour Legislation of the USSR and Union Republics*, Moscow, 1972, page 89.
10. *The Observer*, London, 24 April 1977.
11. RSFSR Corrective Labour Code, Article 43.
12. *Commentary to the Fundamentals of Corrective Labour Legislation of the USSR and Union Republics*, Moscow, 1972, page 35.
13. Valentyn Moroz, "Report from the Beria Reservation", in *Boomerang: The Works of Valentyn Moroz*, Smoloskyp Publishers, Baltimore, 1974, page 55.
14. Kuznetsov, *Prison Diaries*, page 216.

# CHAPTER 6

# Relations between Prisoners and Administrators

Soviet corrective labour institutions are in the jurisdiction of the MVD (the Ministry of Internal Affairs) and are staffed by its personnel.

The MVD and its camp and prison administrations have exercised the discretion allowed them by the corrective labour legislation in such a way as to make conditions of imprisonment considerably more severe than is required by the already harsh legislation. Prisoners of conscience are singled out in many respects for especially harsh treatment, although apparently prisoners of conscience whose cases have come to public attention have generally been spared many of the cruelties sometimes perpetrated against ordinary criminal prisoners.

According to the law the Procuracy and public organizations called "Supervisory Commissions" (*nablyudatelnye komisii*) are empowered to investigate the treatment of prisoners and to take or initiate measures against breaches of law and other abuses by the administrations. In practice, these bodies seem to have little authority over the MVD apparatus.

Furthermore, the country's newpapers and other news media do not subject the treatment of prisoners to serious scrutiny or exposure. This, together with the severe restrictions imposed by the law on prisoners' rights to visits and correspondence, enables the corrective labour system to operate not only as a virtually closed system but in almost complete secrecy, except insofar as prisoners of conscience have succeeded in exposing their conditions of imprisonment.

## Security, Discipline and Prisoners' Rights

Soviet law stipulates that the first requirement of corrective labour institutions is the maintenance of security. The law and the unpublished decrees of the MVD establish, in addition to the constraints aimed at preventing escapes and commission of crimes by prisoners, a strict order of discipline. Prisoners are given to understand clearly that their well-being is entirely in the hands of the administration. It is almost unheard of for prisoners to have visits from their lawyers.

Prisoners are allowed only a very few possessions. They are not permitted to have money or valuables and may have only five books and journals at any one time. Such items as television sets, radios and typewriters are forbidden; nor may they have artists' materials such as paints, crayons and brushes.

Prisoners may legally be subjected at any time to a body search or a search of their possessions and cell or sleeping place. The unlimited right to search is very frequently used to confiscate personal items from prisoners. Numerous instances have been recorded in which the authorities have confiscated prisoners' personal writings, books, writing paper, religious literature of various sorts and crucifixes. Apart from depriving prisoners of their few comforts, such searches serve as a pretext for harassing them and frequently provide grounds for subjecting them to punishment.

Other routine practices frequently violate the legal requirement that imprisonment must not aim at "degrading human dignity". Under the Rules of Internal Order (see Chapter 3) prisoners must stand up when they meet a member of their camp or prison administration, take off their caps (in the warm seasons) and greet them as "citizen". Numerous instances are known of prisoners of conscience being punished for not obeying this rule.

Under the Rules of Internal Order prisoners must wear a patch on their clothing showing their surname and serial number. Prisoners in certain categories (including those in special regime camps) must wear striped clothing. In addition to having to line up daily for roll-call, prisoners must march in rank to and from work and meals. As a matter of routine prisoners are shaved bald and, under MVD Decree (*prikaz*) Number 0125 of 30 May 1975, their moustaches and beards may be forcibly shaved off. This is especially degrading for prisoners for whom the wearing of a beard or moustache has some national or religious significance.

According to the law, prisoners may receive an unlimited number of letters. The quantity they may send out (not including letters of complaint, on which the law places no numerical restriction) are three a month (intensified regime), two a month (strict regime) and one a month (special regime). Inmates of prisons may send one letter per month when they are on ordinary regime and one every two months when on strict regime. The law does not limit the numbers of letters which inmates of ordinary regime camps may send (Articles 62-70, RSFSR Corrective Labour Code).

All letters to and from the prisoner must be censored by the authorities. The official criteria for confiscating a letter or obliterating part of its contents are laid down in an unpublished MVD directive Number 040/56.[1] According to this directive a letter may be confiscated if it contains information which is a "state secret": for example, about the location and organization of a corrective labour institution, the number and types of inmates or other details about the internal operations of a camp or prison. The directive calls for the confiscation of letters which include "anti-Soviet expressions or a distorted view of internal and international life", or that are simply "suspicious in content".

These and other provisions of the MVD directive allow camp or prison authorities to confiscate any letter that contains information about the treatment of prisoners or that otherwise displeases them. Almost all the information that prisoners of conscience have been able to send out of prisons and camps about their treatment has been dispatched by other means, clandestine and subject to heavy punishment. Although in imposing censorship on prisoners' correspondence the authorities aim primarily to suppress the flow of information, they have frequently confiscated letters to and from prisoners that did not infringe even these strict rules but were purely personal. In a number of such cases the authorities have repeatedly refused to inform prisoners or their relatives or friends of the grounds for confiscation or non-delivery of a letter, forcing people to write their letters again and again without knowing which passages were impermissible.

In numerous other cases, the authorities have simply seized letters without informing the correspondents that they had done so.

As far as is known, neither the published law nor any MVD directive imposes any special restriction on letters to prisoners from abroad. Yet mail from abroad to prisoners is systematically held back in the overwhelming majority of cases. Over the years Amnesty International adoption groups have sent thousands of letters to Soviet prisoners of conscience, but although it is known that in numerous cases such mail has arrived at camps and prisons the administrations have only rarely handed it over to the addressees. Correspondence between prisoners and close relatives abroad have a much better chance of getting through, but here too there are many known instances of letters disappearing.

As a consequence of the authorities' systematic disruption of the prisoners' exercise of their rights to correspondence, which is already very restricted by law, prisoners of conscience sometimes go for months without being able to send or receive any mail at all.

Another ground for censorship and obstruction is the language in which a letter is written: letters in any language other than Russian may first be sent to the capital of the appropriate Union Republic, where they are officially translated and returned to the colony censor, a process that may take up to several months. For political prisoners from non-Russian republics (many of whom are serving sentences on charges of nationalist activities and who use their own language on principle – which is not an infringement of any law) this is a particularly humiliating form of censorship.

Prisoners' right to receive parcels provides another form of contact with relatives and friends outside places of imprisonment. According to the law, prisoners may receive parcels only after they have served half their sentences, no matter how long they are. Thereafter prisoners on ordinary regime may receive three parcels a year, those on reinforced regime two parcels a year, those on strict regime and those on special regime one parcel a year. Inmates of prisons may not receive any parcels. The maximum weight of such parcels is five kilograms. In addition, prisoners in camps of all regimes and in prisons may receive two smaller packets (*banderoli*) of up to one kilogram in weight each year.

Depriving prisoners of conscience of their right to receive a parcel is one of the most frequently used punishments for disciplinary offences. Furthermore, the Rules of Internal Order specifically define what parcels and packets may contain. Particular attention is given to ensuring that packages do not contain food sufficient to alter the basic regime of hunger in corrective labour institutions.

The law requires that prisoners be allowed a certain number of visits each year. Two types of visits are provided for. Brief visits may last up to four hours and take place under the supervision of guards in a visiting hall. Prolonged visits by near relatives may last up to three days. Prolonged visits are officially declared to be valuable in maintaining family ties. They are meant to take place in private in rooms fitted out for personal family relations. No more than two adults, together with the prisoners' children (minors), may come for any visit, whether brief or prolonged.

In ordinary regime camps prisoners are permitted four brief and two prolonged visits a year; in reinforced regime camps, three brief and two prolonged visits; in strict regime camps, two brief and one prolonged visit; in special regime camps, one brief and one prolonged visit. Inmates of prisons who are on ordinary regime may receive two brief visits a year, and those on prison strict regime may receive no visits at all.

By any standards Soviet law permits only very limited personal contact between prisoners and their families. This is one of the worst sufferings inflicted on prisoners, especially on those in the stricter regimes in corrective labour camps and prisons, since these prisoners are often serving sentences of many years' imprisonment.

MVD directives and the camp and prison authorities impose still more restrictions on prisoners' limited visiting rights. For example, the RSFSR Corrective Labour Code stipulates that prisoners may have brief visits from "relatives and other people" and does not suggest any restrictions as to who may come for such visits. According to the Commentary to this Code, however:

The Rules of Internal Order interpret "other persons" as persons whose
visit would not, in the opinion of the administration of the corrective
labour institution, have a negative influence on the convicted person.[2]

The Commentary goes on to list certain categories of people who may be categorized as "other people" to whom visits may be granted. Among these are "distant relatives" of the prisoner. Thus, the corrective labour administrations not only have complete discretion to refuse visits by people who are not family members, but may also refuse visits by "distant relatives" as well, although neither of these restrictions is mentioned in the law itself. In practice, both brief and prolonged visits are granted only to near relatives. Therefore, prisoners who do not have any near relatives alive in the USSR, or whose relatives have broken away from them, receive no visits at all. For example, Vladimir Balakhonov, who was sentenced in 1973 to 12 years' imprisonment for "treason" in the form of failure to return to the USSR from abroad, had had no visits by mid-1979. Once Malva Landa, a Moscow human rights activist who specializes in helping forgotten prisoners of conscience, came to see Balakhonov, but was turned away. Nikolai Budulak-Sharygin, also imprisoned for "treason", received only two visits during his entire 10-year term of imprisonment from 1968 to 1978.

Frequently, visits have been cancelled as a punishment or on some other pretext. During 7 years' imprisonment (1969-1976) for "anti-Soviet agitation and propaganda" the Jewish prisoner of conscience Yury Vudka was allowed only one prolonged visit from his mother and none from his wife. Yury Fyodorov saw his wife and mother a total of five times during the first seven years of his current 15-year sentence for taking part in a plan to steal an aircraft with which to leave the country in 1970.

In a number of cases relatives have not been informed of the cancellation of a scheduled visit and have travelled great distances at considerable personal expense and difficulty only to be turned back without seeing the prisoner. In other cases, prisoners of conscience have been moved from one camp to another immediately before a visit without the family being told of the change.

Another restriction imposed on prisoners' rights concerns length of visits. The corrective labour legislation stipulates the maximum duration of brief and prolonged visits, but not the minimum. According to the Commentary to the RSFSR Corrective Labour Code, the camp or prison administration may decide on the length of the visit, taking into account such factors as the prisoner's behaviour and "attitude to work".[3] However, the Commentary adds, brief visits should never be for less than two hours, and prolonged visits never for less than two days. In practice, camp and prison administrations have frequently granted even shorter visits. For example, Svyatoslav Karavansky, a Ukrainian prisoner of conscience who has served almost 30 years' imprisonment (and who is due for release in 1979) did not have a single prolonged visit between 1966 and 1976. Between 1972 and 1976 he did not have any brief visits either, since his wife, Nina Strokata, was also serving a sentence of imprisonment for "anti-Soviet agitation and propaganda". In February 1976 the authorities finally granted him a prolonged visit, but limited it to one day.

The authorities have also commonly cut short visits on the grounds of some real or alleged violation of the visiting regulations by prisoners or their visitors. For example in 1977 the mother of the imprisoned Baptist conscientious objector Anatoly Koplik travelled thousands of kilometers from the Ukraine to visit him in his ordinary regime camp near Blagoveshchensk, near the Soviet-Chinese frontier. The visit was scheduled to last three days, but was cut short after one day when guards discovered that she had slipped him a small quantity of garlic and onion to take back into his barracks.

Similarly, in 1978 relatives of the Ukrainian prisoner of conscience Ivan Hel (serving 15 years' imprisonment and exile for "anti-Soviet agitation and propaganda") arrived at the special regime camp in Mordovia to visit him. They were at first told that the visit had been cancelled for disciplinary reasons, but after they went on hunger-strike they were eventually told that they could have a prolonged visit with him. The visit was cut short after one day when guards found he was in possession of the ink cartridge of a pen.

Brief visits have often been cut short because the prisoners and their visitors spoke in a language other than Russian or because the prisoners embraced their spouses or children (which is forbidden during brief visits) or because the guards suspected that forbidden information was being communicated.

As part of the official effort to prevent information from being passed in or out of camps and prisons, the guards prevent the prisoners and their visitors from discussing matters such as conditions in the place of imprisonment. Prisoners and their visitors (who are invariably close relatives) are forbidden to make physical contact of any sort with each other. Both prisoners of conscience and their visitors are often stripped and subjected to a humiliating body search both before and after the visit. On one recent occasion a group of prisoners went collectively on hunger-strike after the small child of a prisoner of conscience was subjected to such a search after her father had embraced her during a brief visit. In another incident, the sister of Boris Mukhametshin (sentenced in 1975 to seven years' imprisonment and exile for possessing and circulating "anti-Soviet" literature), was not only forced to strip but was forced to vomit because the guards suspected that the prisoner had slipped her a letter.

156

Mikhail Osadchy

Vyacheslav Chornovil

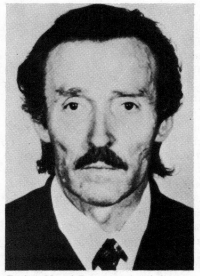

Father Vasyl Romanyuk while in
exile in 1979 after 7 years in a special regime corrective labour camp

Vladimir Balakhonov

## *Punishments*

The corrective labour legislation establishes a series of punishments for violations of discipline by prisoners.

Prisoners of conscience have regularly been subjected to the full range of these punishments. Particularly affected have been those prisoners who have sought to resist or expose ill-treatment.

One of the main forms of protest by prisoners has been collective hunger-strikes or work strikes. In the camps in Perm and Mordovia, and in Vladimir prison, participants in such collective actions have been punished *en masse*. Prisoners known or suspected to have been involved in smuggling information out of their camps or prisons have similarly been punished virtually automatically.

Prisoners of conscience have regularly used their legal right to submit complaints to the authorities about ill-treatment and violations of the law by the camp and prison administrations. In law prisoners cannot be punished for making complaints, but the administrations have punished them for using "unacceptable" ("slanderous" or "insulting" or "anti-Soviet") language or for making "unfounded allegations" in their complaints. The authorities have used a broad and unreasonable interpretation of these concepts as a basis for punishing prisoners.

The Uzbek prisoner of conscience, Babur Shakirov, imprisoned for "anti-Soviet agitation and propaganda", was punished for using the words "political prisoner" in a complaint. The Jewish prisoner Yakov Suslensky (serving 7 years' imprisonment for "anti-Soviet agitation and propaganda") was punished because "in one complaint he contrasted the conditions in which he and his fellow inmates were being kept with Lenin's conditions when he was living in internal exile". Alexander Sergiyenko was punished for describing beatings of prisoners which he said had taken place with the connivance of the prison authorities. Three other prisoners (Gunnar Rode, Yury Vudka and Alexander Chekalin) were punished for complaining that prisoners had been given inedible fish to eat. A number of other prisoners, Vitold Abankin, Alexei Safronov and Vladimir Bukovsky, were punished along with Babur Shakirov because they had created a disturbance and eventually virtually broken down their cell door in an effort to summon medical attention for a cell-mate who had become violently ill. All these people were punished for these "offences" in Vladimir prison in 1975.

These grounds for punishment all relate more or less directly to a conflict between administrators and those prisoners who are struggling to protect their rights and the rights of other prisoners. However, prisoners of conscience who do not recant their views or otherwise cooperate with the authorities have in very many cases been punished on diverse pretexts. The following is a random sample of other grounds on which prisoners of conscience have repeatedly been punished:

"not wearing regulation clothing" (the Ukrainian poet Ihor Kalynets was caught walking with his collar button undone; the Ukrainian Stepan Sapeliak was found with his cap in his pocket instead of on his head);

- "possessing forbidden literature" (the Baptists Grigory Kostyuchenko and Peter Peters, in separate ordinary regime camps, were each found in 1978 to be in possession of a Bible);
- "walking out of line" from the camp dining-room (the Ukrainian philosopher Vasyl Lisovoi in 1978);
- "inducing other prisoners to take part in religious ceremonies" (the Baptist Ivan Pauls in 1976);
- not fulfilling output norms at work;
- drinking tea outside of normal meal times;
- failing to greet camp officials properly by rising and doffing the cap;
- taking food into the work area;
- refusing to report for work;
- "simulating illness";
- refusing to speak to the administration in Russian (the Lithuanian Petras Plumpa Pluira in 1977);
- turning up late for roll-call;
- refusing to shave off one's moustache, or resisting forcible shaving;
- trying to communicate with prisoners in other cells;
- failing to attend political education classes;
- refusing to work on an unsafe machine (the Armenian Bagrat Shakhverdian in 1976).

Article 53 of the RSFSR Corrective Labour Code lists the punishments for these and many other "offences". Some of the punishments most frequently imposed on prisoners have been dealt with in this report: deprivation of a visit; deprivation of a parcel; prohibition on purchasing food in the camp or prison shop for up to one month.

Other punishments are frequently imposed on prisoners of conscience. Inmates of prisons may be placed on strict regime for up to six months or put for up to 15 days in a punishment cell (*kartser*). Inmates of special regime camps may be transferred to a solitary confinement cell for up to one year. Inmates of ordinary, reinforced and strict regime camps may be put in a punishment-isolation cell (*Shtrafnoi Izolyator*, or *SHIzo*) for up to 15 days, or put for up to six months in a prison within the camp, known as "cell-type premises" (*Pomeshcheniye Kamernogo Tipa*, or PKT). Finally, an inmate of a camp of any regime may, by decision of a court, be ordered transferred for disciplinary reasons to a camp with a more severe regime or to a prison.

Each of these punishments inflicts considerable suffering on prisoners. Each involves reduction in the prisoner's already inadequate food rations as well as other deprivations. Because of this, and because they have been applied routinely to a high proportion of prisoners of conscience, it is important to examine each in some detail.

Inmates of prisons who are put on strict regime are confined separately from prisoners on ordinary regime and subjected to several deprivations. They may send only one letter every two months (instead of one every month as do prison inmates on ordinary regime). Their daily exercise period is reduced from one hour to 30 minutes. They may spend only 2 rubles (instead of 3) each month in the prison shop.

The main element of strict regime punishment is reduction of food. Prisoners on strict regime receive a diet including around 1750 calories instead of the ordinary regime prisoners' meagre diet of around 2000 calories (see Chapter 4). Moreover, in their first month on strict regime prisoners are kept on special reduced rations of around 1300 calories.

According to Soviet corrective labour law, inmates of prisons may be put on special regime for from two to six months. Prisoners who are transferred from a camp to a prison are automatically put on prison strict regime on their arrival there.

Inmates of prisons may also be subjected to up to 15 days in a punishment cell. Although the Commentary to the RSFSR Corrective Labour Code treats this as a less severe punishment than transfer to strict regime, the punishment cell involves gross ill-treatment of prisoners.

The law stipulates that prisoners may not be placed in a punishment cell for longer than 15 days. Prisoners have complained that in a number of cases inmates have been held in the punishment cell for longer than this on the grounds that while in the punishment cell they have committed some new breach of discipline. In effect, there is no upper limit on the period a prisoner can be held in a punishment cell. An anonymous 1975 *samizdat* document from a number of inmates of Vladimir prison reported that in 1975 two prisoners had been confined to punishment cells for 70 and 25 days respectively. A report by the Moscow Helsinki monitoring group in July 1975 listed a number of similar cases.

A prisoner in a punishment cell is held in solitary confinement, as is stipulated by the law. Article 54 of the RSFSR Corrective Code provides the following details about conditions in punishment cells:

While in a punishment cell. . . the prisoner is not allowed to have visits, to send letters, to purchase food or items of prime necessity, to receive parcels or packets, to use table games or to smoke. In the punishment cells. . . bedding is not given out and the prisoner confined there is not taken out for exercise.

The Commentary to the RSFSR Corrective Labour Code envisages that before sending a prisoner to a punishment cell the director of the prison must have a "thorough personal conversation" with him or her.[4] By no means is this practised in the regular subjection of prisoners of conscience to this punishment.

Although the conditions prescribed by law are rigorous, prisoners in punishment cells in Vladimir prison have been subjected to still more deprivations that effectively constitute a real threat to the health of the prisoners.

In 1975 the Initiative Group for the Defence of Human Rights in the USSR, an unofficial group based in Moscow, reported:

A punishment cell is a kind of stone dungeon — damp, cold and airless. Often there is an unbearable stench in the punishment cell — the stink from an open sewer pipe. . . (The ventilation system is such that when it is turned on it sucks in the stench from the sewer. The switch is in the corridor; and the guard sometimes threatens a prisoner with the words, "If you make any trouble, I'll turn on the fan".)

It is almost always dark in the punishment cell, with only a very feeble light from a bulb that is almost completely covered over. One's bed — a kind of wooden box with iron cross-pieces — is issued only for the night. There is no bedding except for the prisoner's light cotton blanket, which does not keep him warm. There is nothing to sit on. (True, there is a narrow brick ledge in the wall, but it is virtually impossible to sit on it.)

There are around 50 punishment cells in Vladimir prison. A report (July 1976) by the Moscow Helsinki monitoring group gives this description:

The walls and floor are cement. The walls are covered with cement "fur" — sharp protuberances, spurs. The floor is dirty and damp — it is the same in other punishment cells.

Deep in the meter-thick wall there is a blind window; part of the window is broken and has been stuffed with strips of newspaper. (In other cells the window opening is blocked up with a fine mesh — you can't even get your finger through it. In several the window is completely stopped up, bricks have been laid in.) There is practically nothing to sit on. There is a specially-equipped protuberance from the wall: a vertical half-cylinder with a radius of around 20 or 25 cm and a height of around 50 cm. The top is covered entirely with a board covered at the edges with iron. It is impossible to sit on such a contraption. The muscles of the legs and back are quickly overstrained and begin to hurt. The sharp spurs of the cement "fur" stick into the back.

In other punishment cells there are approximately similar constructions, on some of which it is likewise impossible to sit. At night time they throw in a bed — a low wooden box turned upside-down. (Sometimes the bottom is criss-crossed with iron.) It is impossible to lie on bare boards and iron. But the cold does not allow the prisoner to sleep. Often it is even impossible to lie down. The penetrating cold makes it necessary to keep moving all the time.

The area of punishment cell number 1 is around 3 square meters. (The area of other punishment cells is usually less—around 2.5 or 2.2 square meters.)

Before being put in a punishment cell prisoners are forced to hand over their normal clothing and are dressed instead in a thin cotton garment for the duration of their punishment. They may not wear any additional clothing even at night.

Prisoners in the punishment cell of a prison are fed differently on alternate days: one day they receive a piece of bread, hot water and some salt; the next day they are fed at the "norm 9b" ration, which provides 1300 or 1400 calories and often consists of inedible or spoiled products. This is a starvation diet.

In its July 1976 report the Helsinki Group gave a statistical survey of the application of punishments by strict regime and punishment cell in Vladimir prison between 1 August 1975 and mid-July 1976. Although the Helsinki Group qualified their estimate by saying that there might have been other cases of which they had not heard, their estimate corresponds to information available to Amnesty International from other sources.

In that period of 11½ months the Helsinki Group catalogued 32 cases of political prisoners in Vladimir prison being punished with strict regime (in each case with the first month being on the special reduced rations) and 31 cases of political prisoners there being put in a punishment cell (the shortest period in the punishment cell having been 6 days, the longest 45 days).

This punishment can be imposed repeatedly on a single prisoner. In one such case, Vitold Abankin, sentenced to 12 years' imprisonment for trying to cross the border while doing military service, spent 205 days in punishment cells during his three years in Vladimir prison from 1974 to 1977. Often those on prison strict regime have been sent to punishment cells and after two weeks or more there have been returned straight to strict regime.

Prisoners in special regime camps are normally held in cells in groups of up to five. They may be punished by transfer for up to one year to a solitary cell. There they may still be required to work. If so, they receive reduced rations of around 1700 calories (Norm 9a). If they don't work, they may be fed at Norm 9b: around 1300 calories.

Prisoners of conscience in camps with strict, reinforced or ordinary regimes have frequently been punished – often repeatedly – by a spell in a punishment-isolation cell (*SHIzo*). Conditions in punishment-isolation cells resemble closely those in the punishment cells in prisons described above. The main difference is that more than one prisoner may be put into the same punishment-isolation cell. The maximum duration of such a punishment is 15 days, according to the law. However, in many cases the punishment is renewed at the end of 15 days.

According to the official Commentary to Article 54 of the RSFSR Corrective Labour Code:

> Putting prisoners in a punishment-isolation cell is a very severe measure
> of punishment. Besides being isolated from other prisoners, people in
> punishment cells are subjected to a whole series of other restrictions: they
> are not permitted to have visitors, to send letters, to obtain food and basic
> necessities, to receive parcels, packages and packets, to use table games or
> to smoke. Bedding is not issued to people in punishment-isolation cells.
> Those subjected to this punishment are not taken out for exercise. They
> receive food at reduced norms. Prisoners confined to punishment-isolation
> cells are kept in closed cells.[5]

Mikhail Kheifets, a Leningrad writer who was sentenced in 1974 to 6 years' imprisonment and exile, gave the following description of the punishment-isolation cells in Mordovia camp 19 in 1977:

> The typical cooler is a damp room with the plaster peeling off, and when
> we were put in one it was whitewashed. It has wooden bunks held up by
> chains. In the daytime the bunks are bolted to the wall. There is a tiny
> table with two or four stump seats, 15-18 cm in diameter, which are
> painful to sit on. We lie on the wooden floor. Once one of the present
> "status"-adopters – Budulak – fasted for 18 days, but got himself
> assigned to a floor with wooden boards over cement. They don't issue

a bed — we put slippers wrapped in a handkerchief under our head. They feed us on a reduced norm, ie. on soup that is completely without fat or thickening, and that's only on alternate days. On the other day it's bread and water. There's no limit on salt. We're forbidden to read. They take us out of our cells only half an hour in the morning — to wash and go to the toilet. For daytime and night-time needs it's the close-stool. There's not enough chloride of lime so the cell stinks. Because of the dampness it's cold in the cell at night, even in the warm time of year.[6]

According to *samizdat* sources, at the time he made the above statement Mikhail Kheifets was punished in this way three times within six weeks, spending 30 days during that time in punishment-isolation cells for going on a work strike.

Female prisoners of conscience too have not been spared this sort of punishment. Nadezhda Svetlichnaya said in an interview with Amnesty International staff in 1978 that she regarded the time she spent in punishment-isolation cells as her worst experience during her 4 years' imprisonment. Once when she was subjected to this punishment it was December but she was permitted to wear only a thin cotton garment and, in accordance with the law, she was not issued with any bedding.

Prisoners confined to punishment-isolation cells may be required by order of the camp director to work during normal working hours while on punishment. In such cases, they work in a specially converted cell in the punishment block.

Prisoners of conscience in corrective labour colonies with ordinary, reinforced and strict regime have also frequently been transferred to "cell-type premises" (PKT) within their camps. By law, the maximum duration of this punishment is six months. According to recent reports, the unpublished "Rules of Internal Order" which came into effect in March 1978 removed this limit by allowing prisoners to serve consecutive terms of this punishment without any interval.

The essence of this punishment is that the prisoner is moved from barracks-type accommodation to a cell, where normally he or she is kept with one or more other prisoners. According to official sources, prisoners in "cell-type premises" are subjected to the same conditions as inmates of prisons who are punished by being put on strict regime (see above), including the same reduction of rations to around 1750 calories per day. Prisoners in "cell-type premises" are expected to work either in their own cells or in specially converted cells in the punishment block. Invariably the work given them must be done by hand. In the mid-1970s prisoners of conscience in "cell-type premises" in the Perm camps were put to work cutting bolts by hand. Those in "cell-type premises" in the Mordovian camps in the mid-1970s worked at fine polishing wooden clock cases. If prisoners do not work, their rations are further reduced. Each of these punishments undermines the health of prisoners already weakened by years of imprisonment under "normal" conditions.

The corrective labour legislation does not specify that prisoners must undergo any medical test before being punished. However, according to unofficial sources, until 1977 a prisoner could not be subjected to certain punishments, such as being put in a punishment cell in a prison, without the agreement of the doctor as well as the administration, and the doctor could also in theory have a prisoner removed from punishment and sent to hospital. Reportedly the rules were changed in 1977 so that the doctor's consent was not needed for punishing prisoners in these ways, and so that only the prison or camp director could have a prisoner removed from punishment on grounds of illness.

This change in the rules merely formalized the previous situation, in which camp and prison doctors did not in practice prevent even seriously ill prisoners from being confined to punishment cells or subjected to similar punishments. In numerous well-documented incidents prisoners of conscience with heart conditions, ulcers, bowel disorders, tuberculosis and other ailments have been subjected to these punishments. In one recorded case a paralysed prisoner had to be taken in to the punishment cell on crutches. Vladimir Bukovsky reported after his release in 1976 that the walls of the punishment cells of Vladimir prison were stained with "gobs of bloody saliva" from prisoners with tuberculosis who had been confined there. According to other prisoners, no effort was made to disinfect the cells after they had been occupied by prisoners with infectious diseases.

The effects of such practices were indicated in one report from prisoners in Perm camp 35 in late 1978:

I. Popadichenko has been transferred from the "cell-type premises" in camp 36 and is now in the camp hospital. In three years the administration of camp 36 has been able to turn this strong young sportsman into an invalid. Because of his constantly being in the punishment cells he has begun to develop tuberculosis and his digestive tract no longer functions properly.

Furthermore, prisoners on hunger strike have in many cases been sent to punishment cells (for example, Vasyl Fedorenko in the third month of his hunger strike in Vladimir prison in 1976).

The treatment of the prisoner of conscience Alexander Sergiyenko in Vladimir prison is typical. Sergiyenko suffers from tuberculosis. Nonetheless between May 1975 and April 1976 he was put in the punishment cells of Vladimir prison four times for a total of 50 days. In response to one of numerous appeals by Sergiyenko's mother a doctor in the Medical Administration of the MVD reportedly said in 1976 that it was not within the competence of the medical personnel to alter his conditions of confinement, and that the doctors could not interfere in such administrative matters as the imposition of punishments for disciplinary offences.

It is also difficult for people in punishment cells, punishment-isolation cells and similar places of punishment to obtain any medical treatment. This report has already referred to cases where other prisoners have had to create a disturbance in order to get a doctor or other medical personnel to come to look at prisoners who had fallen ill. In numerous cases doctors have not offered any help to ill prisoners in punishment cells even when they have come to have a look at them. For example, the Moscow Helsinki monitoring group reported in 1978 that Egor Davydov was confined to a punishment cell in Vladimir prison that year in spite of the fact that he suffered from radiculitis and rheumatic carditis. He was able to see a prison doctor and asked her if he could be allowed to wear an extra pair of underwear, since the temperature in the punishment cell was only 11°C. However, the doctor said that she could not authorize this, since it was a "regime matter". She passed the request on to the administration, which several days later refused it.

In other cases administrations have directly overriden recommendations by doctors that prisoners undergoing punishment be given treatment. For example, Yury Pavlovich Fyodorov reported in 1977 in a statement to the United Nations Commission on Human Rights that when he fell ill while confined to an isolation cell in the Mordovia special regime camp the camp doctor asked that he be sent to a hospital for examination. The administration ordered that he complete his punishment before going to the hospital.

According to the law, the most severe punishment which may be imposed on a prisoner for disciplinary offences is transfer to a corrective labour institution with a more strict regime than that initially assigned by the court. Because this punishment represents a change in the prisoner's sentence, it may be imposed only by a court, invariably the court nearest his or her place of imprisonment. A court hearing to decide whether a prisoner should be transferred to a camp with a more severe regime or from a camp to a prison is initiated at the request of the camp administration. According to Article 364 of the RSFSR Code of Criminal Procedure the court "as a rule" summons the prisoner to the hearing, but may proceed without him or her. In some cases prisoners of conscience have had this punishment imposed on them without being present at the court hearing. Prisoners are not often given a copy of the charges against them, they have no right to defence counsel under these proceedings and in practice have no possibility of appeal to a higher court.

Most of the prisoners of conscience known to have been affected by this type of punishment have been prisoners in strict regime camps, almost always in Perm and Mordovia. They have usually been transferred to Vladimir prison. One prisoner of conscience (Kirill Podrabinek, in 1978) is reported to have been transferred from an ordinary regime camp to a prison in Lipetsk region.

According to Article 53 of the RFSFR Corrective Labour Code the maximum term for which a prisoner may be transferred from a camp to a prison is three years. Transfer of prisoners of conscience from camps to Vladimir prison was especially common during the early and mid-1970s. Almost 50 prisoners of conscience are known to have been transferred there as a punishment during 1975 and 1976 alone. However there was a sharp decline in the frequency of such transfers thereafter. According to all accounts this was because the inmates of Vladimir prison had succeeded in organizing collective resistance to the authorities there and in smuggling out a great deal of information on the activities and composition of the administration.

According to the law, transfer to a prison may be imposed only for "malicious" violation of discipline. The grounds on which a court ruled in 1973 that Alexander Sergiyenko be transferred to Vladimir prison were typical: "On 6 December he sang Christmas songs in the lavatory; . . . he had six books—one more than is permitted — in his night table; . . . he did not fulfil his output norms; . . . he did not attend political classes".

In addition to applying these disciplinary punishments, the authorities may bring fresh criminal charges against prisoners for actions committed while serving sentences of imprisonment. A number of prisoners of conscience have been charged with "anti-Soviet agitation and propaganda" or similar offences and brought to trial instead of being released (see Chapter 1). Prisoners of conscience who persistently campaign for their rights have frequently been threatened with fresh charges and sentences.

Another threat occasionally made to prisoners of conscience is that because of their collective actions such as hunger-strikes, they will be charged with "actions disrupting the work of corrective labour organizations" (Article 77-1 of the RSFSR Criminal Code.) This article, which was added to the criminal codes in 1962, carries a possible death penalty. While it has not in recent years been applied to any known prisoners of conscience, it has been applied to criminal prisoners who have taken part in camp or prison revolts. *Samizdat* sources and former prisoners have reported a number of serious disturbances by criminal prisoners in recent years. Two such disturbances, in Mordovia in 1977 and in Omsk in 1977, are reported to have been protests against systematic beatings of prisoners by guards and prisoners favoured by the administrations. According to issue 48 of *A Chronicle of Current Events* two of those put on trial for the Mordovia riot, Vladimir Aitman and Nikolai Agafonov, both about 20 years old, were sentenced to death.

## Beatings and Physical Ill-Treatment of Prisoners

A number of prisoners of conscience have been subjected to beatings and other physical ill-treatment while serving their sentences. Among political prisoners known to have been beaten by guards in recent years are Pyotr Vins, Zoryan Popadyuk, Mikhail Shtern, Father Vasyl Romanyuk, Stepan Sapeliak, Mikhail Osadchy, Vyacheslav Chornovil, Bohdan Rebrik and Yury Pavlovich Fyodorov.

There are also numerous accounts of handcuffs being applied to prisoners as punishment in such a way as to cause great pain, although the law states explicitly that they may be used only to restrain violent prisoners.

There have also been numerous recorded instances of physical attacks on prisoners of conscience by criminal prisoners, acting with the connivance or protection of the authorities. Relatives and sympathizers have expressed particular concern about the possibility of physical attacks on prisoners of conscience when they are held in ordinary camps for criminals where there are no concentrations of political prisoners able to protect each other by collective actions and smuggling out of information.

Sender Levinson, a Jewish would-be emigrant sentenced in 1975 to 6 years' imprisonment, subsequently reduced to 4½ years, for "currency speculation", described after his release in 1978 the physical dangers from other prisoners in his ordinary regime camp:

> The enraged and embittered prisoners lived according to the rule of the jungle, with no compassion for the weak. The weak were raped and beaten. When I went down the mine at first I did not know that it was dangerous to walk down there alone. After about a week three men came up before me in a dark passage, pushed the torch out of my hand and tried to rape me. There are no women in the camp and weak men are therefore raped.

This was the first time that I had to defend myself against this sort of thing. I was saved by the fact that I used to do wrestling and fought them off by force. The camp lives by laws of its own. That was how I became familiar with them. . .

. . .I was again taken from prison to prison, from one transfer cell to another. Again it was "Black Marias" [the *voronok*, see Chapter 4—*AI note*] , prison carriages, violence, rape, card games in the cells. The guards did whatever they felt like. . .

The streams of blood spilled, the violence that I witnessed during that trip, both in the transit prisons and the trains, was incredible. In Odessa and Kharkov we were beaten with wooden hammers for our complaints about the lack of sanitary conditions and poor quality food. In Ruzaevka we were made to take showers with luke-warm water in a bath-house that had broken windows — in winter. In Ulyanovsk a group of juvenile delinquents were placed in our train carriage (they were being transferred to the regular camps) and half of them were raped. They were children who were starting to live and so many of their lives were already broken. In Kharkov someone got a metal picket thrust into his stomach because he did not want to give away a shirt. . .[7]

However, beatings of prisoners of conscience are not routine. Those whose cases have been known abroad and become the subject of publicity, and especially those in the political camps in Perm and Mordovia, have evidently been spared some of the worst excesses of physical brutality which many criminal prisoners have had to endure. There have been numerous cases of such prisoners being subjected to a permanent reign of terror by other prisoners and guards. Among recorded cases of physical ill-treatment of criminal prisoners is one from a camp in the Komi ASSR in 1974 where the camp director who ordered the beating of a prisoner by guards subsequently wrote a record of the incident, saying: "In connection with the fact that all measures of re-education applied to the prisoner Brechko have been without result, measures of physical influence were applied to him." He reportedly gave this to the prisoner and asked him to sign it.

Among other accounts of beatings by guards or by prisoners acting for them is a document by an anonymous inmate or former inmate of a prison in Andizhan in the Uzbek republic which arrived outside the USSR in 1979. This prisoner recounted:

On the day they brought me to Andizhan prison the deputy director Umayukulov and the head of the special section Azimov summoned me. They began to torment me and threatened me with physical reprisals: "You'll find that this isn't some camp in Bukhara — we have cells here such that if we put you there you'll renounce both your opinions and your life." Later I found out that there really are such cells, where bandits are kept, their agents.

After describing how criminal prisoners were employed to beat other prisoners, the anonymous author went on to describe beatings by guards themselves, which he witnessed after he was brought back from a failed escape attempt with five other prisoners:

After my escape I found myself under investigation in cell number 139. Opposite me, in cell number 137, the guards murdered the prisoner [blank space in document – AI note] known as "Boxer". I saw the assault on this prisoner from beginning to end with my own eyes. This happened either in January or early February 1977. The guard who killed him was named Yury, nicknamed "Hooligan" by the prisoners. Azimov and Yumayukulov were there too. They didn't kill him at once – his torture lasted four days.

The incident described in the following account (confirmed in a number of other accounts by prisoners there) took place in Vladimir prison, which is not only one of the country's central corrective labour institutions but one which the authorities might be expected to supervise especially carefully because the prisoners of conscience there have managed to make it a subject of international attention.

On 23 November 1975 they put the criminal prisoner Tikhonov into cell number 1-13. (He was more than 50 years old, an invalid of the Second World War, missing his left arm and suffering from a stomach ulcer. He was receiving diet food.) When he was put in this cell, the criminal prisoners there, Vagrov, Yury Varinov and another known as "The Tartar" said that there was an irreconcilable enmity between them and Tikhonov. In spite of this the guards shoved Tikhonov into the cell. The prisoners started to beat Tikhonov. The beating last a whole day (several days, according to some accounts). A number of criminal prisoners in the neighbouring cell 1-14 heard his cries and demanded that the administration put an end to the beating. This had no effect. When they were taken out for their exercise and were returning from exercise the prisoners from cell 1-14 (amongst them Vladimir Khoroshkov, born in 1933) appealed to the head of the operations section, Ugodin, and the operations officer, Senior Lieutenant Khripunov, who watched the beating through the eye-hole of cell 1-13. Then the prisoners asked again that the beating be ended. Ugodin replied: "No one is being beaten – he's just shouting like that."

The account continues to say that eventually the prisoner was taken from the cell and died shortly thereafter. "On his body there wasn't one place untouched, they'd broken his ribs and smashed his kidneys and liver."

Rivalries and reprisals of this sort are common among criminal prisoners in the USSR, but in this case as in others the administration itself evidently played a part. While the three prisoners named in the account as the direct perpetrators of the murder were reportedly tried and received additional sentences for this, apparently no one from the administration was called to account. Ugodin was subsequently promoted to director of the prison.

## Legal Controls over Colony and Prison Administrations

The legal reforms which were enacted piecemeal in the USSR after 1953 were accompanied by efforts to restore the rule of law in Soviet prison institutions. Although new corrective labour codes were not promulgated until after 1969, during the mid-1950s institutional changes were made providing for legal supervision over colony and prison administrations. Most important was the 1955 Statute on the Supervisory Powers of the USSR Procuracy which is still in effect. According to Article 35 of this statute, officers of the Procuracy have an unlimited right to visit colonies and prisons to check documents related to prisoners' cases and to check the legality of all orders and directives of the administrations of corrective labour institutions. Article 36 of the statute requires the Procuracy to give timely consideration to complaints and petitions by prisoners. In addition, public supervisory commissions were established in 1957 throughout the USSR to act "as organs of public control over observance of legality in the activity of corrective labour institutions".

In the present corrective labour legislation, the Procuracy and public supervisory commissions are retained as the two channels for supervision of observance of legality in Soviet corrective labour institutions.

Article 11 of the RSFSR Corrective Labour Code stipulates that the Soviet Procuracy and its subordinate procuracies are to ensure "exact observance of the laws" in prison institutions. They are to prevent and punish violations of the law "from whomsoever these violations may emanate". In numerous places in the code it is stated that the MVD is to cooperate with the Procuracy in determining certain details of the operation of prisons and colonies. Article 11 of the RSFSR Corrective Labour Code also states that camp and prison administrations "are obliged to fulfil" the instructions of the Procuracy about observing the laws. To ensure that prisoners can bring abuses to the attention of the Procuracy (and other organs and institutions), the Fundamentals of Corrective Labour Legislation assures them of the right to lodge complaints in writing. According to the Commentary to the Fundamentals of Corrective Labour Legislation of the USSR and Union Republics:

> The right of convicted persons to make complaints is regarded as one of the
> important guarantees for provision of legality during the execution of
> punishment. . . The drawing up and sending of complaints is not limited
> by any norms whatever.[8]

However, the authorities commonly infringe the right of prisoners to lodge complaints. Only those letters of complaint sent by prisoners to the Procuracy are exempt from obligatory censorship by the colony or prison administration. This means that prisoners' complaints, unless addressed to the Procuracy, are censored by the very officials who are the subjects of the complaints.

Prisoners' complaints to ministries and other bodies are not only read by the colony or prison administration, but also are often forwarded to the central corrective labour administration within the MVD.

Given the power which camp and prison administrations have to change conditions for any prisoner, they have considerable scope for taking revenge on prisoners who lodge complaints. Sometimes revenge and intimidation are given the appearance of legality, as the following account from a Perm colony in 1973 or 1974 illustrates:

> The camp administration informed the prisoners that there is a special
> instruction according to which the administration is authorized to

censor prisoners' complaints and to decide whether they contain slander or whether they are objective. In the first case, that is if they find slander in the complaint, the camp administration has the right not to send on the complaint and the right to punish the prisoner for giving false information or for the presence of improper expressions in the letter. In this manner a number of prisoners were punished for sending complaints by punishment cell and by deprivation of parcels and visits.

According to reports from prisoners in Perm camp 35 in late 1978, the new Rules of Internal Order which came into effect in March 1978 forbid prisoners to submit collective complaints or complaints about the treatment of other prisoners. This important change in the rules was introduced almost certainly because of the collective efforts of prisoners of conscience to expose administrative abuses, and the prisoners themselves have described it as "taking away prisoners' rights to protect one another". The change derives no authority from any published legislation.

Despite its sweeping authority, the Procuracy has only very rarely responded positively to prisoners' complaints by ruling that the administration of a camp or prison had acted illegally. Usually procurators reply to prisoners' complaints by saying simply that the administrative practice or action about which the prisoner had complained was "not illegal" or that the particular improvement which the prisoner requested was "not authorized". Often the Procuracy is technically correct in saying this, since the corrective labour legislation is phrased very broadly in most places and leaves a great deal regarding the treatment of prisoners to the discretion of camp and prison administrations. However, many administrative practices constitute cruel and degrading treatment, and if the Procuracy were genuinely impartial or authoritative it could rule that such abuses contradict the spirit if not the letter of corrective labour legislation. To Amnesty International's knowledge no procurator has ever made such an important ruling.

Furthermore, numerous administrative practices and actions, including some described in this report, are clearly illegal, but have continued without intervention by the Procuracy.

A further indication of the lack of willingness of the Procuracy to exercise its authority was made by one of two officials (Drozdov and Obraztsoy) of the Vladimir Regional Procurator's Office in a meeting with some prisoners in Vladimir prison in 1976. According to a report in issue 42 of *A Chronicle of Current Events*:

> The political prisoners in one of the cells raised with them the issue of observance of legality. Drozdov said that this would be too expensive for the state.

As an official told hunger striking political prisoners in a Perm camp in 1974: "You can complain but you'd better learn that no procurator can help."

The public supervisory commissions provide the second means of supervising the observance of legality in colonies. These commissions are attached to local Soviets of Workers' Deputies at region, city and district level. According to

Article 110 of the RSFSR Corrective Labour Code, their membership is composed for the most part of "deputies of soviets and representatives of trade unions, Young Communists and other public organizations and workers' collectives". Workers of the MVD, Procuracy and courts are barred from being members of the supervisory commissions.

The supervisory commissions are legally entitled to concern themselves with all aspects of the functioning of corrective labour institutions. They are authorized to help in the re-education of prisoners. On the basis of their own evaluation of prisoners' records, they can seek early release of prisoners through the courts or their transfer from one type of regime to another. Their agreement is legally required before any prisoner can be punished by transfer to a more severe type of corrective labour institution or by being put on strict regime in a prison or into "cell-type premises" in a camp.

The supervisory commissions are required to participate "in the implementation of public control" over the activity of corrective labour institutions. They are therefore endowed with broad rights to visit colonies and prisons to hear prisoners' complaints and to demand presentation of relevant documents by the administration.

The gap between these legal provisions and the actual practice is wide. There is almost no reference to the supervisory commissions in accounts by prisoners and former prisoners. They apparently do not function all the time and prisoners have little possibility of maintaining contact with them. Amnesty International knows of no case where a supervisory commission has intervened on behalf of a prisoner of conscience who had complained to them or vetoed an administrative decision to punish a prisoner. The supervisory commissions also play no active role in obtaining early release of prisoners of conscience.

The Soviet jurist M.D. Shargorodsky wrote in 1973 that the view is still held tenaciously among the Soviet public that "the more severe the punishments applied the more effective will be the struggle with crime".[9] If in their operations the supervisory commissions reflect this view, it might be one explanation for their lack of effectiveness in easing prison conditions.

However, the public supervisory commissions do not operate independently of government organs. They are obliged to respect the principles and goals of the authorities charged with administering the prison system. Whatever the accuracy of Shargorodsky's statement of Soviet public attitudes, contemporary corrective labour legislation itself reflects a punitive, retributive attitude toward imprisonment which is certainly characteristic of those who administer its application. It is this attitude that determines the operations of the public supervisory commissions.

## *Notes*

1. For a partial text of this directive see Number 46 of *A Chronicle of Current Events*.
2. *Commentary to the RSFSR Corrective Labour Code*, Moscow, 1973, page 67.
3. *Ibid*, page 66.
4. *Ibid*, page 178.
5. *Ibid*, page 140.
6. Mikhail Kheifets, "A Letter from a Camp", in Mikhail Kheifets, *Mesto i vremya*, YMCA Press, Paris, 1978, page 202. See also Number 47 of *A Chronicle of Current Events*, page 109.
7. *Jews in the USSR*, London, 12 April 1979.
8. *Commentary to the Fundamentals of Corrective Labour Legislation of the USSR and the Union Republics*, Moscow, 1972, page 100.
9. M.D. Shargorodsky, *Punishment, Its Goals and Effectiveness*, Moscow, 1973, page 49.

# CHAPTER 7

# Compulsory Detention in Psychiatric Hospitals

Amnesty International knows of more than 100 people who were forcibly confined to psychiatric hospitals for exercising their human rights rather than for authentic medical reasons between 1 June 1975 and 31 May 1979. This figure does not include the many known prisoners of conscience who were put into psychiatric hospitals prior to 1 June 1975 and who in many cases remained confined after that date. Nor does this figure include cases on which Amnesty International regards the available information as inadequate for categorizing the confined person as a prisoner of conscience.

A great deal of new evidence on political abuse of psychiatry in the USSR has become available since 1975. A number of victims have emigrated, been met by foreign psychiatrists and other individuals and given detailed accounts of their treatment. Other victims have been released from psychiatric hospitals and their accounts of their treatment have circulated in *samizdat*. Several psychiatrists have emigrated from the USSR and been able to add information about their professional experience to what is known of the abuses.

Most important, the work of human rights activists inside the country in chronicling cases and practices of political abuse of psychiatry has become more efficient and better informed. To the reporting of *A Chronicle of Current Events* and other unofficial sources has been added the prolific documentation of the Helsinki monitoring groups and the Working Commission for the Investigation of the Use of Psychiatry for Political Purposes, an unofficial group set up in Moscow in early 1977. The Working Commission produced 16 *Information Bulletins* (comprising more than 500 pages) and numerous separate appeals and statements in its first two-and-a-half years of existence. Friends and relatives of victims came frequently to Moscow to inform members of this group about individual cases, and the group's members supplemented this flow of information by trips to the provinces to obtain facts on the spot. The accuracy and scope of the research carried out by the Working Commission were strengthened by the close collaboration of two Moscow psychiatrists and a lawyer.

The authorities have continued to imprison and otherwise persecute human rights activists who attempt to expose political abuses of psychiatry.

In spite of repeated denials by the Soviet authorities that people have been confined to psychiatric hospitals in the USSR because of their exercise of their human rights, international psychiatric associations have authoritatively condemned the abuses. In August 1977 the subject was discussed at the Sixth Congress of the World Psychiatric Association, whose General Assembly subsequently adopted the following resolution:

That the World Psychiatric Association take note of the abuse of psychiatry for political purposes and that it condemn those practices in all countries where they occur and call upon the professional organizations of psychiatrists in those countries to renounce and expunge those practices from their country and that the WPA implement this resolution in the first instance in reference to the extensive evidence of the systematic abuse of psychiatry for political purposes in the USSR.

The week before, the World Federation of Mental Health had approved a similar position and drawn it to the attention of the WPA.

At its Sixth Congress the WPA also decided to set up a Committee to Review the Abuse of Psychiatry for Political Reasons for monitoring individual cases.

## Formal Procedures for Compulsory Confinement

There are three formal procedures for forcibly confining people to psychiatric hospitals: (1) the civil procedure, applicable to those not accused of a criminal offence prior to being confined to a psychiatric hospital; (2) the criminal procedure, applicable to those accused of a criminal offence; (3) the procedure whereby individuals convicted of a criminal offence are transferred from their place of imprisonment to a psychiatric hospital. (The third of these procedures has been dealt with briefly in Chapter 4.)

Both the civil and the criminal procedures provide inadequate protection against wrongful confinement to a psychiatric hospital. In particular, they facilitate the arbitrary subjection of dissenters to psychiatric measures and make difficult the defence of such people through legal means.

However, in one important respect the established procedures offer a protection which, if respected by the authorities, would at least make wrongful confinement of political and religious dissenters and others rare. Under both the civil procedure and the criminal procedure even if individuals are diagnosed as mentally ill they may be confined to a psychiatric hospital only if they are shown to be dangerous to themselves or others.

In hundreds of cases of forcible confinement of dissenters to psychiatric hospitals there has been no suggestion, even by the authorities, that the subjects were physically violent or dangerous to themselves or others. In their persistent denials of political abuses of psychiatry Soviet officials, propagandists and spokesmen for the psychiatric profession have not addressed themselves to this most elementary principle of psychiatric practice, insisting invariably that well-known dissenters who had been confined were mentally ill, but rarely attempting to show that they were in any way "violent" or "dangerous".

The following is a sampling of the types of actions which the authorities have used as grounds for confining people to psychiatric hospitals: giving song recitals in one's own flat (Pyotr Starchik, 1976); criticizing the government in the presence of workmates and other private citizens (Vladimir Rozhdestvov, 1978); trying to cross the border to another country without official permission (the brothers Alexander and Mikhail Shatravka, in the mid-1970s); persistently making religious craft articles (Valeriya Makeyeva, 1978); bringing personal complaints to high government offices in Moscow (Nadezhda Gaidar, 1976);

publicizing one's demand to emigrate by carrying a placade in front of the Bolshoi Ballet (Valentin Ivanov, 1977) or a foreign embassy (Anatoly Uvarov, 1976); hanging up pictures of dissenters over one's sleeping place in a hostel (Mikhail Kukobaka, 1977); persistently seeking official permission to emigrate (Anatoly Glukhov in 1978 as well as twice previously); surreptitiously taking down Soviet flags in Lithuania on the anniversary of the October Revolution (Egidius Ionaitis, 1977); distributing leaflets containing "anti-Soviet slander" (Vyacheslav Zaitsev, 1978); writing complaints to government authorities (Anatoly Ponomaryov, 1977); trying to meet with a foreign correspondent (Vasily Zhigalkin, 1976).

The fact that the authorities have systematically confined non-violent individuals to psychiatric hospitals against their will is itself clear evidence that psychiatry has been abused for political purposes.

## Criminal Procedure for Compulsory Psychiatric Confinement

The Code of Criminal Procedure for each Union Republic dedicates a separate chapter to criminal cases where the mental health of the accused is called in question. (In the RSFSR Code of Criminal Procedure this is Chapter 33.)

Under the criminal procedure, the accused loses virtually all of his or her procedural rights, and is left only with the passive right to an honest psychiatric examination and a fair court hearing, a right which in practice is unenforceable.

It is the investigator who decides whether the accused should be subjected to a psychiatric examination. When the investigator comes to such a decision, the accused is examined by a forensic psychiatric commission, usually in a psychiatric hospital or institution but sometimes also or instead in the investigation prison.

The investigator need not even inform the accused that such an examination is to be carried out "if his mental state makes this impossible".[1] The accused also has no right to be told the results of the psychiatric examination or the recommendations made by the psychiatrists.[2] Furthermore, the accused loses the right to be informed of any fresh charges against him or her, to be told of the results of the criminal investigation of the case or to be shown the materials compiled in the investigation.[3] The law does not grant any special right to such people to have visits from their families. Normally dissenters subjected to psychiatric examination have no visits from their families until after their cases have been heard in court. Hearings usually occur between six and 12 months after the arrest.

In one of the very few procedural guarantees for accused whose mental health is called in question, the law states that participation of defence counsel is "mandatory" at court hearings in such cases.[4]

However, this provision of the law is as grossly violated in such cases as in other cases involving prisoners of conscience (see Chapter 2).

Commonly prisoners of conscience subjected to psychiatric diagnosis, and their families, have not been permitted to meet their lawyers or have any say in their selection. For example, in June 1977 the case of the Ukrainian dissenter Iosif Terelya was heard by a court in the Ukraine without the accused even being assigned a lawyer. The court ordered that he be confined to a special psychiatric hospital. In an unusual development, the court's decision was subsequently annulled on the grounds that the accused had no legal representation. However, Terelya's wife was not informed of the name of the lawyer assigned to her husband for the second hearing. A month later she was told that the second hearing had been held, with the same outcome as the first.

If the psychiatric commission conducting the forensic expert examination finds that for reasons of mental illness the suspect is "not accountable" (a term sometimes translated as "non-responsible") for his or her offence, this finding is submitted to a court together with a recommendation as to what medical measures should be applied to the subject. Instead of a trial there is a court hearing on the case in which the court decides: a) whether the accused committed a socially dangerous action (ie. committed an act defined as criminal by the criminal code), b) whether to accept the expert psychiatric commission's findings as to the subject's accountability and c) what measures to apply to him or her.

The following is the definition of "non-accountability" (*nevmenyaemost*) used in Soviet criminal law, set forth in the most recent official Commentary to the RSFSR Code of Criminal Procedure:

Non-accountability is a concept having two criteria, the medical and the juridical. The medical criterion of non-accountability requires the establishment of chronic mental illness, temporary mental derangement, feeble-mindedness or other condition of mental illness in a person who has committed a socially dangerous act. This is in the exclusive competence of the expert — the forensic psychiatrist.

The juridical criterion of non-accountability requires that it be established that the person who has committed a socially dangerous act could not as a consequence of mental illness account for his actions or control them. It is the court (the investigator) which establishes whether the judicial criterion of non-accountability is satisfied, proceeding not only from the conclusion of the expert psychiatrists but also from other evidence.[5]

According to Article 407 of the RSFSR Criminal Code, it is left to the court to decide whether to permit the accused to attend the hearing of his or her case. In very few cases have prisoners of conscience been permitted to attend the court hearings which ruled on whether or not they were accountable. Furthermore, the accused does not have any legal right to send a written statement to the court.

As the Moscow lawyer Sofia Kallistratova said in an unofficial report on the court hearing of Vladimir Rozhdestvov in November 1977, at which the accused was, *in absentia*, ordered confined to a special psychiatric hospital:

Thus, neither the judge nor the people's assessors nor the procurator nor the defence lawyer, ie. *none* of the trial participants, *saw the man in question*.

This is particularly impermissible in view of the fact that the defence disputed the findings of the forensic psychiatric expert examination regarding Rozhdestvov's sanity and responsibility.

How could the court carefully and impartially resolve the dispute between the procurator (who supported the findings of the psychiatric examination) and the defence counsel (who contested the findings) without seeing and hearing Rozhdestvov in court?[6]

Earlier in this report it was pointed out that Soviet courts invariably convict dissenters brought to trial for political or religious reasons. Dissenters diagnosed as mentally ill fare little better. The courts have heard such cases without taking remedial action against flagrant violations of legality by the investigation organs and psychiatrists. The Ukrainian cyberneticist Leonid Plyushch, for example, was held in detention for one year before his case came to court, in direct violation of Article 34 of the USSR Fundamentals of Criminal Procedure. During the whole of this period, and for six months thereafter, he was not allowed to meet his wife or a lawyer.

Furthermore, the courts themselves have frequently added their own procedural violations to those committed by the investigating officials. Often such court hearings are held *in camera*. In Plyushch's case, Judge Dyshel classified as a state secret the court hearing on Plyushch's state of mind and ordered that the hearing be held *in camera*, although the case did not fall into the categories where this might be lawful (see Chapter 2).

Judge Dyshel also refused to allow court witnesses to give evidence in favour of the defendant. Finally, the judge did not allow Plyushch's legal representative (his wife) to participate in the hearing. Consequently:

> The courtroom was empty; neither the accused, nor his legal representative, nor a psychiatric expert, nor the accused's relatives were present. So great was the isolation of the hearing from the outside world that the police detachment guarding the empty hall refused (with threats of arrest) to allow on to the steps of the court building the citizens wishing to attend the hearing. It was only after many requests that the accused's wife and sister were allowed (on account of the severe cold) to await the end of the hearing in the vestibule.[7]

When in June 1978 the Donetsk regional court ordered that the coal miner and labour rights activist, Vladimir Klebanov, be confined to a special psychiatric hospital, neither he nor his relatives were informed in advance of the court hearing.

The most important criticism that can be made of court hearings of such cases is their uncritical attitude toward the psychiatric diagnoses submitted. The psychiatric diagnoses cited below, and others, are at the very least questionable as recommendations for court action. One course of action which is available to courts presented with unclear, incomplete or contested diagnoses is to call for a second psychiatric opinion. This is rarely done, and when courts do ask for a second opinion it is always from officially-appointed psychiatrists, never psychiatrists nominated by the accused or their families. Soviet courts in political cases almost invariably accept not only the findings of forensic psychiatric commissions, but also their recommendations as to what should be done with the accused.

If, as normally happens, the court accepts the psychiatric commission's diagnosis and recommendations, it must then release the accused from criminal responsibility or punishment and order measures that are both conducive to the individual's medical recovery and protective of society.

The court has three options: it may order that the accused be placed in the care of relatives or a guardian; confined for an indefinite period to an ordinary psychiatric hospital; or confined indefinitely to a special psychiatric hospital.

Putting the accused in the care of relatives or a guardian does not entail incarceration. In no known political case has a court exercised this option.

If the court, advised by a forensic psychiatric commission, decides that the accused requires compulsory in-patient medical treatment, it orders that he or she be confined either to an ordinary or a special psychiatric hospital for an indefinite period. According to the RSFSR Criminal Code, ordinary psychiatric hospitals are intended for those who have not committed especially serious crimes; the special institutions are designed for people who "represent a special danger to society". A 1966 official textbook on Soviet criminal law cited as its example of a person sent by court to an *ordinary* psychiatric hospital a certain "B", a Leningrad woman

> who during an argument with her neighbour slashed her in the face with a
> large table knife and, after dislodging several teeth, inflicted less serious
> wounds to her body.

It has been common for courts to order that dissenters be confined to special psychiatric hospitals in the absence of any record of violence on their part, let alone any effort on the part of psychiatrists or the courts to show that they represented a "special danger" to other people or to society.

Two cases where courts have made a ruling that differed from the recommendation of the forensic psychiatric commission were those of Vyacheslav Igrunov and Nikolai Sorokin.

Vyacheslav Igrunov, an electrician, was arrested in Odessa in 1975 and charged with "anti-Soviet slander" after police found *samizdat* writings in his possession. A forensic psychiatric commission in Odessa could not reach agreement as to his mental condition so he was sent for a second examination to the Serbsky Institute in Moscow, which prepared a report saying that he was suffering from "schizophrenia" and that he was "of great social danger". The Institute recommended that he be confined to a special psychiatric hospital. The court in Odessa which heard the case in March 1976 accepted the Institute's findings that Igrunov was "not accountable", but ruled that he be confined to an ordinary psychiatric hospital rather than a special psychiatric hospital. The Serbsky Institute psychiatrist who testified at the trial said that Igrunov's mental condition had improved since he had been diagnosed and that therefore the recommendation of the psychiatric commission at the Institute could be rejected.

In the case of Nikolai Sorokin, a worker from Voroshilovgrad, a court applied a tougher measure than was recommended by psychiatrists. Sorokin was arrested in 1977 and charged with "anti-Soviet slander" after police found in his possession "various notes libelling the Soviet political and social system". A forensic psychiatric commission concluded that he was "not accountable" because of "schizophrenia" and recommended that he be confined to an ordinary psychiatric hospital. The local court overruled this recommendation and ordered that he be confined instead to a special psychiatric hospital.

In some cases courts have ordered that dissenters be sent for forensic psychiatric examination even though forensic psychiatrists had already examined the subject and concluded that he or she was "accountable". For example, this happened in March 1979 to Vladislav Bebko, who was charged with "malicious hooliganism" for tearing down an official poster celebrating the anniversary of the October Revolution and "anti-Soviet slander" for making "oral propaganda" and distributing documents of the Czechoslovak human rights group Charter 77. Bebko was subsequently ruled "accountable" again and sentenced to 3 years' imprisonment for "anti-Soviet slander".

## Civil Procedures for Forcible Commitment

Under the *civil commitment procedure* (sometimes referred to as the "administrative" procedure) people who have not committed criminal offences but who are diagnosed as mentally ill and are likely to commit socially dangerous acts may be forcibly confined for treatment on the authority of a psychiatrist and with the subsequent agreement of a commission of three psychiatrists. Those committed under this civil procedure are normally confined in ordinary psychiatric hospitals.

The civil commitment procedure is laid down in a directive ("On Emergency Confinement of Mentally Ill Persons Who Represent a Social Danger") issued on 26 August 1971 by the Ministry of Health in agreement with the Procurator General and the MVD. The text of this directive is not published in any easily available Soviet publication and it is virtually a secret document.[8]

The directive states that mentally ill people may be confined to a psychiatric hospital without their permission or that of the family if they are an "evident danger" to themselves or those around them. To guide psychiatric practitioners and law enforcement agencies, the directive lists a number of symptoms which are to serve as criteria for application of this measure. The list has been criticized by human rights activists and foreign psychiatrists because of the obscurity and lack of medical precision of the symptoms listed. The terms used are so broad as to cover almost any dissident or nonconformist behaviour: for example, among the symptoms listed are "a hypochondriac delusion, causing an abnormal aggressive attitude in the ill person towards individuals, organizations and institutions" and "a systematic syndrome of delusions with chronic deterioration if it results in behaviour dangerous to society". The directive does not give even a rough explanation of what is meant by "social danger".

As if deliberately to invite the forcible confinement of peaceful citizens, the directive states that any of the enumerated conditions of "mental illness"... "may be accompanied by externally correct behaviour and dissimulation".

The directive states that emergency confinement may be effected by medical personnel, and that the police must render assistance if there is a "possibility" that the subject will resist or if he or she shows aggressive behaviour or hides, or if the subject's family refuses or resists his or her being taken away.

The doctor who first orders the person's confinement must submit to the psychiatric hospital a report justifying this, and within one day of being confined the subject must be examined by a commission of three psychiatrists who are to decide whether the forcible confinement was justified and if there is a need for further confinement. The subject must be re-examined by a commission of three psychiatrists at least once a month. The commission must order the subject's release "upon improvement of the patient's mental condition or such change of the picture of the illness that he is no longer a danger to society". In discharging a person from confinement, the psychiatric hospital must inform the local psychiatric dispensary at his or her place of residence, and the released person must be placed on a "special list" and receive "systematic preventive treatment".

The directive does not provide for any involvement of a court or other judicial agencies. The regulations do not indicate any right of the confined person to have access to a lawyer; Amnesty International knows of no case where a dissenter confined in this way has been permitted to see a lawyer. The only agency outside the psychiatric service which is given a formal role under these procedures is the police, which is administered by the MVD. In practice, the KGB has in many cases played a major part at various stages between confinement and release.

Dissenters have been forcibly confined to psychiatric hospitals in a great variety of circumstances, a common feature being the direct link between the dissenters' exercise of their human rights and the official decision to have them confined to a psychiatric hospital. It is quite common for dissenters to be forcibly confined without having been seen first by a psychiatrist.

Dissenters have been picked up and taken directly to psychiatric hospitals from work, school, home, or off the streets. The abruptness of the procedure is illustrated by the case of Valeria Novodvorskaya, a linguist, who was detained at her place of work in a Moscow library on 24 November 1978 less than a month after she was publicly involved in the formation of an independent trade union group (see Chapter 1). According to a *samizdat* account of her detention:

> At 5.45 pm on the day of her hospitalization a man came into the room
> where she was working and asked her to help him take away some books.
> She took a package of books, went out and did not return. A colleague who
> was working with her in the same room waited for a long time and then
> became apprehensive and raised the alarm. After lengthy searching her friends
> found her in Psychiatric Hospital Number 15 (telephone number 114-53-89).

In a number of instances dissenters have been summoned on some pretext to a hospital, militia headquarters or other public building, where, to their surprise, they were taken to a psychiatrist who had them committed to a psychiatric hospital. For example, in July 1976 Alexander Argentov, a participant in a religious seminar in Moscow which had been labelled "anti-Soviet" by state security officials, was unexpectedly summoned to a local Military Commission, a body which deals with military conscription. The Military Commission told him that he must report to a district psychiatric clinic to obtain a medical certificate. Although Argentov had never been under psychiatric treatment or observation, the clinic already had a file card about him. Two doctors there questioned him (mainly about his religious views) and had him immediately committed to Moscow Psychiatric Hospital Number 14.

A number of people have been detained and forcibly confined to psychiatric hospitals when they brought personal complaints to the highest organs of government. A startling indication of the extent to which this happens came in October 1976, when the Moscow Helsinki monitoring group reported:

Every day the police sends to the duty psychiatrists approximately 12 people from the reception room of the USSR Supreme Soviet alone; besides these, another two or three of those people who try to get into an embassy; still others who are picked up from other places, including directly off the streets. Of these about half are subsequently hospitalized.

One person who was confined in this way was Ivan Kopysov, a war veteran who had been denied work and been harassed by the state security authorities after writing letters to Alexander Solzhenitsyn. In a subsequent letter to the Presidium of the USSR Supreme Soviet, Kopysov described his detention as follows:

On 10 November 1976 I decided to take my complaint to the Presidium of the USSR Supreme Soviet. In the reception hall I was received at 10.00 am in consulting room number 10 by a most respectful and sympathetic woman. She questioned me sensitively and I frankly told her of all my misadventures. Then she said: "Wait for ten minutes in the corridor." I was so happy! I was convinced that now everything would be fixed up. They would help me get back to a normal way of life... But when I went back to the cabinet there were three men there, looking like bouncers. They took me by the arms and dragged me through a back door to an ambulance. My "good" fairy tenderly smiled after me. They soon had me undressed in psychiatric hospital number 7 in Moscow city. Later they took me to the Orlovka psychiatric hospital in Voronezh region.

Kopysov has reported also that while he was in Moscow Psychiatric Hospital Number 7 he saw people "from all over Moscow" who had been picked up and taken to psychiatric hospitals when they submitted complaints " in the reception rooms of ministries and central offices and even in the reception room of the Central Committee of the Communist Party of the Soviet Union".

People who are forcibly confined for submitting complaints are commonly diagnosed as suffering from a "mania for litigation".

Violations of the regulations laid down in the 1971 directive governing civil confinement have been common. Frequently the relatives of the confined person have not been informed within 24 hours of what has happened, as is required by the directive. Often the subjects have been examined by a psychiatrist only after they were forcibly confined to a psychiatric hospital. In many cases dissenters have not been examined by a psychiatric commission within one day of being detained, as is required by the directive, but only days or weeks later; and in a number of cases confined dissenters have not had any psychiatric examination at all.

Frequently confined dissenters have not been examined every month by a psychiatric commission, as the directive requires. When Yevgeny Nikolayev was confined to the Kashchenko Psychiatric Hospital in Moscow in 1978, he asked his doctor why he was not being examined by a commission each month. According to Nikolayev's subsequent account, their conversation went as follows:

Doctor: "I will not call a commission."

Nikolayev: "Why not? "

Doctor: "Because even without a commission it is obvious that you need treatment."

Nikolayev: "But a Directive of the USSR Ministry of Health calls for a regular summoning of a commission, at least once a month."

Doctor: "We cannot call the commission together just for the sake of form. We have about three thousand patients in this hospital and we can't call a commission for each of them."

## *Diagnosis*

Under both the criminal and civil procedure the psychiatric diagnosis is invariably carried out by officially appointed psychiatrists. Dissenters have never been able to obtain the appointment of psychiatrists of their own choice to the psychiatric commissions that decide whether or not they should be hospitalized. In a number of cases officially-appointed psychiatrists are known to have concealed their names from the people they were diagnosing.

Under both procedures diagnoses are generally perfunctory and even in formal terms are based on inadequate examination of the subject. Dissenters who have been sent under the criminal procedure to the Serbsky Institute of Forensic Psychiatry in Moscow, officially regarded as the country's leading centre for forensic psychiatric diagnosis, have reported that their diagnosis has consisted of several conversations with a psychiatrist assigned to their case and then a few minutes (as a rule "10 or 15 minutes", according to Alexander Podrabinek) in front of the psychiatric commission whose task it is to establish whether the subjects are accountable and to recommend on the measures to be applied to them. Both in the Serbsky Institute and elsewhere, psychiatrists base their diagnoses almost exclusively on "subjective" observations (from conversations with the subjects, from visual observation of their behaviour, and from their record) and make little use of objective testing methods.[9] As mentioned above, sometimes dissenters have been confined to psychiatric hospitals under the civil procedure without any psychiatric diagnosis at all.

The following features are common to those cases of confinement of dissenters to psychiatric hospitals mentioned in this report:

(1) In each case the subject had exercised his or her human rights in a manner which was not approved of by the authorities and which has often been punished in other cases by imprisonment under criminal law. The most common forms of behaviour which have been punished by forcible psychiatric confinement have been: expressing views critical of government practices, whether in written or in oral form; submitting to government authorities complaints against government officials; engaging in public demonstrations for purposes disapproved-of by the authorities; belonging to unofficial groups informally labelled "anti-Soviet" or "illegal" by state security or other

government officials; participating in religious activities; making persistent efforts to gain official permission to emigrate from the country; trying to leave the country without official permission. In many cases the forcible psychiatric confinement of the subject took place only after the authorities had tried by other means to deter him or her from engaging in such activities. In many cases it was exactly such exercise of human rights which officially-appointed psychiatrists labelled as symptomatic of mental illness.

(2) Neither the subject nor his or her relatives, friends and sympathizers believed the subject to be in need of forcible in-patient psychiatric treatment. Many prisoners of conscience have been permitted to emigrate after being released from psychiatric hospitals, and have been seen by psychiatrists and other individuals abroad who formed the view that their psychiatric confinement was not justified on medical grounds. Foreign psychiatrists have reached similar conclusions after examining former victims during visits to the USSR. During the period from 1977 to 1979 Dr Alexander Voloshanovich, a Moscow psychiatrist who lent his expert services to the unofficial Working Commission for the Investigation of the Use of Psychiatry for Political Purposes, gave in-depth psychiatric examinations to 36 dissenters who feared they might be forcibly confined to psychiatric hospitals. Most of the 36 had previously been forcibly confined to psychiatric hospitals. Dr Voloshanovich concluded that none of them required forcible hospitalization on any grounds nor had they required this in the past.

(3) The subjects were not known to have any record of violence nor did the authorities or the psychiatrists involved demonstrate how they were dangerous to themselves or others.

Yet between mid-1975 and mid-1979 in more than 100 known such cases officially-appointed psychiatrists ruled that dissenters were mentally ill to such a degree that compulsory in-patient psychiatric treatment was necessary.

A simple indication of how psychiatric diagnoses have been used for political persecution is that often when Soviet citizens have associated together in activities, which, though not illegal, were not approved of by the authorities, several of the participants have been officially diagnosed as mentally ill and forcibly confined to psychiatric hospitals — as though the group's participants were mentally ill *en masse*. The following are cases in point.

In 1971 seven members of an unofficial group advocating Marxist-Leninist views different from those enforced by the Communist Party of the Soviet Union were arrested in Leningrad and charged with "anti-Soviet agitation and propaganda". Four of them were ruled mentally ill and confined to psychiatric hospitals: Vyacheslav Dzibalov, Sergei Purtov, Andrei Kozlov and Mariya Musiyenko.

In 1971 Alexei Kotov, who had reportedly spent some 40 years in camps and psychiatric hospitals for propagating his Orthodox religious beliefs, was released from a psychiatric hospital in Vladimir region into the guardianship of Faina Komarova, a cleaner at the psychiatric hospital and herself a religious believer. Reportedly, both were detained a year later, ruled mentally ill and confined to special psychiatric hospitals, he to the one in Sychyovka and she to the one in Kazan.

In 1972 nine people were arrested in Siberia for organizing and participating in a "secret Buddhist sect". Four of them were ruled mentally ill and ordered confined to psychiatric hospitals: Yury Lavrov, Vladimir Montlevich, Alexander Zheleznov and Donatus Butkus.

During the mid-1970s two brothers, Alexander and Mikhail Shatravka, were arrested while trying to cross the border into Finland without permission from the Soviet authorities. Both were subsequently ruled mentally ill and ordered confined to special psychiatric hospitals.

In 1976 an entire family of religious believers (both parents and two daughters) were confined to a psychiatric hospital in Byelorussia on account of their religious faith, according to a prisoner of conscience who was himself held there at the time.

In 1974 a group of Russian Orthodox believers in Moscow organized a seminar to discuss religious and philosophical matters. Officials subsequently told participants that the seminar was "anti-Soviet". Of at least eight people who have been arrested since 1976 in connection with the seminar, four (Alexander Argentov, Edward Fedotov, Alexander Kuzkin and Alexander Pushkin) were confined to psychiatric hospitals under the civil procedure and another (Sergei Yermolayev) was confined to the Serbsky Institute for diagnosis under the criminal procedure, but subsequently ruled accountable.

A number of workers grouped together in Moscow in 1976 to protest collectively at violations of their labour rights. By early 1978 no less than five of the groups leading members had been confined to psychiatric hospitals: Vladimir Klebanov, Yevgeny Nikolayev, Gavriil Yankov, Gennady Tsvyrko and Varvara Kucherenko. (Another member was sentenced to imprisonment.)

In late 1978 another group announced that they were forming a similar unofficial trade union group. Within three weeks one founding member, Valeriya Novodvorskaya, was confined to a psychiatric hospital. (Four other members of this group were arrested, tried and sentenced to imprisonment or exile after announcing their participation in it.)

In November 1978 Vladislav Bebko, a student, was arrested in Kuybyshev and charged with tearing down an official poster celebrating the October Revolution. He was subsequently charged with "anti-Soviet slander" as well after police found in his possession tape recordings of foreign radio broadcasts and documents of the Czechoslovak human rights group Charter 77. In March 1979 a court ordered him sent for an in-patient psychiatric examination. Later in the same month, Anatoly Sarbayev and Victor Ryzhov, two of Bebko's associates who had appeared as witnesses at the court hearing, were also confined to psychiatric hospitals in Kuybyshev.

Since the early 1970s enough has been known about the nature of diagnoses by officially-appointed psychiatrists in cases of political and religious dissenters to identify a number of common features.

First, such diagnoses usually give only a vague, generalized explanation of the mental illness from which the subject is purportedly suffering and the nature of the symptoms. Professor Andrei Snezhnevsky, Director of the Institute of

Psychiatry of the USSR Academy of Medical Sciences and, through him, the Serbsky Institute of Forensic Psychiatry in Moscow have provided a strong lead for the country's psychiatrists in making such diagnoses. Snezhnevsky's most distinctive contribution to Soviet psychiatry has been his extremely broad definition of schizophrenia, an illness which in his interpretation need not be accompanied by external symptoms even when it is serious enough to justify forcible hospitalization. Schizophrenia, often in its "sluggish" form, has been the diagnosis most commonly made of dissenters. Alexander Kuzkin, a young Orthodox Christian, has reported that while he was confined to a Moscow psychiatric hospital in late 1978 and early 1979 the hospital's chief doctor, R.D. Smirnov, told him "that Christ and all his apostles were schizophrenics and that this had long ago been proved scientifically".

The following are examples of how officially-appointed psychiatrists have characterized the mental illness of dissenters: "nervous exhaustion brought on by her search for justice" (Nadezhda Gaidar in 1976); "psychopathic paranoia with overvalued ideas and tendencies to litigation" (Mikhail Zhikharev in 1974); "schizophrenia with religious delirium" (Alexander Voloshchuk in 1977); "reformist delusions" or "reformist ideas" (Yevgeny Nikolayev in 1978); "psychopathy with tendency to litigation" (Alexander Komarov in 1978); "delusional ideas of reformism and struggle with the existing social political system in the USSR" (Vladimir Rozhdestvov, 1978); a "mania for reconstructing society" (Mikhail Kukobaka, 1976).

Another common characteristic of official diagnoses of dissenters is that "seemingly normal" people have often been labelled "dangerously mentally ill". The broad rejection of "apparent normality" as an obstacle to forcible hospitalization derives authority both from the theories of Professor Snezhnevsky and the Serbsky Institute and from the 1971 directive governing civil commitment to psychiatric hospitals (summarized above). The view that only a select group of officially-appointed psychiatrists are able to judge correctly people's mental health was put succinctly in 1973 in a statement by a group of the most prominent Soviet psychiatrists. The statement was widely publicized within the USSR and sent to foreign newspapers for publication:

There is a small number of mental cases whose disease, as a result of a mental derangement, paranoia and other psycho-pathological symptoms, can lead them to anti-social actions which fall into the category of those that are prohibited by law, such as disturbance of public order, dissemination of slander, manifestation of aggressive intentions, etc. It is noteworthy that they can do this after preliminary preparations, with a "cunningly calculated plan of action", as the founder of Russian forensic psychiatry V.P. Serbsky, who was widely known for his progressive views, wrote. To the people around them such mental cases do not create the impression of being obviously "insane". Most often these persons are suffering from schizophrenia or a paranoid pathological development of the personality. Such cases are well-known both by Soviet and foreign psychiatrists.

The seeming normality of such sick persons when they commit socially dangerous actions is used by anti-Soviet propaganda for slanderous contentions that these persons are not suffering from a mental disorder.10

The consequences of dismissing "seeming normality" as a decisive criterion in psychiatric analysis are well illustrated by the case of Olga Iofe. Born in 1950, she became involved in the distribution of *samizdat* in 1966 and was arrested in 1969 on charges of "anti-Soviet agitation and propaganda". She was diagnosed by a psychiatric commission at the Serbsky Institute, which declared that she was suffering from "creeping schizophrenia". When her case was heard in court on 20 August 1970, the court rejected a defence petition to allow her to be present in person at the hearing, but allowed her parents to represent her. According to *A Chronical of Current Events*, "all the witnesses" testified in court that in their opinion she was of sound mind and of good character. To Dr Martynenko, chairman of the psychiatric diagnosis commission, this was irrelevant, as is indicated by the following exchange between Olga Iofe's defence counsel, Yury Pozdeyev and the doctor:

Question: "Exactly what physiological tests were carried out to establish that she was suffering from an illness?"

Answer: "Such physiological tests are carried out on everybody without exception. The absence of symptoms of an illness cannot prove the absence of the illness itself."

Question: "On the basis of exactly what remarks did the commission establish that her thought-processes were functioning on different levels? Describe even one of the tests administered to Olga by means of which major disturbances of her thought-processes were established, or give even one remark by her which suggested such disturbances."

Answer: "I am unable to give a concrete answer, and if the court requires one it will be necessary to send to the Serbsky Institute for the history of the illness. However, her reaction to being taken to the Serbsky Institute may serve as an example of her behaviour. She knew where she had been taken and realized what this meant, but she showed no sign of emotion, the tone of her voice didn't even change."

Question: "Do you not ascribe Olga's behaviour to her self-control, strength of will and serenity, of which the witnesses have spoken?"

Answer: "It's impossible to control oneself to that extent."

Question: "How do you explain the fact that the presence of an illness, which, according to the diagnosis, has been developing in O. Iofe since she was 14, did not prevent her from successfully graduating from the mathematical school and entering the university?"

Answer: "The presence of this form of schizophrenia does not presuppose changes in the personality noticeable to others."

Despite the absence in Olga Iofe of obvious symptoms of mental illness and despite the absence of any indication that her behaviour was physically dangerous, the psychiatric commission recommended that she be sent to a special psychiatric hospital: that is, an institution legally designated for people who represent "a special danger to society".

In their *Handbook on Psychiatry for Dissidents*, a *samizdat* document prepared in a Perm corrective labour colony in 1974, the prisoners of conscience Semyon Gluzman, a psychiatrist, and Vladimir Bukovsky, a former victim of psychiatric abuse, discussed the absence of any clear demarcation between "normal" expression of opinions and manifestations of "creeping schizophrenia" and "pathological development of the personality" as formulated by Soviet psychiatrists in the Serbsky Institute:

> ...the demonstrability of this sort of illness ("creeping schizophrenia" and "pathological development of the personality") is very limited. Conversely, try to prove that your opinion about the occupation of Czechoslovakia or about the absence of democratic freedoms in the USSR is not a mistaken opinion but on the contrary has a real basis. Or that the shadowing of you and your near ones is not "persecution mania". Or that your subjective evaluation of domestic political life in the USSR is not immaterial when related to actual facts. Or that your "release" from your job after you added your signature to a "statement of protest" is an infringement of your rights.

This handbook advised people threatened with compulsory detention in a psychiatric hospital how best to convince examining psychiatrists of their sanity:

> It is fatal to emphasize the moral qualities of the dissidents: truthfulness, honour and sympathy, because that would mean giving truthful responses which harm oneself and provide the psychiatrist with the symptoms he needs.

Bukovsky and Gluzman recommended that political dissenters tell the psychiatrists that their political activities were due to ignorance of the possible consequences and by desire for fame. If, nonetheless, they were confined to a psychiatric hospital, they should use "every possible tactical trick" to convince the psychiatrists that they had changed their political views.

Another feature of official psychiatric diagnoses of dissenters is that they have commonly focused precisely on the subjects' exercise of their human rights as symptomatic of mental illness. When subjects have refused to accept that their behaviour was brought on by mental illness, psychiatrists have often described this as "lack of criticism". Typical of this was the case of Pyotr Starchik, who was diagnosed in 1973 as suffering from "creeping schizophrenia" and confined to a special psychiatric hospital. The symptoms identified by an officially-appointed forensic psychiatric commission included his religious belief and his "rudeness" to the investigators of his case. After his release in 1975 Starchik, an amateur composer, held concerts of his songs in his Moscow flat which were attended by large audiences. In the summer of 1976 state security officials warned him that if he continued to hold these concerts he would be confined to a psychiatric hospital again. In September 1976 he was forcibly committed to an ordinary psychiatric hospital in Moscow. Reportedly the hospital's admittance journal explained his forcible commitment thus:

> S.D. [socially dangerous]. Was an in-patient in the psychiatric hospital in Kazan for compulsory treatment under Article 70. Recently he has been composing songs of anti-Soviet content and has been holding gatherings of 40 or 50 people in his flat. On examination he was well-orientated. There were no major disturbances of his consciousness. His contact was formal. He

was suspicious. He answered questions monosyllabically. He does not deny having composed the songs, and said "I have my own world views." Lacks critical faculty.

When the Orthodox believer Alexander Argentov was examined by two psychiatrists in a Moscow psychiatric clinic in July 1976, the diagnostic session opened as follows, according to Argentov's subsequent account:

— "So you believe in God? "
— "Yes, I believe in God", answered Argentov.
— "And you go to church? "
— "I go to church."
— "But how can you believe in God in this age? ... And pray to icons? "

Still according to Argentov's account, one of the two psychiatrists continued: "In our age of the flowering of space technology it is impossible to believe in God. That is forgiveable only for illiterate old people." The psychiatrists ordered Argentov's forcible commitment to a psychiatric hospital. According to Argentov: "The parting words of the doctor at the clinic was that in the hospital they would 'beat all this nonsense out of me', meaning my religious faith."

Another case in point is that of Mikhail Kukobaka, a worker who was arrested in 1970 and charged with "anti-Soviet slander". He was ruled "not accountable" and was confined first to the Sychyovka Special Psychiatric Hospital, then to an ordinary psychiatric hospital until mid-1976. After his release he wrote an account of the inhuman conditions in the Sychyovka institution, and this document circulated in *samizdat*. In October 1976 he was again confined to a psychiatric hospital, this time an ordinary psychiatric hospital in Mogilev, near his place of residence in the Byelorussian Republic. According to his subsequent account, the doctors stated that a symptom of his "mental illness" was that he had hung over his bed in the hostel where he was living a religious icon and photographs of two dissenters, Academician Sakharov and General Pyotr Grigorenko. Kukobaka reported in a letter to a friend:

The doctor treating me, Nadezhda Matveyevna Drabkina of the third section, told me: "Hanging up icons and pictures of such people as Academician Sakharov and General Grigorenko is contrary to our accepted way of life, and so it is abnormal."

The case of Vladimir Rozhdestvov is also illustrative of the way in which official diagnoses of dissenters have seen the subject's beliefs as symptomatic of mental illness. Rozhdestvov was confined to a psychiatric hospital in Kaluga in September 1977, charged with "anti-Soviet slander" and diagnosed as suffering from "schizophrenia" by a forensic psychiatric commission which recommended that he be confined to a special psychiatric hospital. The grounds for this diagnosis were indicated by the psychiatrist L. Tronina, the expert witness at Rozhdestvov's court hearing, in response to questioning by Rozhdestvov's defence lawyer, N. Ya. Nemerinskaya.

Defence Counsel: "In what way was the behaviour of Rozhdestvov delirious? "
Expert: "All his remarks and his behaviour bore the mark of anti-Soviet

views."

Defence Counsel: "What form did his delirium take? "

Expert: "He did not respond to correction."

Defence Counsel: "What does that mean? He had written that he would be true to his convictions until death. Is that delirium? "

Expert: "He expressed ideas about reorganization, anti-Soviet remarks."

Defence Counsel: "But these ideas can be those of a healthy person. How can you confirm that these ideas are not anti-Soviet but delirious? "

Expert: "They do not respond to correction. I do not wish to add anything further."

Defence Counsel: "You are not able to or you do not wish to? "

Expert: "I do not wish to."

Defence Counsel: "Apart from the delirious ideas of reform, did Rozhdestvov have any other delirious ideas, for instance, of persecution? "

Expert: "Not yet."

Defence Counsel: "What characteristics of Rozhdestvov's psychology give grounds for putting him in a special psychiatric hospital? "

Expert: "Long-term treatment of the illness, its incurable nature, that is, it does not respond to treatment."

The court accepted the conclusion and recommendation of the forensic psychiatric commission and ordered Rozhdestvov confined to a special psychiatric hospital.

Another characteristic of the diagnosis of dissenters by officially-appointed psychiatrists is that very often the state security authorities have played a direct role in the decision-making of the psychiatrists, often to the extent of deciding themselves what the diagnosis should be.

One of the many documented illustrations of this comes from the case of Anatoly Ponomaryov, a Leningrad engineer who has been repeatedly confined to psychiatric hospitals throughout the 1970s for his *samizdat* writings and his open protests to the authorities. When in October 1975 he was forcibly confined for the fourth time, another well-known dissenter, the historian Mikhail Bernstam, accidentally learned of it at once and went to see Dr L.D. Fedoseyeva, the deputy chief doctor of the psychiatric clinic where Ponomaryov had been diagnosed and ordered committed. The psychiatrist told Bernstam that the reason for Ponomaryov's hospitalization was his protest letters, which "hindered the work of public bodies". She added that the fact that Ponomaryov's behaviour was "otherwise normal" did not indicate that he was mentally healthy. Their conversation then took the following turn:

Bernstam: "What sort of letters were they? "

Dr Fedoseyeva: "Neither I nor the doctor treating him has read the letters but we know their contents. They are the letters of an ill man. They aren't anti-Soviet but in them he expresses a low opinion of the Soviet government and in general writes cynically about our leaders."

Bernstam: "If you haven't read the letters how do you justify Ponomaryov's hospitalization? "

Dr Fedoseyeva: "We possess the information and an evaluation from the competent authorities."

Bernstam: "Which authorities do you mean? "

Dr Fedoseyeva: "Surely you understand... "

Bernstam: "Nonetheless? "

Dr Fedoseyeva: "Well, officials of the KGB."

Bernstam: "You said the letters were a symptom of an aggravation of the patient's illness. But are KGB officials really competent to make such judgments?"

Dr Fedoseyeva: "They make a political judgement and phone us, advising us to intern Ponomaryov. For us to make a medical diagnosis it's enough simply to know of the existence of anti-government letters. There's no need to read them."

Soviet psychiatrists have frequently told the subjects of their diagnoses: "Nothing depends on us."

## Treatment in Psychiatric Hospitals

The conditions of imprisonment of prisoners of conscience or others who are ruled mentally ill depends in large measure on whether they are confined to special psychiatric hospitals or ordinary psychiatric hospitals. Special psychiatric hospitals are more secretive institutions and partly because of this are characterized by more severe ill-treatment of their inmates than are most ordinary psychiatric hospitals. Inmates of both types of institutions are commonly given arbitrary treatment with drugs and other psychiatric methods.

## Special Psychiatric Hospitals

Special psychiatric hospitals (SPHs) are designated in Soviet law for the forcible confinement of mentally ill persons who are "especially dangerous". *Samizdat* sources have mentioned the following such institutions: the Dnepropetrovsk SPH, the Chernyakhovsk SPH, the Leningrad SPH (sometimes called the *Arsenalynaya*), the Oryol SPH, the Kazan SPH, the Sychyovka SPH, the Smolensk SPH, the Talgar SPH (sometimes called Alma-Ata SPH), the Tashkent SPH, the Kzyl-Orda SPH, the Blagoveshchensk SPH and the Rybinsk SPH.

People forcibly confined to a special psychiatric hospital normally spend several years there, and in some cases up to 15 or 20 years.

There is no legal code governing conditions of detention in such hospitals as there is for corrective labour institutions. Commentaries on the passages in the criminal and civil legislation which deal with this form of detention practically ignore conditions in and functioning of the special psychiatric hospitals, which are evidently regulated by ministerial regulations.

The only published directive on the operation of psychiatric hospitals and the only one cited by official Soviet sources dates from 14 February 1967. It is entitled "Directive on the System of Application of Compulsory Treatment and Other Measures of Medical Character in relation to Mentally Ill Persons who have Committed Socially Dangerous Acts". This document contains only 30 brief articles, and a large proportion of its contents is devoted to repetition of general clauses in the criminal and civil procedural codes. As for the actual operation of psychiatric hospitals, the 1967 directive is almost exclusively devoted to the system of documentation of inmates' cases and to their pension rights. This directive in no way regulates conditions of detention. Whereas the corrective labour codes are open to criticism for failing to provide sufficiently detailed published regulations, no published regulations at all are available regarding conditions in special psychiatric hospitals.

This situation reflects and perpetuates the most important and disadvantageous peculiarity of the position of inmates of psychiatric hospitals: withdrawal of their status as rational subjects of the law. This status is specifically granted to inmates of corrective labour institutions: they formally retain the rights of Soviet citizens, with limitations, and they have the formal right to protest at violations of the law to which they have been subjected. Individuals committed to psychiatric hospitals are apparently not formally denied their status as citizens with the right to claim legal redress in the event of such violations. However, the omission in law of specific guarantees of retention of this status has opened the possibility for its complete removal in practice.

A most important consequence of this is that inmates of Soviet special psychiatric hospitals have no guaranteed process by which to seek redress of psychiatric and juridical errors or abuses. They may write letters only at the discretion of their doctors, and then usually only to relatives. They are normally not allowed to have writing materials except at specific times for writing letters. Doctors can, in the course of prescribing treatment, forbid an inmate to read or write.

In a number of cases dissenters in special psychiatric hospitals have been punished for describing their conditions in letters or secret messages to people on the outside.

Inmates of special psychiatric hospitals are permitted visits only with close relatives, usually twice a month for up to two hours, according to unofficial accounts. In most cases these visiting privileges cannot be used much, as dissenters are commonly sent to hospitals far from their homes, often several thousand kilometers away. They have no contact with legal authorities. Although, as far as Amnesty International knows, they are not forbidden by law to consult a lawyer, it is extremely rare for an inmate to have any contact with a lawyer while in detention. Nor are they allowed to write to the Procuracy, although the Procuracy is legally charged with supervision of psychiatric institutions.

Throughout their confinement in a special psychiatric hospital, inmates are virtually cut off from the outside world, and are "at the disposal" of the authorities who administer the institutions and the psychiatrists who staff them.

Special psychiatric hospitals operate under the direct authority of the MVD rather than of the health authorities. They are operated like prisons. Several of them (the Oryol, Chernyakhovsk and Dnepropetrovsk SPHs) are housed in former prison buildings, while the Sychyovka SPH is located next to a corrective labour colony. They are heavily guarded with watchtowers, barbed wire, armed and uniformed MVD personnel and dogs.

According to all accounts, not only the security and administrative staff but also virtually all the leading medical personnel of special psychiatric hospitals hold rank in the MVD. One of the main complaints about these institutions is that considerations of security and discipline are given complete priority over considerations of the medical well-being of the inmates. Inmates are subject to a strict regime. Their correspondence, visits, receipt of parcels, access to toilets and smoking areas, daily exercise and personal possessions are strictly regulated and may be arbitrarily taken away. They are under constant supervision. Lights are on all night in the wards. They are expected to obey any orders given them by any of the staff. This policy is made particularly dangerous and inhumane by the heinous practice of recruiting convicted criminal prisoners from the corrective labour institutions to serve as orderlies in such hospitals.

According to an anonymous "witness" who spent time in the Sychyovka corrective labour colony in the early 1970s, at any given time 200 prisoners from that colony worked as orderlies in the adjacent psychiatric hospital. Other accounts indicate that this practice obtains in all other special psychiatric hospitals in the USSR.

Arbitrary, often sadistic and sometimes fatal beatings of inmates in a number of special psychiatric hospitals have been reported time and again. By all accounts, not only the criminal orderlies but also administrative and medical staff have ferociously beaten helpless and non-violent inmates.

The most detailed accounts in recent years have concerned the Sychyovka Special Psychiatric Hospital, which stands apart from any other institution of imprisonment in the USSR for the horror with which it is regarded by dissenters and prisoners of conscience.

Prisoners of conscience who have been held in the Sychyovka Special Psychiatric Hospital (Mikhail Kukobaka, Iosif Tereliya, Yury Belov) have said that staff members there refer to beatings of the inmates as treatment with "*kulazin*", an amalgam of the Russian word for fist (*kulak*) and the name of the drug aminazin.

In the mid-1970s an eye-witness recounted the following conversation with a prisoner from the corrective labour colony at Sychyovka who had worked as an orderly in the special psychiatric hospital there:

— "It's good to work in the nuthouse: there's always someone to hit in the mouth."

— "But why hit people? "

— "Here's why. You're standing in the middle of a corridor. A fool comes along, slinking against the wall. You're bored, you see. You just give him one in the mouth, and it cheers you up."

Another orderly, a tall, husky, healthy fellow, complained:

— "My hands hurt today."

— "Why do they hurt? "

— "I cudgelled a fool."

Mikhail Kukobaka reported of his stay in the Sychyovka Special Psychiatric Hospital in the mid-1970s:

I do not remember one case in 32 months when someone's health improved instead of the opposite. A typical example was that of a certain Ovanesiyan, an Assyrian from somewhere near the Black Sea. He was in for murdering his mother. The old-timers said that when he was brought into the hospital he was a confident man. He had an imposing appearance, his teeth were capped with gold, he was well-dressed... Any psychiatric disturbances in him were unnoticeable, or almost so, even to specialists. Because of countless beatings and huge doses of various tablets he developed a stomach disorder, he became almost unable to walk, and when he did move about he held on to the walls. He carried out every demand of the orderlies without question, whether it was to swallow a frog or a beatle, or to suffer with tears in his eyes while the orderlies put a bee on his nose or his lips and were amused when his face twisted up from the sting.

It is interesting that when talking with Ovanesiyan one was struck by the sensibility and logic of his speech and at the same time by his absolute indifference to himself and his situation. It was a depressing sight when they finally released him, ruling him to be "not socially dangerous", and took him to the bus. He was a formless hulk, scarcely resembling a human being, trudging along with difficulty, hardly moving his feet and supported on both sides by nurses.

Iosif Terelya, a Ukrainian Uniate believer who served imprisonment on various charges from 1962 onwards, was charged with "anti-Soviet agitation and propaganda" in 1972, ruled "not accountable" and sent to the Sychyovka Special Psychiatric Hospital, where he remained until 1976. After his release he wrote an "open letter" to Yury Andropov, Chairman of the KGB, recounting his experiences in camps, prisons and the Sychyovka Special Psychiatric Hospital. Of the Sychyovka hospital he said in part:

For anything at all the orderlies beat and tormented the "loonies", especially the Jews. Beginning in 1972 a secret persecution of Jews in the camps and prisons – humiliations, beatings – was sanctioned by the camp and prison administration. Whereas until recently we, Ukrainian nationalists, had been characterized as "spies", we now all at once became "Yids", since only "Yids" want the collapse of the state. They took away "loonies' " parcels. For a laugh they would make mentally ill people eat live frogs. They raped patients to satisfy their sexual appetites – and all this for a laugh! Thus in 1965 the head of the orderlies of Ward 3 murdered the young patient Surganov when the latter asked to be taken to the toilet. What happened? They transferred the murderer to another camp.

In the spring and early summer of 1973 on the order of the head of Ward 9 Yelena Leontevna, they tortured the patient Smirnov for two months. The "orderlies" and wardens beat him every night, as a result of which he died.

In 1977 Terelya was arrested again and confined to a special psychiatric hospital, this time the one in Dnepropetrovsk. KGB officials indicated to his wife that this was because of his "open letter" to Andropov.

Psychiatrist Semyon Gluzman, before his arrest in 1972 (left) and in exile, after serving seven years' imprisonment in the strict regime camps in Perm region

Alexander Argentov in Moscow Psychiatric Hospital No 14 in 1976

Josif Terelya

The Serbsky Institute of Forensic Psychiatry in Kropotkin Lane in central Moscow

The Oryol Special Psychiatric Hospital

Vladimir Klebanov

The Russian Orthodox nun Valeriya Makeyeva

The Talgar Special Psychiatric Hospital

## Ordinary Psychiatric Hospitals

According to a 1979 report by the unofficial Moscow-based Working Commission for the Investigation of the Use of Psychiatry for Political Purposes there are "several hundred ordinary psychiatric hospitals in the country, including in-patient facilities at psychiatric clinics and psychiatric wards in normal hospitals."

In the cases known to Amnesty International dissenters confined to such institutions have normally spent a shorter time in them — usually anything from a few days to up to over a year — then have those held in special psychiatric hospitals.

Ordinary psychiatric hospitals are under the jurisdiction of the health authorities and are staffed by civilian personnel. They are generally much less secretive than the special psychiatric hospitals. Inmates may correspond more freely and may be visited by people other than relatives, although correspondence and visits have frequently been cancelled at the discretion of the administration and medical staff. Prisoners of conscience held in ordinary psychiatric hospitals have invariably been kept under lock and key, often in wards set aside for violent inmates.

While ordinary psychiatric hospitals are generally characterized by better treatment of inmates than the special psychiatric hospitals, this varies considerably, both within any given hospital and among different hospitals.

Former inmates and psychiatrists who have emigrated from the USSR have reported that unhygienic conditions and severe overcrowding are common in ordinary psychiatric hospitals. One former inmate has remarked that the psychiatric hospitals in Moscow have a reputation for better conditions than such institutions elsewhere in the country.

Among prisoners of conscience who experienced conditions in ordinary psychiatric hospitals similar to those in special psychiatric hospitals was Victor Borovsky. He was confined to psychiatric hospitals twice before emigrating from the USSR in 1977. In 1975, reportedly after he had mentioned Alexander Solzhenitsyn's book *GULag Archipelago* in a university thesis, he was confined for three months to an ordinary psychiatric hospital in the town of Slavyansk, in Donetsk region in the Ukraine. He subsequently told human rights activists in Moscow about conditions in the hospital:

> The orderlies, often in a drunken condition, constantly beat the patients,
> sometimes savagely. (Especially savage were Yury Slepets and Arkady
> Mikhailovich Zhuravsky, who was "treating" Borovsky.) Furthermore,
> they set the patients to fight one another and laid "bets" on them; they
> woke patients up during the night and forced them to sing.

## Treatment with Psychiatric Methods

Inmates of Soviet psychiatric hospitals have no influence over the selection of the psychiatrist assigned to treat them. Psychiatrists are not even obliged to tell their patients or relatives their names, and in a number of known cases such information has been kept secret. Neither the patients nor their families have any influence over the type of psychiatric measures applied to them.

Most of the prisoners of conscience mentioned in this chapter, and most others known to Amnesty International who have been forcibly confined to psychiatric hospitals, have been arbitrarily treated with drugs.

The drugs most commonly used on dissenters are the powerful tranquilizers (commonly referred to as neuroleptic drugs) aminazin, haloperidol and triftazin; insulin and sulphazin. Among other drugs which have been applied to prisoners of conscience and other inmates are tizertsin, sanapax, etaperazin, phrenolon, trisedil, mazheptil, seduksin and motiden-depo. These drugs have been administered by various means, including injections, solutions for drinking and tablets.

The most commonly used of the neuroleptic drugs are also used in other countries, and it is worthwhile indicating their approved names in other countries.[11] Aminazin is known in western European countries as chlorpromazin, chloractil or largactil. Haloperidol is known also as haldol or serenace. Triftazin is known as trifluoperazin.

Each of these tranquilizers is used in many countries for treatment of a variety of psychiatric disorders. However in accepted medical practice their use is carefully regulated. First, each is intended for treatment of specific disorders. Application of any of these drugs to people not suffering from the medically-indicated symptoms causes harm.

Second, each of these drugs can cause serious negative side-effects, among them skin and blood disorders, disorders associated with pigmentation and the sensitivity of the eyes to light, gain or loss in weight, dryness of the mouth, reduced blood pressure and jaundice. A characteristic negative side-effect, and the one which victims regard as the greatest threat to their sanity, is the "parkinsonism" or "extra-pyramidal derangement" often induced by these drugs. This side-effect is characterized by muscular rigidity, paucity and slowness of body movement, physical restlessness and constant desire to change the body's position.

In accepted medical practice these negative side-effects are countered by careful determination of the dosage, simultaneous administration of other drugs which counteract these side-effects, careful observation of the patient to ensure that the drugs are not contra-indicated by some characteristic of the patient's condition and cessation of treatment with the drug if it causes too much discomfort.

From numerous accounts it is plain that in Soviet psychiatric hospitals, both the ordinary and special ones, these drugs are administered indiscriminately and routinely to patients, without attention to the size of the dosage, the characteristics of the subject's physical or psychiatric condition or the harm caused by the drugs. They are often used without the accompaniment of any counteracting drugs, and they are frequently applied to persons for whose condition they are contra-indicated.

In a number of known cases dissenters have been treated with these drugs on arrival at ordinary psychiatric hospitals without even being diagnosed by a psychiatrist. Even when dissenters have been lucky enough to be released from an ordinary psychiatric hospital within a few days, they have as a rule received treatment with these drugs before their release.

In a number of cases dissenters have challenged their psychiatrists to explain why they were giving these drugs to them, and received the reply that it was necessary to justify their being treated in a psychiatric hospital. In known cases aminazin, haloperidol, triftazin and similar drugs have been applied at the request of, or even by decision of, entirely untrained orderlies recruited from among convicted criminals.

These drugs are frequently, indeed routinely, applied as a means of punishing inmates for violations of discipline and as a form of pressure on dissenters to renounce their disapproved-of beliefs and behaviour. The effects on the physical and mental health of the victim are well-illustrated from the case of Leonid Plyushch, a Ukrainian cyberneticist who was arrested in 1972, charged with "anti-Soviet agitation and propaganda" and confined to the Dnepropetrovsk Special Psychiatric Hospital from July 1973 to January 1976. The doctors in the hospital began to treat him with haloperidol a month after his arrival. When on 22 October 1973 his wife, Tatyana Zhitnikova, visited him, she found him in the following condition after two months of treatment with haloperidol:

> When they brought Leonid Ivanovich into the visiting room, it was impossible to recognize him. His eyes were full of pain and misery, he spoke with difficulty and brokenly, frequently leaning on the back of the chair in search of support. His effort at self-control was evident as from time to time he closed his eyes, trying to carry on a conversation and to answer questions. But his inner strength was exhausted. Leonid Ivanovich began to gasp, to awkwardly unbutton his clothing . . . , his face was convulsed and he got cramp in his hands and legs . . . It was evident that from time to time he lost his hearing . . . Leonid Ivanovich could not control himself, and it was he who asked that the meeting be ended 10 minutes ahead of time. They took him away.

When after the visit she asked her husband's doctor (who refused to give her family name, identifying herself only as "Lidiya Alekseyevna") why he was being treated with haloperidol, the doctor replied: "Why do you have to know? We'll give him whatever is necessary."

When Plyushch's wife next visited him (6 November 1973) his state had further deteriorated. He told her that he was incapable of writing letters to her and that he did not want her to send him any more scientific books since he was incapable of reading them. She again approached the psychiatrist in charge of his case, asking why her husband had not at least been given medication to counteract the negative effects of haloperidol. The psychiatrist replied that she would divulge nothing, either about the diagnosis or about the treatment.

In February and March 1974, doctors ceased giving Plyushch haloperidol and instead began to administer insulin to him, apparently in large doses. At a meeting with his wife on 4 March 1974, he was, by her account, unrecognizable:

> Great dropsical swelling had occurred, he moved with difficulty, and his eyes had lost their liveliness.

Possibly on account of Plyushch's serious physical condition, doctors temporarily ceased to give him drugs at least twice in 1974: in April and May, and in late June. Each time, his physical and mental condition improved.

In November 1974 the psychiatrists began to administer large doses of triftazin to him. At the end of 1974, they again stopped giving him drugs, and when his wife visited him on 3 January 1975, his condition was improved. However, in a five-line note later that month Plyushch said that he was physically incapable of replying to her letters.

Throughout this period Plyushch was under constant pressure from his psychiatrists to renounce his political views.[12]

Among numerous other examples of the administration of drugs to dissenters as a form of punishment is the case of Vladimir Titov, a one-time KGB officer who was arrested in 1969, sentenced to 5 years' imprisonment for "anti-Soviet agitation and propaganda" and subsequently transferred to the Sychyovka Special Psychiatric Hospital, and from there in 1976 to an ordinary psychiatric hospital in Kaluga. *A Chronicle of Current Events* reported his treatment in the Kaluga hospital:

> Valentin Sergeyevich Yakovlev, the doctor in charge of Titov's treatment, told him: "I'll treat you, an anti-Soviet, all the way. I'm going to make you into a real lunatic." They have forcibly treated Titov with haloperidol, aminazin, motiden-depo. When he refused to take medication voluntarily, they tied him to his bed for a week.

Reportedly, Titov was released in December 1976, still suffering from convulsive twitching brought on by the drugs.

Former inmates of Soviet psychiatric hospitals have pointed to many individual cases in which inmates were subjected to great suffering and even lost their lives through arbitrary application of neuroleptic drugs.

Another type of psychiatric treatment to which dissenters have often been subjected is insulin shock therapy. This method consists of administering increasing doses of insulin over a period of days. The dosage is increased until the subject goes into "hypoglycaemic coma" and shock. A course of insulin shock therapy in Soviet psychiatric hospitals usually consists of 25 or 30 such shocks. One dissenter, Mikhail Bernstam, was reportedly subjected to three courses of this treatment involving 60 shocks.

The drug sulfazin was at one time used in a number of countries for treating schizophrenia and other ailments in certain circumstances but has generally gone out of use long ago because it was shown not to be useful. However sulfazin causes great physical discomfort — raging fever so intense that the patient is virtually incapacitated for up to three days after an injection. Most former inmates of Soviet psychiatric hospitals who have been in a position to give an account of their conditions of incarceration have reported that sulfazin is regularly used as a punishment for violation of discipline, with the victims sometimes being subjected to injections of it every day for several days. As with the other treatments mentioned above, the medical personnel administering this drug have often done so without proper assessment of whether the subject was physically able to stand the treatment.

Incidents like the following, reported by Leonid Plyushch after his release from the Dnepropetrovsk Special Psychiatric Hospital in 1976, appear in numerous accounts by former prisoners of conscience:

One of the patients called the doctors Gestapoists [*sic*]. They prescribed injections of sulphur. (After an injection of sulphur your temperature goes up to 40°, the place where you had the injection is very painful, you cannot get away from the pain. Many people get haemorrhoids as a result of sulphur injections.) This patient groaned loudly for 24 hours, mad with pain he tried to hide himself under the bed, in despair he broke the window and tried to cut his throat with the glass. Then he was punished again and beaten up. He kept asking everyone "Am I going to die?" And only when he really did begin to die and another patient noticed it did they stop the sulphur. And for two days they gave him oxygen and brought him various medicines. They saved him. As I understood the use of sulphur was contra-indicated for him.

Another psychiatric measure which is regularly applied as a disciplinary measure to inmates of Soviet psychiatric hospitals is fixation, the immobilization of the patient. In its simpler form, this consists simply of strapping the patients tightly to their beds and leaving them there. Former prisoners of conscience have reported cases of patients who had shown no violence but had somehow irritated hospital staff being tied to their beds for a week or longer and neglected. A more complicated form of fixation is the "wet pack" or "dry wrap", in which the inmate is tightly wrapped in strips of wet sheeting. The sheeting tightens as it dries, causing great pain. In reported cases, hospital staff have repeated the process several times on the same patient. Unlike the simpler methods of fixation and the other psychiatric measures described above, the wet pack has apparently not been commonly used against known prisoners of conscience during the late 1970s, although evidently it has not gone out of use.

## Release and After Release

Under both the criminal and the civil procedures, forcible confinement to a psychiatric hospital is indefinite. Confined individuals may be released only when their psychiatric condition is judged to have improved to such an extent that they are no longer a public danger.

The criminal procedure codes stipulate that when the administration of the psychiatric institution, supported by the findings of a commission of doctors, recommends a person's release or transfer to a different type of psychiatric hospital, this proposal shall be considered by a court. Ministerial instructions specify that each patient shall be examined by a psychiatric commission at six-monthly intervals. This commission can recommend release, transfer to a different type of hospital or continued confinement for treatment in the same institution. Participation of a legal authority (ie someone from the procurator's office) in sessions of such commissions is apparently optional, but does not appear to have occurred in any of the cases well-known outside the USSR.

These psychiatric commissions have been marred by the same abuses as those involved at the initial stages of diagnosis and confinement. For one thing, the psychiatric commissions often do not examine inmates every six months, as required by the regulations, but at longer intervals.

The work of the commissions is also determined by political considerations. As a rule the commissions are subject to the authority of the Serbsky Institute in Moscow, no matter where in the country the inmate is confined. Frequently doctors in special psychiatric hospitals have told inmates or their relatives that they have no influence as to whether the inmates are to be recommended for release, since it is the Serbsky Institute that decides such matters. Dissenters regard the Serbsky Institute as an instrument for carrying out decisions of the state security organs concerning the confinement of dissenters to psychiatric hospitals. Natalya Gorbanyevskaya, a poet who had herself been confined to a special psychiatric hospital in 1971, went to visit the prisoner of conscience Yury Belov in the Sychyovka Special Psychiatric Hospital in the mid-1970s. She was not permitted to see him, but discussed his case with the doctor in charge of his treatment:

> I asked the doctor: "Well, how are things with Yury? Are there any hopes for the next commission?" She spread her hands helplessly. "We have no complaints about him here, but as you know we are not the ones who take the decision. It's the Serbsky Institute that decides." I already knew that the Serbsky Institute decides. On a previous occasion a woman doctor had told Yury: "We regard your religious convictions as pathology." Another time the same woman had said: "Belov, of course, is healthy, but he hasn't been in long enough." And if you speak to her, the lady from the Serbsky, she too will spread her hands and say: "You know, it is not our decision."

In a number of cases where details are known about the way in which the six-monthly psychiatric commissions have examined dissenters, the questions put to them concerned only their political or religious views and behaviour, and release was made conditional on some form of recantation.

The role of psychiatric commissions in the case of Boris Yevdokimov illustrates the predominance of political considerations. Yevdokimov, a Leningrad journalist, was arrested in 1971 and charged with "anti-Soviet agitation and propaganda" on account of some articles he had written for publication abroad. He was ruled "not accountable" and confined to a special psychiatric hospital. He later stated that he had simulated mental illness to avoid a long term of imprisonment. After a spell in the Leningrad Special Psychiatric Hospital, he was moved to the similar institution in Dnepropetrovsk, and from there he was transferred in 1978 to the Kazan Special Psychiatric Hospital. Throughout this period psychiatric commissions repeatedly refused to recommend his release. In 1977 human rights activists in Moscow reported:

> In May 1977 doctors in the commission considered it necessary to order his release, but then a woman psychiatrist arrived from the Serbsky Institute and began to scream at and threaten both Yevdokimov and the doctors. She resorted to methods which are incompatible with the obligations of a doctor: psychological pressure and blackmail (she told Yevdokimov that his wife had renounced him, she insulted him and threatened that he would never leave imprisonment). At the commission she stated: "You should be grateful that you are alive at all — what more do you need?"

According to the same sources, the commission which examined him in 1978 put only political questions: "Did Yevdokimov wish to emigrate?

What were his political opinions? What was he going to do after his release?" At around this time the doctor in charge of Yevdokimov's ward in the Kazan Special Psychiatric Hospital told him that he would not be released unless he retracted his statement that at the time of his psychiatric examination in 1972 he had simulated mental illness. Yevdokimov was finally released in 1979, after he was found to be suffering from cancer from which he died later in the year.

The arbitrary character of official decisions on the release of inmates of special psychiatric hospitals was also illustrated in the case of Victor Rafalsky, a Ukrainian writer who has been confined in such an institution since 1968 when police confiscated from him the manuscript of a book he had written which the authorities regarded as "anti-Soviet". Rafalsky had previously been confined to psychiatric hospitals twice for his links with unofficial Marxist circles. According to accounts by Leonid Plyushch after his release from the Dnepropetrovsk Special Psychiatric Hospital in 1976, the deputy director of that institution said in the early 1970s: "As long as I work here Rafalsky will not leave this hospital."

Often when a six-monthly psychiatric commission has recommended the release of a dissenter from psychiatric hospital, the courts have rejected the recommendation and ordered the subject's continued confinement.

Usually, the courts do not order the release of dissenters but instead order them transferred from a special psychiatric hospital to an ordinary psychiatric hospital, where they may spend several more years as prisoners of conscience awaiting release. Mykola Plakhotnyuk, a Ukrainian medical doctor confined to a special psychiatric hospital after being arrested in 1972 for "anti-Soviet agitation and propaganda", was transferred in 1978 to an ordinary psychiatric hospital in the town of Smela, in Cherkassy region in the Ukraine. In 1979 human rights activists in Moscow reported that a doctor in the hospital had recently told Plakhotnyuk that "until the Olympic Games have taken place there can be no rush in your case."

A number of cases are known of prisoners of conscience who have spent decades in special psychiatric hospitals. The prisoners involved were confined before systematic human rights reporting and *samizdat* developed in the Soviet Union, and so their cases have not been well-known abroad or within the country. One such prisoner is Vasily Shipilov, who was first arrested in 1939 while studying in a religious seminar and sentenced to 10 years' imprisonment for "counter-revolutionary activities." After his release in 1949 he was re-arrested and faced with a similar charge, but was ruled mentally ill ("schizophrenia") and confined to the Kazan Special Psychiatric Hospital. Shipilov's case became known only in 1978, when the unofficial Working Commission for the Investigation of the Use of Psychiatry for Political Purposes reported it. The following passages from their report resemble accounts about other long-term prisoners of conscience in psychiatric hospitals:

> As a result of beatings and treatment with insulin he began to suffer from fits. They changed his diagnosis to "epilepsy" and began to treat him for his fits. In the course of 29 years Shipilov has repeatedly been beaten

because he crossed himself and fasted. They sought to force him to give up his religious beliefs. Since 1960 Shipilov has been held in the Sychyovka Special Psychiatric Hospital, where the head of the 9th section, Elena Leontievna Maximova, has told him repeatedly: "You'll be here until you renounce your religion, unless they kill you." Professor Elizaveta Kholodkovskaya of the Serbsky Institute, in charge of the commission for discharging patients, constantly told Shipilov that no one knows or ever will know about him, and therefore "anything can happen" to him.

According to the civil procedure for release from psychiatric hospital, a commission of three psychiatrists must examine every inmate every month and has complete authority to order the subject's discharge. In cases of prisoners of conscience this procedure too has been abused as regards the regularity of the examinations, the influence of political considerations on the psychiatrists' deliberations and the common practice of promising release only if the subject retracts his or her political views or behaviour.

Individuals who have been released from psychiatric confinement under either the civil or the criminal procedure bear the stigma of mental illness for the rest of their lives. Often they are officially qualified against their wishes as "invalids." If they are political dissenters, they face especially severe job discrimination and in many cases have been unable to find any work at all. They are registered on lists of people diagnosed as mentally ill and are normally required to report regularly to psychiatric clinics for examination and out-patient treatment. The influence of Professor Andrei Snezhnevsky's theories are important here too, since in Snezhnevsky's accepted view schizophrenia is a permanent condition and anyone diagnosed as suffering from it may require repeated courses of in-patient treatment. The existence of a psychiatric record on dissenters provides the authorities with the most convenient of pretexts for confining them again and again for their nonconformist behaviour or simply as a "prophylactic" measure at times of public celebrations or important public events.

## Notes

1. RSFSR Code of Criminal Procedure, Article 184.
2. *Commentary to the RSFSR Code of Criminal Procedure*, Moscow, 1976, page 277.
3. RSFSR Code of Criminal Procedure, Article 404.
4. RSFSR Code of Criminal Procedure, Article 405.
5. *Commentary to the RSFSR Criminal Code*, Moscow, 1976, page 604.
6. *Information Bulletin, (Moscow)*, Number 6, 1 February 1978, Working Commission for the Investigation of the Use of Psychiatry for Political Purposes.
7. Tatyana Khodorovich (editor), *Istoriya Boleznyi Leonida Plyushcha*, Herzen Foundation, Amsterdam, 1974, page 168. This *samizdat* collection of documents on the Plyushch case has been published in English under the title *The Case of Leonid Plyushch*, C. Hurst and Company, London, 1976.
8. For the text of this directive in English see *A Chronicle of Human Rights in the USSR*, Khronika Press, New York, Number 26.
9. On the diagnostic methods used in the Serbsky Institute see especially Victor Nekipelov's account of his confinement there in 1974: *House of Fools*, Harcourt, Brace, Jovanovich, New York, 1979.
10. *The Guardian*, London, 29 October 1973.
11. Reference here is to the *Glossary of Terms, Tests and Drugs Used in Psychiatric Practice*, Lancashire Area Health Authority, United Kingdom, 1976 and 1978.
12. On Plyushch's treatment see his memoirs, *Dans le Carnaval de l'Histoire*, Seuil, Paris, 1977; his testimony in 1976 before the Subcommittee on International Organizations of the Committee on International Relations of the United States House of Representatives, *Psychiatric Abuse of Political Prisoners in the Soviet Union—Testimony by Leonid Plyushch*, U.S. Government Printing Office, Washington, 1976; and Khodorovich, *op cit*.

# INDEX

Abankin, Vitold 125, 157, 161
Abel, Erhard 18
"Actions Disrupting Work of Corrective Labour Institutions" 86, 165
Administrative Detention 22, 41, 65-66, 77
Administrative Surveillance, see Surveillance, Administrative
Adventists, see Religious Believers
Agafonov, Vladimir 165
Airikian, Paruir 17
Aitman, Vladimir 165
Akhov, A. 35
Akinkin, Ivan 30
All-Union Church of True and Independent Seventh Day Adventists 39
All-Union Council of Evangelical Christians and Baptists 39
Alma-Ata Special Psychiatric Hospital, see Talgar Special Psychiatric Hospital
Altman, Anatoly 145
Aminazin 197-199
Amnesties 78, 79, 84-85
Amnesty International, Moscow adoption group 16
Anashkin, G.Z. 5
Andropov, Yury 192
"Anti-Soviet Agitation and Propaganda" 5, 9-19, 21, 22, 30, 31, 60, 61, 62, 66, 70, 72, 73, 75, 77, 78, 79, 99, 100, 108, 109, 119, 125, 126, 130, 138, 139, 144, 145, 146, 147, 148, 154, 155, 157, 165, 182, 183, 185, 186, 188, 198, 199, 201
"Anti-Soviet Slander", see "Dissemination of Fabrications known to be False which Defame the Soviet State and Social System"
Antonov, Ivan 59
Appeals from Court Decisions 82-83
Argentov, Alexander 21, 179, 183, 187
Armenian Apostolic Church, see Religious Believers
Armenians, see Nationalities
Arrest 65-71
Arsenalnaya Special Psychiatric Hospital, see Leningrad Special Psychiatric Hospital
Arutyunian, Edward 20
Association of Free Trade Unions of Workers in the USSR 21-22, 183

Bagdasarian, Zaven 87
Baitullayev, Yakob 51
Balakhonov, Vladimir 49, 131, 154
"Banditry" 86
Banishment 50, 78, 79, 101-102, 103-104
Baptists, see Religious Believers
Barin, Yekaterina 41
Barladyanu, Vasyl 112, 124, 143-144
Bashkirov, Pavel 16, 72
Beatings of Prisoners 68-69, 109-110, 121, 148, 157, 165-167, 191-192, 196, 202-203
Bebko, Vladislav 178, 183
Begun, Joseph 46, 59-60
Bekirov, Lyufti 51
Belov, Yury 130-131, 191, 201
Berdnyk, Oles 20
Bergen, Boris 44
Bernstam, Mikhail 188-189, 199
Blagoveshchensk Special Psychiatric Hospital 189
Bleile, Anton 46
Bolonkin, Alexander 60, 69
Bondarenko, Joseph 58
Borovsky, Victor 48, 196
"Box" Cells 68, 110
Brezhnev, Leonid Ilyich 4, 17
Brusilovsky, Lazar 46
Buddhists, see Religious Believers
Budulak-Sharygin, Nikolai 120, 154, 161
Bukovsky, Vladimir 119, 121, 125, 157, 163, 186
*Bulletin of the Council of Relatives of Imprisoned Evangelical Christians and Baptists* 40
Butkus, Donatus 183
Buzinnikov, Yevgeny 18, 107

Camps, see Corrective Labour Institutions
Capital Punishment, see Death Penalty
Cell-type Premises (*PKT*) 114-115, 129, 158, 162-164, 170
Chamovskikh, Victor 63
Charter 77, 178, 183
Chekalin, Alexander 157
Chernyakhovsk Special Psychiatric Hospital 189, 190
Children, 40, 43, 84, 155
China, People's Republic of 146

Chistopol Prison, see Corrective Labour
Institutions
Chornovil, Vyacheslav 103, 165
"The Christian" Printing House 44
Christian Seminar on Problems of Religious
Rebirth 21, 183
*Chronicle of Current Events* 15, 16, 41, 42-
44, 50-51, 68, 109, 119, 127, 131, 136,
138, 165, 169, 172, 185, 199
*Chronicle of the Lithuanian Catholic Church*
15, 30
Code of Criminal Procedure of the RSFSR
7, 8, 65-88, 164, 174, 176
Colleges of Advocates 71, 72, 73, 74
*Commentary to the Code of Criminal
Procedure of the RSFSR* 9, 175
*Commentary to the Corrective Labour Code
of the RSFSR* 9, 89-104, 113, 129-130,
135, 137-138, 140, 154, 155, 159, 161
*Commentary to the Criminal Code of the
RSFSR* 9-12, 36-38
*Commentary to the Fundamentals of
Corrective Labour Legislation of the
USSR and Union Republics* 9, 89-104,
135, 137, 146
Committee of State Security (KGB) 8, 65,
66, 67, 72, 73, 74, 87, 126, 147, 148,
179, 189, 192
Communist Party of the Soviet Union 4, 17,
38, 40, 72, 127, 145, 180, 182
*The Community (Obshchina)* 21
Conclusion to Indict, see Indictment
Conditional Release from Places of
Imprisonment with Obligatory Induction
to Labour 85-86
Conditional-early Release from Punishment
85
Conditional Sentence 82
Conditional Sentence of Imprisonment with
Obligatory Induction to Labour 18, 50,
78, 82, 104
Conditions of Confinement in Psychiatric
Hospitals 14-15, 189-204
Conditions of Imprisonment in Corrective
Labour Institutions:
Accommodation 99-100, 101, 110-112,
159-161, 161-162
Clothing 112, 152, 157, 160, 163-164
Correspondence and Parcels 17, 98, 100-101
121, 124, 151, 152-153, 155, 158-159,
161, 168-169
Food 91-92, 98, 100, 101, 107,112-122,
129, 134, 140, 144, 155, 157, 158, 159,
160, 161, 162

Labour 91, 94, 97, 98, 101, 114,
115-116, 120, 121-122, 124, 125, 127,
134, 135-145, 155, 158, 162
Medical Treatment 86, 97-98, 121-132,
137-138, 144-145, 157, 162-164
Political Education 134-135, 145-148, 158,
164
Punishments 91, 97, 98, 114-116, 120,
121, 124, 125, 126, 129, 138, 146, 151-
171
Reeducation 91, 92-94, 134-150
Right to Submit Complaints 98, 157,
168-169
Transport of Prisoners 106-110, 122,
128
Visits 97, 98, 100, 151, 153-155, 158,
159, 161
Conscientious Objectors 4, 17, 38, 45, 46,
51-56, 155
Constitution of the USSR (1936) 3, 5
Constitution of the USSR (1977) 3-64,
84, 96
Constitution of the RSFSR 84
Corrective Labour Code of the RSFSR 60,
86; 89-104, 110, 112, 113, 129-131, 135,
136, 137, 138, 139, 140, 143, 154, 158,
164, 168, 170
Corrective Labour Institutions:
Colonies (Camps) 78-79, 99-101, 152,
153-154
Mordovia 31, 101, 106, 107, 109, 111,
116, 120, 122, 123, 124, 125, 127, 128,
131, 135, 136-137, 138, 139, 143,
144-145, 148, 149, 155, 157, 161-162,
164, 165, 166
Perm 101, 107, 116, 119, 120, 122, 123,
125, 126, 127, 128, 130, 131, 137, 146,
147, 148, 149, 157, 162, 163, 164, 166,
168-169
Others 100, 112, 114, 116, 127, 136,
138-139, 143, 155, 158, 164, 165-
166, 190, 191
Prisons 78, 98-99, 115-116, 152, 154,
158, 158-161, 164, 170
Chistopol 99, 111, 124, 136, 139
Vladimir 99, 110-111, 116, 119, 121,
125, 126, 127, 128-129, 130, 136, 143,
148, 154, 157, 158-161, 163, 164, 167,
169
Others 99, 108, 164, 166-167
see also Investigation-Isolation Prisons,
Transit Prisons, Conditions of Imprisonment
in Corrective Labour Institutions
Corrective Work without Imprisonment
50, 78, 82, 101-102, 104

Council of Churches of Evangelical Christians and Baptists 34, 35, 39
Council of Ministers of the USSR 33, 38, 60, 102, 103, 113
Council of Relatives of Imprisoned Evangelical Christians and Baptists 40
Council of Religious Affairs attached to the USSR Council of Ministers 33, 34, 38, 39
Courts 8, 13-64, 65-88, 129-131, 164, 175-179, 200, 202
Courts, Administrative Sessions of 70
Courts, Jurisdiction of 75-76
Crimean Tartars, see Nationalities
Criminal Code of the RSFSR 7-64
Custody before Trial 65-88 see also Investigation, pre-Trial and Investigation-Isolation Prisons

Davydov, Egor 163
Davydov, Georgy 108
Death Penalty 48, 73, 78, 86-87, 108, 110, 165
Detention, Administrative, see Administrative Detention
"Dissemination of Fabrications known to be False which Defame the Soviet State and Social System" ("Anti-Soviet Slander") 5, 9-19, 22, 30, 39 44, 46, 47, 51, 60, 70, 75, 77, 146, 155, 157, 177, 178, 183, 187, 188
Dnepropetrovsk Special Psychiatric Hospital 49, 189, 190, 192, 198-200, 201, 202
Dolgotyor, Yakov 45
*Dopusk* (clearance) 72, 73
Drabkina, Dr N.M. 187
Drugs, Treatment with in Psychiatric Hospitals 14-15, 196-200
Dyak, Mikhail 130
Dymshits, Mark 87
Dyshel, Judge 176
Dzhemilev, Mustafa 17, 30, 51, 63, 73, 74
Dzhemilev, Reshat 30, 51
Dzibalov, Vyacheslav 182
Dzyuba, Yury 147-148

"Engaging in a Prohibited Trade" 44
Estonians, see Nationalities
Exile, 78-79, 101-103

Fedorenko, Vasyl 163
Fedoseyeva, Dr L.D. 188-189
Fedotov, Edward 21, 183
Fefelov, Valery 20

Feldman, Alexander 72-73
Finland 49
Fixation 199, 200
Fot, Yakov 44
Free Inter-Professional Union of Workers 22, 183
French Communist Party 14
Fundamentals of Corrective Labour Legislation of the USSR and Union Republics 89-104, 122, 134, 135, 168 see also *Commentary*
Fundamentals of Criminal Legislation of the USSR and Union Republics 7, 85, 176 see also *Commentary*
Fundamentals of Criminal Procedure of the USSR and Union Republics 7 see also *Commentary*
Fundamentals of Legislation of the USSR and the Union Republics on Education 37
Fundamentals of Legislation of the USSR and Union Republics on Marriage and the Family 40
Furman, Lily 16, 46
Fyodorov, Yury 63
Fyodorov, Yury Pavlovich 145, 154, 164, 165

Gabai, Ilya 73
Gaidar, Nadezhda 173, 184
Gambarian, Rafik 87
Gandzyuk, Vladimir 103, 108, 131
Gayauskas, Balys 14, 16-17
Georgians, see Nationalities
Germans, see Nationalities
Ginzburg, Alexander 14, 30, 72, 111
Glezer, Ilya 106, 109
Glukhov, Anatoly 48, 174
Gluzman, Dr Semyon 186
Goldstein, Gregory 46, 60
Goncharova, Raisa 41
Gorbanyevskaya, Nataliya 201
Grigorenko, Pyotr 187
Grilius, Shimon 145-146
Grodetsky, Yury 125

Haloperidol 197-199
Harlemann, Albert 46
Hel, Ivan 155
Helsinki Monitoring Groups 20, 30, 41, 57, 60 62, 73, 76, 111, 115, 116, 119, 143, 159, 161, 163, 172, 180
"Hooliganism" 21, 56-58, 70
Hunger Strikes by Prisoners 121-122, 125, 147, 157, 163, 165

208

Igrunov, Vyacheslav 72, 177
"Illegal Exit Abroad and Illegal Entry into the USSR" 48
Indictment 69-71, 75, 77, 78
"Infringement of Person and Rights of Citizens under the Appearance of Conducting Religious Ceremonies" 37-39, 41-42
Initiative Group for the Defence of Human Rights in the USSR 159-160
Institute of Psychiatry of the USSR Academy of Medical Sciences 183-184
Insulin 198, 199, 202
"Insulting a Policeman" 60
Investigation, Pre-Trail 65-88, 174-176
Investigation-Isolation Prisons 67-69, 108
Iofe, Olga 185
Ionaitis, Egidius 174
Ivanov, Valentin 48, 174
Ivanovna, Raisa 31

Jantsen, Yakov 41
Jehova's Witnesses, see Religious Believers
Jews, see Nationalities, Religious Believers
Judicial Review, see Review by Way of Judicial Supervision

Kalafatov, Zubeit 50
Kalandarov, Boris 46, 52
Kalinin, Vasyly 31
Kallistratova, Sofia 72, 175-176
Kalynets, Ihor 157
Kaminskaya, Dina 72, 73
Kampov, Pavel 103
Karavansky, Svyatoslav 155
Kartser see Punishment Cell
Kazakhstanskaya Pravda 135
Kazan Special Psychiatric Hospital 31, 131, 183, 186, 189, 201-203
KGB see Committee of State Security
Khaustov, Victor 30
Kheifets, Mikhail 19, 161-162
Khmara 42
Kholodovskaya, E. 203
Khyrkhara, Sefran 51
Kiirend, Matti 21
Klassen, Alwin 45, 46
Klebanov, Vladimir 22, 176, 183
Klink, Arthur 46, 60
Klink, Valentin 46, 47
Klink, Victor 46, 60
Komarov, Alexander 184
Komarova, Faina 182
Konin, Father Lev 30

Konovalikhin, Vadim 47
Koop, David 44
Koplik, Anatoly 155
Kopysov, Ivan 180
Korizor, Ya. I. 123
Kormushka 110
Korneyev, Victor 56
Kostyuchenko, Grigory 59, 158
Kotov, Alexei 182
Kovalyov, Sergei 14-17, 123, 126
Kozlov, Andrei 182
Kravchenko, Nikolai 55
Kucherenko, Varvara 22, 183
Kukobaka, Mikhail 18, 174, 184, 187, 191-192
Kuroyedov, Vladimir 38
Kuzkin, Alexander 21, 183, 184
Kuznetsov, Edward 87, 135, 146
Kzyl-Orda Special Psychiatric Hospital 189

Labour by Prisoners see Conditions of Imprisonment in Corrective Labour Institutions
Landa, Malva 154
Lapienis, Vladas 30, 138
Latvians see Nationalities
Lavrov, Yury 183
Law on Court Organization of the RSFSR 8
Lawyers 65, 69, 70, 71-74, 77, 96, 164, 174-176, 179, 190
Legal Advice Centres 71
Lenin, V.I. 32, 54, 157
Leningrad Special Psychiatric Hospital 189, 201
Leontiyev, Academician 113
Letters and Parcels to Prisoners see Conditions of Imprisonment in Corrective Labour Insitutions
Leven, Ivan 44
Levinson, Sender 165-166
Levit, Shimon 144
Lisovoi, Vasyl 149, 158
Lithuanians, see Nationalities
Litvin, Yury 20, 127
Lukyanenko, Levko 61-62, 131
Lyubarskaya, Dr L.A. 15
Lyubarsky, Kronid 109, 144

Makarenko, A.P. 45
Makarenko, Mikhail 127
Makeyeva, Valeriya 30, 173
"Malicious Violation of the Passport Regulations" 45, 46-47, 50, 60

Malkin, Anatoly 46, 52, 53
Mamut, Musa 50
Marchenko, Anatoly 63
Marchenko, Valery 119, 124
Markosian, Razmik 120
Martens, Helmut 46, 47
Mattik, Kalja 21
Matulionis, Jonas 30
Matvyuk, Kuzma 144
Maximova, Dr E.L. 203
Medical Treatment of Prisoners, see
Conditions of Imprisonment in Corrective
Labour Institutions
Mennonites 39
Ministry of Internal Affairs, USSR (MVD)
8, 66, 67, 68, 85, 91, 94-98, 102-104,
107, 111, 113, 115, 121, 122, 124, 126,
129, 130, 146, 151, 152, 153, 154, 163,
168, 170, 178, 179, 190, 191 see also
People's Commissariat of Internal Affairs
Ministry of Justice of the USSR 71
Ministry of Public Health of the USSR
129-130, 178, 181, 196
Minyakov, Vladimir 55-56
Moldavians, see Nationalities
Monastyrsky, Boris 17
Montlevich, Vladimir 183
Mordovia Camps, see Corrective Labour
Institutions
Moroz, Valentin 131, 145
Morozov, Mark 22
Moslems, see Religious Believers
MVD, see Ministry of Internal Affairs
Mukhametshin, Boris 155
Musiyenko, Mariya 182
Muslyadinov, Riza 50-51

Naidovsky G.S. 127
Naritsa, Pyotr 58
Natashev, A.Y. 92-93
Nationalities 3, 12-13, 100-101, 153, 158
Armenians 13, 17, 20, 30, 87, 120, 158
Crimean Tartars 13, 17, 30, 49-51, 58,
79, 103
Estonians 13, 21, 79
Georgians 13, 20, 30, 68, 87
Germans 13, 16, 18, 45-58, 60
Jews 13, 45-58, 52-53, 57, 60, 72-73,
86, 87, 106, 114, 144-148, 154, 157,
165
Latvians 13, 18, 49, 58, 79, 123
Lithuanians 13, 14, 15, 20, 30, 79, 101,
108-109, 116, 131, 138, 139, 158, 174

Moldavians 13
Russians 13, 30
Ukrainians 13, 14-15, 20, 30, 57-58,
61-62, 73-74, 79, 101, 103, 108, 109, 119,
120, 123, 125, 126, 130, 144, 147, 148,
149, 155, 157, 158, 174, 192, 198-199,
202
Uzbeks 13, 101, 125, 157
Nekipelov, Victor 72
Nemerinskaya, N. Ya. 187-188
Netzel, Otto 46
Neuroleptic Drugs 197-199
Nikolayenko, Nikolai 108
Nikolayev, Yevgeny 22, 180-181, 183, 184
Novodvorskaya, Valeriya 22, 179, 183
Nudel, Ida 46, 57

Ogorodnikov, Alexander 21, 60
Ogurtsov, Igor 123-124
Okulova, Yuliya ("Yuliya Voznessenskaya")
16, 109-110
Ordinary Psychiatric Hospitals, see
Psychiatric Hospitals
"Organizational Activity Directed Toward
Commission of Especially Dangerous
Crimes Against the State and also
Participation in Anti-Soviet Organizations"
20, 100
"Organizing Group Actions which Violate
Public Order" 44
Orlov, Yury 14, 60, 76, 119, 123
Orthodox Believers, see Religious Believers
Oryol Special Psychiatric Hospital 189, 190
Osadchy, Mikhail 109, 165
Osipov, Vladimir 30
Ovanesiyan 192
Ovsienko, Vasyl 58

Panafidin, Pyotr 44
Parasha 67
"Parasitism" 21, 22, 58-60, 70, 75
Pardon 78, 79, 84, 130
Parental Rights, Deprivation of 40, 43-44
Pargamannik, Yefim 46
Partiinaya Zhizn (Party Life) 4—5
Passport System 46-47, 49-51, 60
Pauls, Ivan 41, 158
Pentecostalists, see Religious Believers
People's Assessors 76
People's Commissariat of Internal Affairs
(NKVD) 8, 94
People's Courts 75-76
Pererva, Vasyly 41-42
Perm Camps, see Corrective Labour
Institutions

Peters, Ivan 46
Peters, Peter 42-44, 158
Peters, Yakov 46
Petkus, Viktoras 20
Petronis, Povilas 30
Piontkovsky, A.A. 7
*PKT*, see Cell-Type Premises
Plakhotnyuk, Mykola 202
Plumpa-Pluira, Petras 30, 101, 158
Plyushch, Leonid 14-15, 67, 176, 198-200, 202
Podrabinek, Alexander 14, 18, 20-21, 181
Podrabinek, Kirill 20-21, 164
Polyakov, Igor 21
Ponomaryov, Anatoly 174, 188-189
Popadichenko, I. 163
Popadyuk, Zoryan 165
Poplavsky, Valentin 22, 60
Pozdeyev, Yury 72, 185
Pranskunaite, Ona 30, 116, 138
Presidia of the Supreme Soviets, see Supreme
   Soviets
Prisons, see Corrective Labour Institutions,
   Conditions of Imprisonment in Corrective
   Labour Institutions, Custody before Trial
   and Investigation-Isolation Prisons
Procuracy 8-9, 66, 69-71, 76, 83, 94-98, 146,
   151, 167-170, 175-176, 179, 190
Procurator General of the USSR 8, 18, 178
   see also Rudenko, Roman
Pronyuk, Yevgen 130
Psychiatric Confinement 6, 14, 17, 18, 20-
   21, 22, 30, 31, 41, 45, 46, 47-48, 49, 60,
   65, 82, 130-131, 172-204
Psychiatric Hospitals 172-204
   Ordinary Psychiatric Hospitals 177-181,
   184, 186, 187, 196-200, 202
   see also Serbsky Institute
   Special Psychiatric Hospitals 14-15, 174-
   175, 176, 177-178, 185, 187, 188,
   189-192, 196-203
Punishment of Prisoners, see Conditions of
   Imprisonment in Corrective Labour
   Institutions, Conditions of Confinement in
   Psychiatric Hospitals
Punishment Cell (*Kartser*) 97, 114, 115, 126,
   129, 158, 159-161, 162-164
Punishment-Isolation Cell (*SHIzo*) 97, 114,
   115, 127, 129, 131, 158, 161-162, 162-164
Purtov, Sergei 182
Pushkin, Alexander 21, 183
Rafalsky, Victor 202
Ravinsh, Maigonis 49, 123
Rebrik, Bohdan 109, 165

Recidivists 78, 98, 100, 101
Record of Conviction (*Sudimost*) 62
Redikop, Heinrich 46
Redikop, Ivan 46
Reimer, Heinrich 16, 46
Release from Psychiatric Hospital 200-203
Release from Punishment on Grounds of
   Illness 86, 129-131
Release from serving Sentence 17, 60-63,
   82-86, 129-131, 146, 164-165
Released Prisoners 59, 60-63, 134, 149, 203
Religious Believers 3, 4, 5, 13, 30-45, 74, 75,
   77, 82, 83, 96, 98, 146-147, 151-152,
   173, 183, 184, 202-203
   Armenian Apostolic Church 30
   Buddhists 183
   Evangelical Christians and Baptists 31, 32-
   45, 46, 53-56, 59, 85, 107, 155, 158
   Georgian Orthodox Church 30
   Jehovah's Witnesses 31, 37
   Jews 147
   Moslems 30
   Pentecostalists 31, 32-45, 46, 53-56
   Roman Catholics 30
   Russian Orthodox 21, 30, 31, 147, 179,
   182, 183, 184, 187
   Seventh Day Adventists 31, 32-45, 53-56,
   76-77
   True Orthodox Christians 31, 99
   True Orthodox Church 31
   Uniate Catholic Church 31, 192
Religious Legislation 3, 4, 5, 31-45
Reshatov, Enver 50
"Resisting a Representative of Authority"
   50, 58
"Resisting a Policeman or People's Guard"
   51, 58
Review by Way of Judicial Supervision
   83-84
Rode, Gunnar 125, 157
Roitburd, Lev 46, 58
Roman Catholics, see Religious Believers
Romanyuk, Father Vasyl 30, 147, 165
Rozhdestvov, Vladimir 173, 175-176, 184,
   187-188
Rudenko, Mykola 73
Rudenko, Roman 8, see also Procurator
   General of the USSR
Rules of Internal Order 97, 120-121,
   146, 152, 153, 154, 162, 169
Russians, see Nationalities
Rybinsk Special Psychiatric Hospital 189
Ryzhov, Victor 183

Sadunaite, Niole 30, 108-109, 139
Safronov, Alexei 125, 157
Sakharov, Academician A.D. 113, 187
Salamakha, Stepan 41-42
Sapeliak, Stepan 148, 157, 165
Sarbayev, Anatoly 183
Schlecht, Ivan 41
Schultz, Ivan 46
Sekach, Gregory 31
Seksyasov 123
Sentences of Punishment Imposed by the
Courts 12, 48-49, 56, 59-60, 78-82, 83,
86-87, 98-104, 164
Serbsky Institute of Forensic Psychiatry
21, 130, 131, 177, 181, 183, 184, 185,
186, 200-201, 203
Serbsky, V.P. 184
Serebrov, Felix 20, 60, 82
Sergiyenko, Alexander 126, 130, 157, 163,
164
Seventh Day Adventists, see Religious
Believers
Shabatura, Stefania 149
Shakhverdian, Bagrat 158
Shakirov, Babur 101, 125, 157
Shargorodsky, M.D. 90, 93, 170
Shatalov, Nikolai 17-18, 47
Shatalov, Tatyana 17
Shatalov, Vasily 17
Shatravka, Alexander and Mikhail 49, 173,
183
Shcharansky, Anatoly 46, 60, 67, 73, 78,
139
Sheliya 123
Shelkov, Vladimir 39, 44, 76-77
Shepilov, Vasily 202-203
Shepshilovich 145
SHIzo, see Punishment-Isolation Cell
Shnirman, Simon 46, 52
Shtern, Mikhail 114, 127, 143, 165
Shveisky, Vladimir 72
Sichko, Petro 20
Sichko, Vasyl 20
Silnitsky, Alexander 46, 52
Sinyavsky, Andrei 145
Skulme, Jurgis 18
Skvirsky, Vladimir 22
Slepak, Maria 46, 57
Slepak, Vladimir 46, 57
Slobodian, Mykola 125
Smirnov, R.D. 184
Smirnov 192

Smogitel, Vadim 57-58
Smolensk Special Psychiatric Hospital 189
Smykhalkov, P.S. 45
Snezhnevsky, A.V. 183-184, 203
Soldatov, Sergei, 21
Solitary Confinement 67, 110, 159-161,
Solzhenitsyn, Alexander 14, 15, 16, 180
Sorokin, Nikolai 177
Sotnikov 127
Special Psychiatric Hospitals, see Psychiatric
Hospitals
Stalin, J.V. 8, 16, 31, 39, 89, 94
Starchik, Pyotr 173, 186
Stasiv-Kalynets, Irina 109, 120
Statute on Advocates of the RSFSR 71
Statute on the Supervisory Powers of the
USSR Procuracy 9, 168
Stephanian, Akop 87
Stolypin Wagon 106-108
Strogovich, M.S. 74
Striltsev, Victor 20
Strokata, Nina 155
Struchkov, N.A. 92-93
Stus, Vasyl 123, 149
Sulfazin 199-200
Superfin, Gavriil 30, 119
Supervisory Commissions 151, 168, 169-170
Supreme Court of the USSR 75, 83
Supreme Courts of the Union Republics
14, 18, 75-76, 82, 83
Supreme Soviet of the USSR 3, 4, 8, 51, 60,
65, 67, 79, 84, 89, 113, 180
Supreme Soviets of the Union Republics
36, 40, 58, 84
Surveillance, Administrative 51, 60-63
Suslensky, Yakov 157
Svetlichnaya, Nadezhda 120, 123, 162
Svetlichny, Ivan 123
Sweden 48
Switzerland 49
Sychyovka Special Psychiatric Hospital 131,
183, 187, 189, 190, 191-192, 199, 201,
203

Talgar Special Psychiatric Hospital 189
Tarakhanov, Yury 48
Tashkent Special Psychiatric Hospital 189
Terelya, Josif 174-175, 191, 192
Terkhova 42
Teurer, Ivan 46, 47
"Theft of State Property" 60
Tikhonov 167
Tikhy, Oles 73

Timokhin, Valery 30
Titov, Vladimir 199
Trade Unions, see Workers Imprisoned
Transit Prisons 108-110
"Treason" 48-49, 60, 66, 72, 73, 79, 100, 154
Treatment of Prisoners, see Conditions of Confinement in Psychiatric Hospitals and Conditions of Imprisonment in Corrective Labour Institutions
Trials 14-64, 65-88
Triftazin 197-199
"The True Witness" Publishing House 44-45
Tsirekidze, Yury 68
Tsvyrko, Gennady 183
Tverdokhlebov, Andrei 14, 16, 30, 73

Ugodin 167
Ukrainians, see Nationalities
Uniate Catholics, see Religious Believers
United Nations Commission on Human Rights 164
United Nations Human Rights Committee 3, 4
United Nations General Assembly 21
United Nations International Covenant on Civil and Political Rights 3, 4, 49
United Nations International Covenant on Social, Economic and Cultural Rights 3
United Nations Secretary General 21
United Nations Standard Minimum Rules for the Treatment of Prisoners 91
United Nations Universal Declaration of Human Rights 3, 18, 45, 49, 145-146
United States of America 39
Usoyeva, Nadezhda 99
Usta, Izek 51
Uvarov, Anatoly 48, 174
Uzbeks, see Nationalities

Valendo, Lidiya 48
Varato, Arvo 21
Vashchenko, Daniil 53-54
Veretennikov, Vladimir 30
Vilik, Alexander 46, 52
Vinarov, Yakov 46, 52
Vins, Georgy 39
Vins, Pyotr 60, 112, 143-144, 165
Vins, Valentin 46
"Violation of Laws on Separation of Church and State and of School and Church" 35-37, 39, 41-42, 45
Visits to Prisoners, see Conditions of Confinement in Psychiatric Hospitals, Conditions of

Imprisonment in Corrective Labour Institutions, Custody Before Trial
Vladimir Prison, see Corrective Labour Institutions
Voevodin, L.D. 5-6
Volokhonsky, Lev 22
Voloshchuk, Alexander 184
Voloshonovich, Dr Alexander 182
Voronok 106, 108, 109, 166
Vorozhbit, Father Mikhail 30-31
"Voznessenskaya", Yuliya, see Okulova, Yuliya
Vudka, Yury 154, 157

Wagner, Ivan 46, 60
Windschuh, Anton 46
Windschuh, L. 46
Wolf, Yakov 45
Women Prisoners, 16, 17, 22, 30, 31, 41, 44, 78, 84, 99, 101, 108-110, 116, 120, 123, 137, 138, 139, 144-145, 149, 155, 162, 173 155, 162, 173
Workers Imprisoned 17, 21-22, 107, 176, 179, 183
Working Commission for the Investigation of the Use of Psychiatry for Political Purposes 20-21, 82, 172, 182, 196, 202-203
World Congress of Peace Forces 4
World Council of Churches 147
World Federation of Mental Health 173
World Health Organization 116
World Medical Association 124
World Meteorological Organization 49
World Psychiatric Association 172-173

Yankov, Gavriil 22, 183
Yermolayev, Sergei 21, 183
Yershov, Mikhail 31
Yevdokimov, Boris 201-202
Yezhov, I.S. 72-73
Yurkiv, M. 45
Yuskevich, Artem 21

Zadikian, Stepan 87
Zaitsev, Vyacheslav 174
Zaitseva, Larissa 44
Zaitseva, Ludmilla 44
Zakharova, Nina and Lena 43
Zalmonson, Israel 147-148
Zalmonson, Sylva 144-145
Zamovskaya (prison doctor) 126
Zavurov, Amner 46, 60, 86
Zheleznov, Alexander 183
Zhigalkin, Vasily 174

Zhikharev, Mikhail 184
Zhiltsov, Alexei 41-42
Zhitnikova, Tatyana 198-199
Zholkovskaya, Irina 111

Zhvania, Vladimir 87
Zolotukhin, B.A. 72
*Znaniye* 35
Zukauskas, Sarunas 126
Zypre, Algirdas 131

# AMNESTY INTERNATIONAL PUBLICATIONS

**Report on Allegations of Torture in Brazil,** A5, 108 pages, first edition September 1972, re-set with updated preface March 1976: £1.20

**Prisoners of Conscience in the USSR: Their Treatment and Conditions,** A5, 154 pages, November 1975: £1.00

**Professional Codes of Ethics,** A5, 32 pages, October 1976: 40 pence

\* **Report of an Amnesty International Mission to the Republic of the Philippines,** A5, 60 pages, first published September 1976, second (updated) edition March 1977: £1.00

\* **Dossier on Political Prisoners Held in Secret Detention Camps in Chile,** A4, March 1977: £1.00

\* **Torture in Greece: The First Torturers' Trial 1975,** A5, 98 pages, April 1977: 85 pence

**Islamic Republic of Pakistan. An Amnesty International Report including the findings of a Mission,** A4, 96 pages, May 1977: 75 pence

\* **Evidence of Torture: Studies by the Amnesty International Danish Medical Group,** A5, 40 pages, June 1977: 50 pence

**Report of an Amnesty International Mission to the Republic of Korea,** A4, 46 pages, first published April 1976, second edition June 1977: 75 pence

\* **The Republic of Nicaragua. An Amnesty International Report, including the findings of a Mission to Nicaragua 10-15 May 1976,** A4, 75 pages, July 1977: 75 pence

\*\* **Indonesia. An Amnesty International Report,** A5, 148 pages, October 1977: £2.00

**Political Imprisonment in South Africa,** A5, 105 pages, January 1978: £1.00

\* **Political Imprisonment in the People's Republic of China,** A5, 192 pages, November 1978, £1.50

\* **The Death Penalty. Amnesty International Report,** 209 pages, September 1979: £2.00

\* **Amnesty International Report 1979,** 220 pages, December 1979, £2.50

**Report of an Amnesty International Mission to Singapore,** A4, 60 pages, January 1980

\* **Testimony on Secret Detention Camps in Argentina,** A4, 66 pages, February 1980

\*also available in Spanish
\*\*also available in Indonesian

In addition to these major reports, Amnesty International also publishes a monthly **Newsletter,** an annual **Report** and a series of **Amnesty International Briefing Papers:**

**Amnesty International Newsletter and annual Report:** The **Newsletter** is an eight-page monthly account of Amnesty International's work for human rights in countries throughout the world and includes a one-page bulletin on the work of the Campaign for the Abolition of Torture. The annual **Report** gives a country-by-country survey of human rights violations which have come to the attention of Amnesty International. Yearly subscription £6.00 (US $15.00) inclusive.

**Amnesty International Briefing Papers**: a series of human rights reference booklets on individual countries, averaging between 12 and 16 pages in A5 format. Briefing Papers Numbers 1—16:

| | | |
|---|---|---|
| Singapore | Guatemala* | German Democratic |
| Paraguay* | Turkey | Republic (GDR)* |
| Iran† | People's Democratic | Morocco |
| Namibia | Republic of Yemen | Guinea* |
| Rhodesia/Zimbabwe | Taiwan (Republic of China) | Peru* |
| Malawi | Czechoslovakia* | Syria+ |

*also available in Spanish †also available in Farsi +also available in Arabic

Subscription price for series of 10 Briefing Papers: £6.00 (US $15.00). Price includes postage and packing. Single copies 40 pence (US $1.00), plus 20 pence (50 cents) for postage and handling.

**AMNESTY INTERNATIONAL PUBLICATIONS** may be obtained from the following national sections:

**Australia**: Amnesty International, Australian Section, Box X 2258, GPO Perth, Western Australia 6001
Branch addresses:
*New South Wales:* Amnesty International, New South Wales Branch, PO Box 2598, GPO Sydney, New South Wales 2001
*Queensland:* Amnesty International, Queensland Branch, 272 Petrie Terrace, Brisbane, Queensland 4000
*South Australia:* Mrs Vira Chawtur, 42 Maple Avenue, Royal Park, South Australia 5054
*Tasmania:* Amnesty International, Box 968K, Hobart, Tasmania
*Victoria:* Amnesty International, Victorian Branch, PO Box 28, 277 Inkermann Street, St Kilda, Victoria 3182
*Western Australia:* Ms V. Payne, Box X2258, GPO Perth, Western Australia 6001
**Austria**: Amnesty International, Austrian Section, Esslinggasse 15/4, A-1010 Wien
**Bangladesh**: Amnesty Bangladesh, GPO Box 2095, Dacca
**Belgium**: *(Flemish-speaking)* Amnesty International, Blijde Inkomststraat 98, 3000 Leuven
*(French-speaking)* Amnesty International, 145 Boulevard Leopold 2, 1080 Brussels

**Canada:** *(English-speaking)* Amnesty International, Canadian Section (English-speaking), PO Box 6033, 2101 Algonquin Avenue, Ottawa, Ontario K2A 1T1 *(French-speaking)* Amnistie Internationale, Section Canadienne (francophone), 1800 Ouest, Boulevard Dorchester, Local 400, Montreal Quebec H3H 2H2

**Costa Rica:** Apartado 72, Centro Colón, San José

**Denmark:** Amnesty International, Frederiksbörggade 1, 1360 Kφbenhavn K

**Ecuador:** Casilla de Correo 8994, Guayaquil, Ecuador

**Faroe Islands:** Anette Wang, Tróndargφta 47, Post Box 23, 3800 Tórshavn

**Finland:** Amnesty International, Finnish Section, Laivasillankatu 10 A, Helsinki 14

**France:** Amnesty International, French Section, 18 rue de Varenne, 75007 Paris

**Germany, Federal Republic of:** Amnesty International, Section of the Federal Republic of Germany, Heerstrasse 178, 5300 Bonn 1

**Ghana:** Dr I.S. Ephson, Ilen Chambers, PO Box 6354, Accra

**Greece:** Amnesty International, Greek Section, 22 Kleitomachou Street, Athens 502

**Iceland:** Amnesty International, Iceland Section, Hafnarstraeti 15, PO Box 7124, 127 Reykjavik

**India:** Amnesty International, Indian Section, D-19 Annexe, Gulmohar Park, New Delhi 110049

**Ireland:** Amnesty International, Irish Section, 8th Floor, Liberty Hall, Dublin 1, Eire

**Israel:** Amnesty International, Israel National Section, PO Box 37638, Tel Aviv

**Italy.** Amnesty International, Italian Section, Sezione Italiana, Viale Mazzini 146, 00195 Roma, Italy

**Ivory Coast:** Section Ivoirienne, 55 Boulevard Clozel, 01 BP 698, Abidjan 01

**Japan:** Amnesty International, Room 74 3-18 Nishi-Waseda 2-chome, Shinjuku-ku, Tokyo 160

**Korea, Republic of:** Amnesty Korean Committee, Fifth floor, Donhwamoon Building, 64-1 Kwonnongdong, Chongnoku, Seoul

**Luxembourg:** Amnesty International Luxembourg, Boîte Postale 1914, Luxembourg-Gare

**Mexico:** Amnistía Internacional, Sección Mexicana, Apartado Postal No. 20-217, Mexico 20 DF

**Nepal:** Amnesty International, Nepal Section, GPO Box 890, 21/242A Dillibazar, Kathmandu

**Netherlands:** Amnesty International, Dutch Section, $3^e$ Hugo de Grootstraat 7, Amsterdam

**New Zealand:** Amnesty International, New Zealand Section, PO Box 3597, Wellington

**Nigeria:** Amnesty International, Nigerian Section, 15 Onayade Street, Fadeyi-Yaba, Lagos

**Norway:** Amnesty International, Norwegian Section, Akersgatan 39, II, Oslo 1

**Pakistan:** Amnesty International, Pakistan Section, 615 Muhammadi House, I.I. Chundrigar Road, Karachi

**Peru:** Casilla 2319, Lima, Peru

**Spain:** *Secretariat:* Columela 2, 1° derecha, Madrid 1
*Barcelona:* Rambla de Prat 21 1°, Barcelona 12
*San Sebastián:* Apartado 1109, San Sebastián

**Sri Lanka:** E.A.G. de Silva, 79/15 Dr C.W.W. Kannangara Mawatha, Colombo 7

**Sweden:** Amnesty International, Smalandsgatan 2, 11434 Stockholm

**Switzerland.** Amnesty International, Swiss Section, PO Box 1051, CH-3001 Bern

**Turkey:** Uluslararasi Af Örgütü, Türkiye Ulusal Subesi, Izmir Cadesi, Ihlamur Sk 6 (Tugay Han, 1/30), Ankara

**USA:** Amnesty International of the USA, 304 West 58th Street, New York, NY 10019
*Western Region:* Amnesty International of the USA, Western Region Office, 3618 Sacramento Street, San Francisco, CA 94118
*Washington Office:* 413 East Capitol Street, S.E., Washington, DC 20003

**United Kingdom:** Amnesty International, British Section, 8-14 Southampton Street, London WC2E 7HF

**Venezuela:** Amnesty International, Venezuelan Section, Apartado 51184, Caracas 105

FOR FURTHER INFORMATION
ABOUT THE WORK OF
AMNESTY INTERNATIONAL
PLEASE CONTACT:

AMNESTY INTERNATIONAL
BRITISH SECTION
TOWER HOUSE
8 – 14 SOUTHAMPTON STREET
LONDON WC2E 7HF
TELEPHONE: 01-836 5621